VRANCKEN   DESBERG

I.R.$.

BLUE ICE

DAMN!

WE'VE BEEN WAITING FOR RICKS TO RESURFACE FOR 12 YEARS NOW, AND HE'S HERE, SOMEWHERE WITHIN ARM'S REACH, TO BUY OUT THE BIGGEST MEXICAN CARTEL...

COLOUR WORK: COQUELICOT

9th CINEBOOK
The 9th Art Publisher

This two-volume book includes:

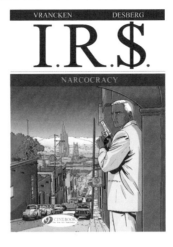

Original titles: Blue Ice – Narcocratie

Original edition: © Editions du Lombard (Dargaud-Lombard SA), 2001 - 2002
by Desberg & Vrancken
www.lelombard.com

English translation: © 2008 Cinebook Ltd

Translator: Luke Spear
Lettering and text layout: Imadjinn
Printed in Spain by Just Colour Graphic

This edition first published in Great Britain in 2009 by
CINEBOOK Ltd
56 Beech Avenue
Canterbury, Kent
CT4 7TA
www.cinebook.com

A CIP catalogue record for this book
is available from the British Library

ISBN 978-1-905460-74-8

CINEBOOK
The 9th Art Publisher

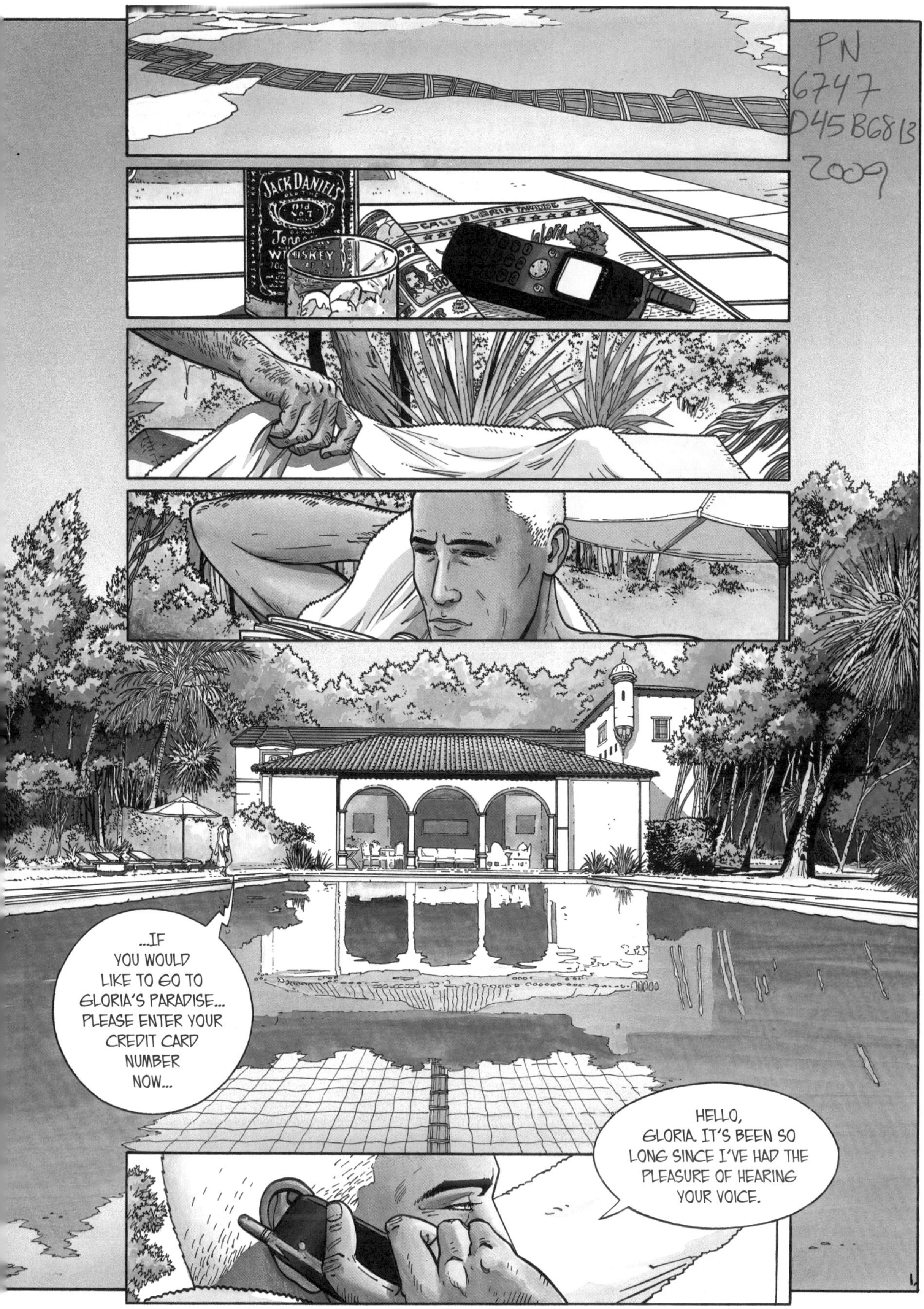
JACK DANIEL'S
Old No. 7
WHISKEY
CALL GLORIA PARADISE
...IF YOU WOULD LIKE TO GO TO GLORIA'S PARADISE... PLEASE ENTER YOUR CREDIT CARD NUMBER NOW...
HELLO, GLORIA. IT'S BEEN SO LONG SINCE I'VE HAD THE PLEASURE OF HEARING YOUR VOICE.

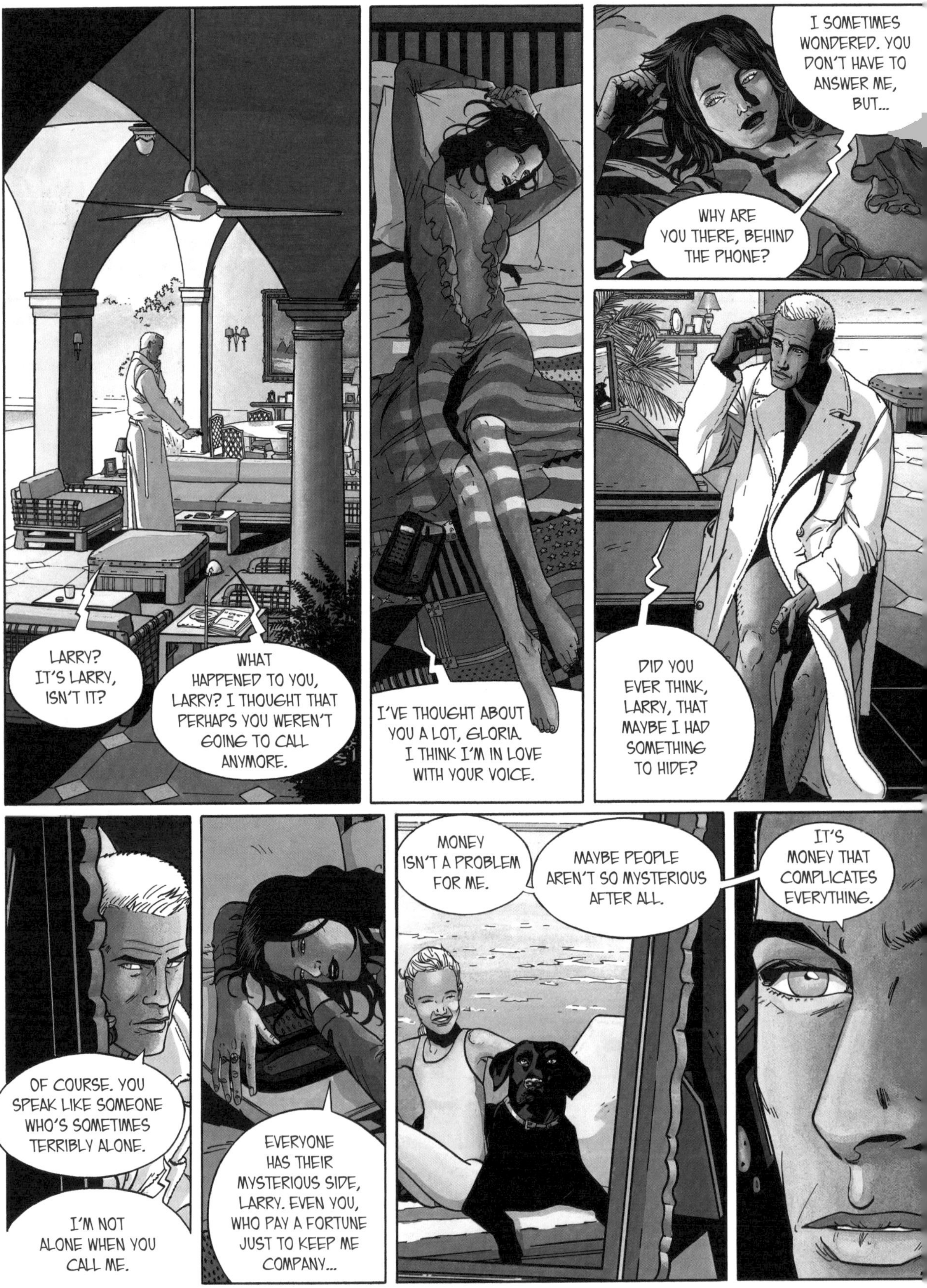
LARRY? IT'S LARRY, ISN'T IT?
WHAT HAPPENED TO YOU, LARRY? I THOUGHT THAT PERHAPS YOU WEREN'T GOING TO CALL ANYMORE.
I'VE THOUGHT ABOUT YOU A LOT, GLORIA. I THINK I'M IN LOVE WITH YOUR VOICE.
I SOMETIMES WONDERED. YOU DON'T HAVE TO ANSWER ME, BUT...
WHY ARE YOU THERE, BEHIND THE PHONE?
DID YOU EVER THINK, LARRY, THAT MAYBE I HAD SOMETHING TO HIDE?
OF COURSE. YOU SPEAK LIKE SOMEONE WHO'S SOMETIMES TERRIBLY ALONE.
I'M NOT ALONE WHEN YOU CALL ME.
EVERYONE HAS THEIR MYSTERIOUS SIDE, LARRY. EVEN YOU, WHO PAY A FORTUNE JUST TO KEEP ME COMPANY...
MONEY ISN'T A PROBLEM FOR ME.
MAYBE PEOPLE AREN'T SO MYSTERIOUS AFTER ALL.
IT'S MONEY THAT COMPLICATES EVERYTHING.

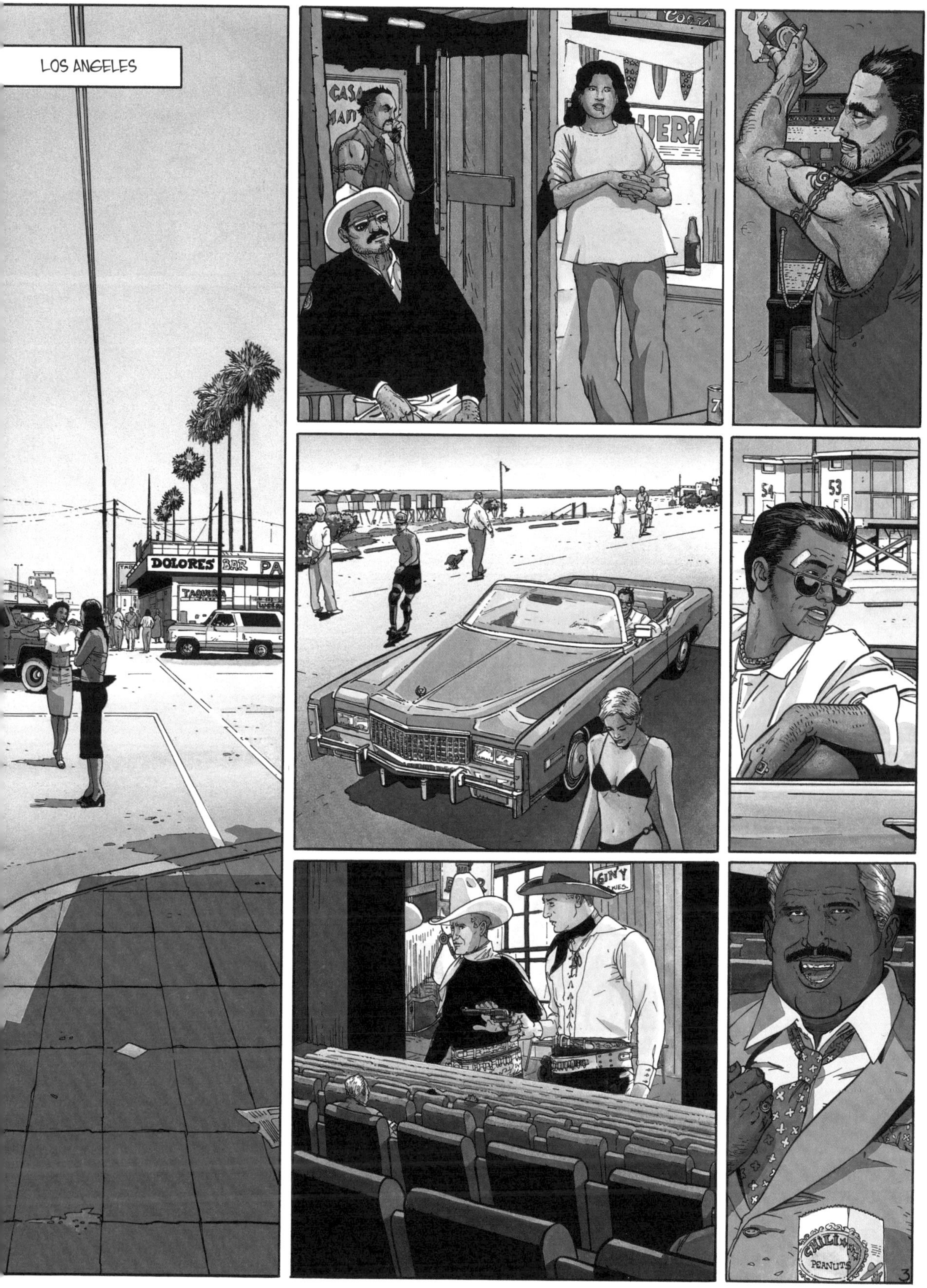
LOS ANGELES
DOLORES' BAR
TAQUERIA
Coors
54
53
PEANUTS

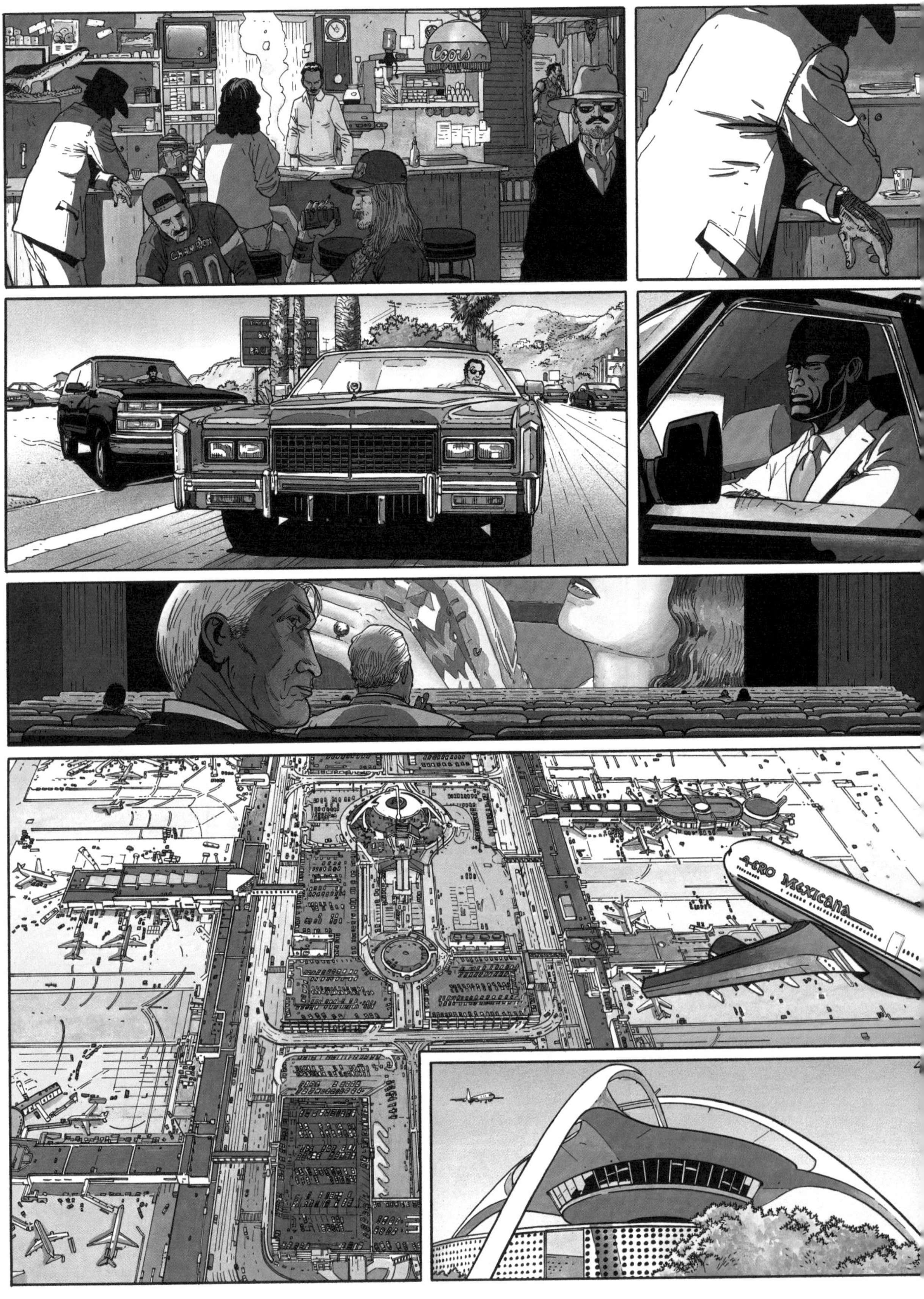
Coors
CHAMPION
AERO MEXICANA

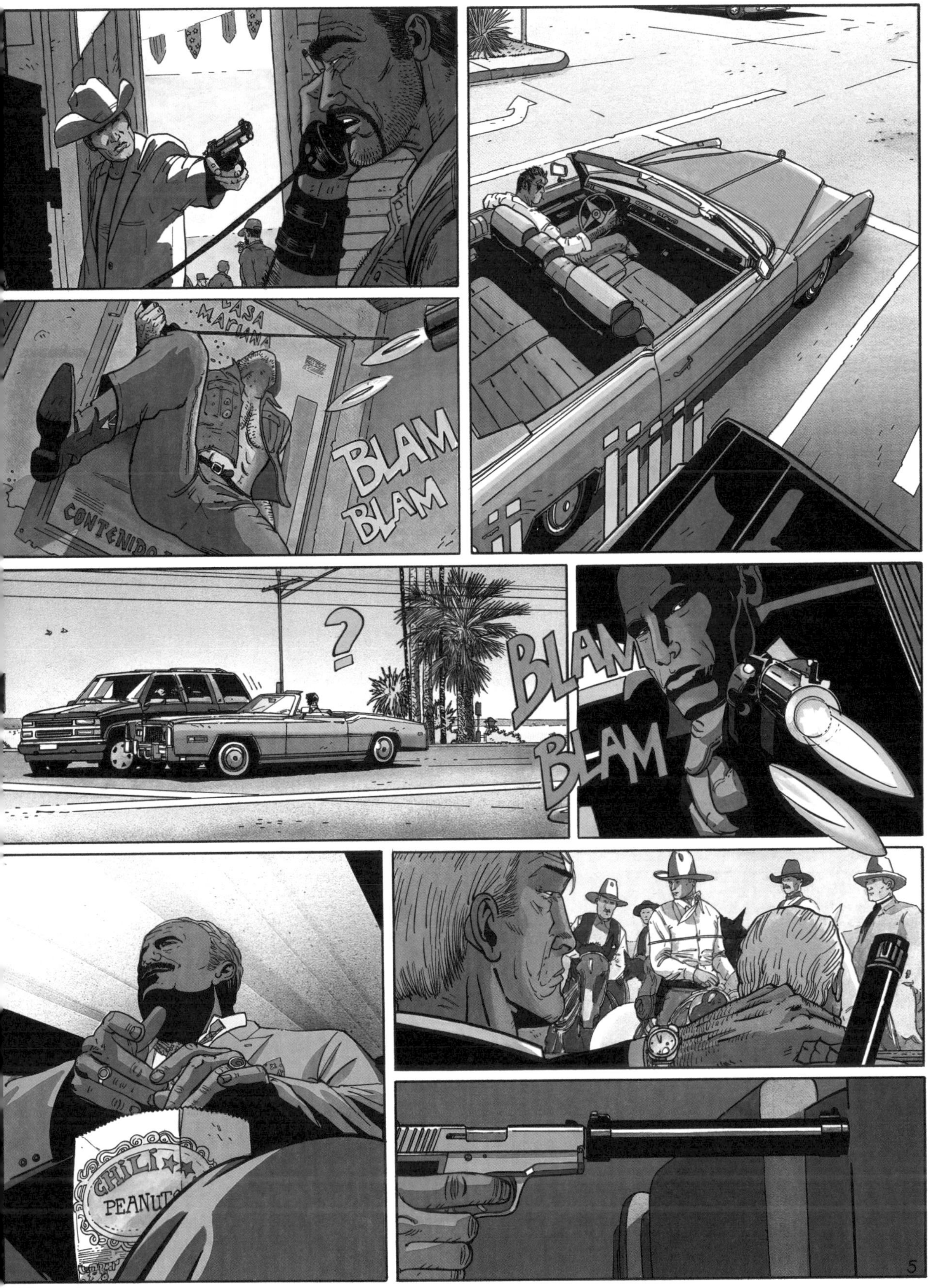
CASA
MARIANA
CONTENIDO
BLAM
BLAM
?
BLAM
BLAM
CHILI
PEANUT
5

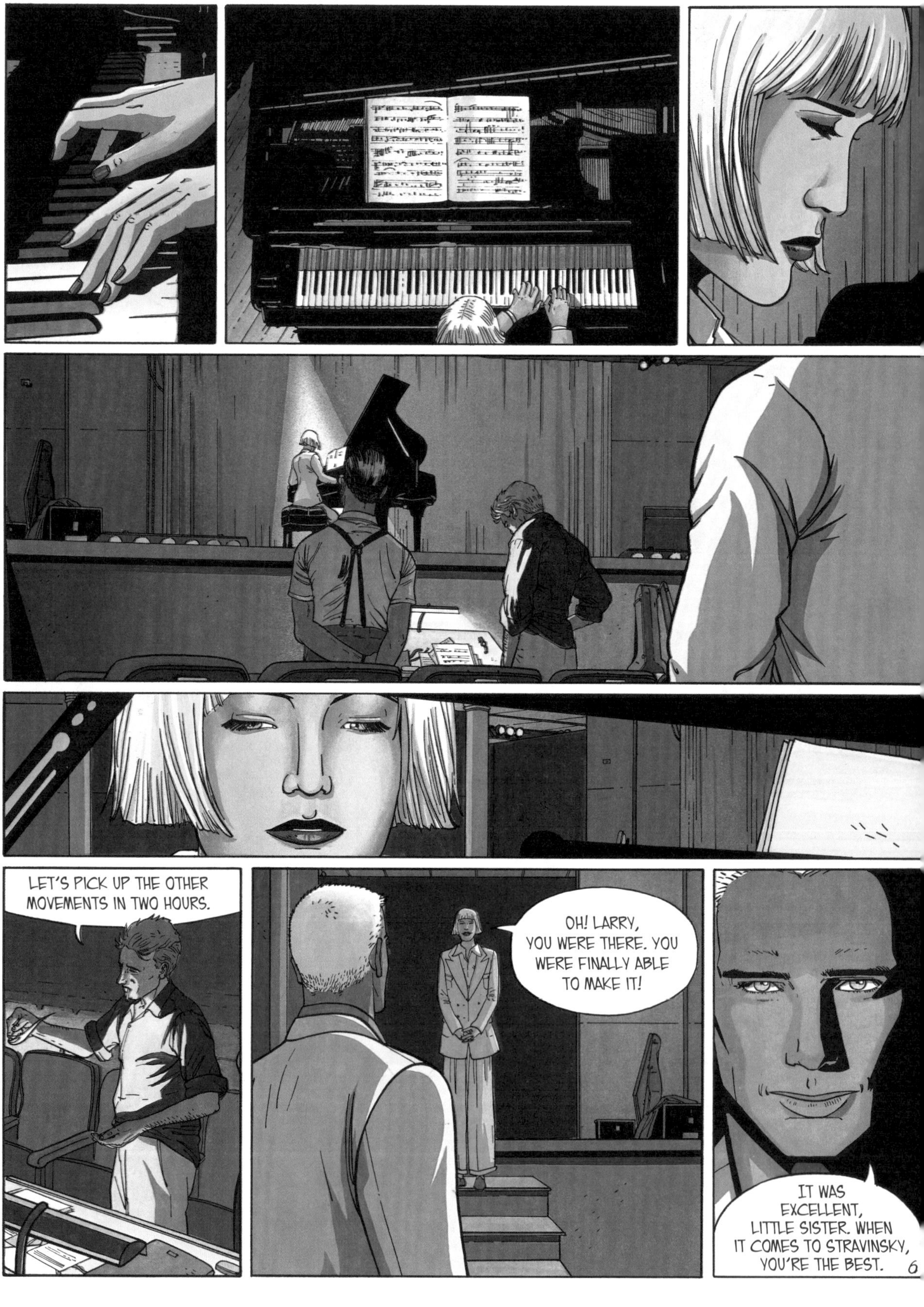
LET'S PICK UP THE OTHER MOVEMENTS IN TWO HOURS.
OH! LARRY, YOU WERE THERE. YOU WERE FINALLY ABLE TO MAKE IT!
IT WAS EXCELLENT, LITTLE SISTER. WHEN IT COMES TO STRAVINSKY, YOU'RE THE BEST.
6

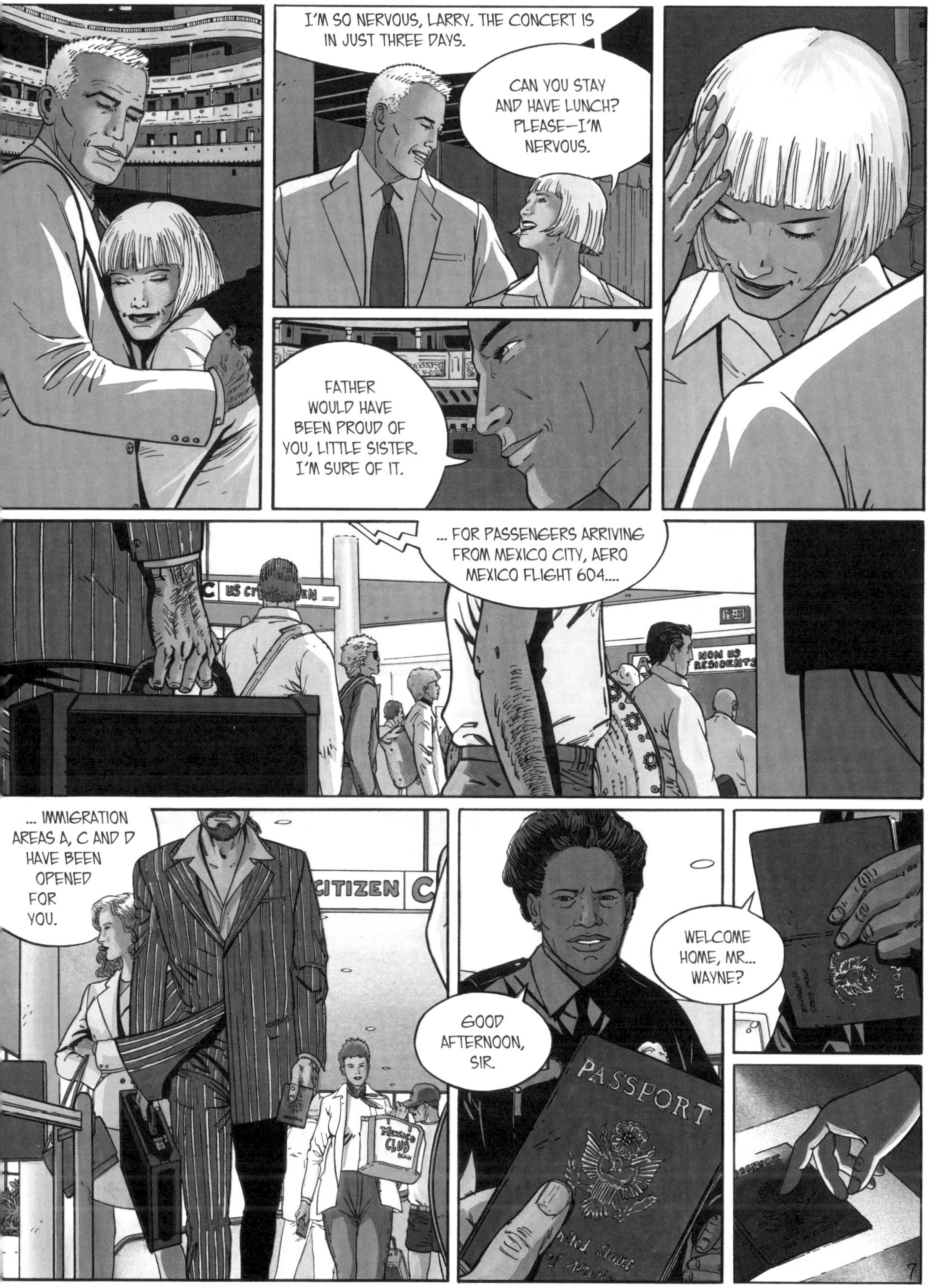
I'M SO NERVOUS, LARRY. THE CONCERT IS IN JUST THREE DAYS.
CAN YOU STAY AND HAVE LUNCH? PLEASE—I'M NERVOUS.
FATHER WOULD HAVE BEEN PROUD OF YOU, LITTLE SISTER. I'M SURE OF IT.
... FOR PASSENGERS ARRIVING FROM MEXICO CITY, AERO MEXICO FLIGHT 604....
NON US RESIDENTS
... IMMIGRATION AREAS A, C AND D HAVE BEEN OPENED FOR YOU.
CITIZEN
GOOD AFTERNOON, SIR.
WELCOME HOME, MR... WAYNE?
PASSPORT
7

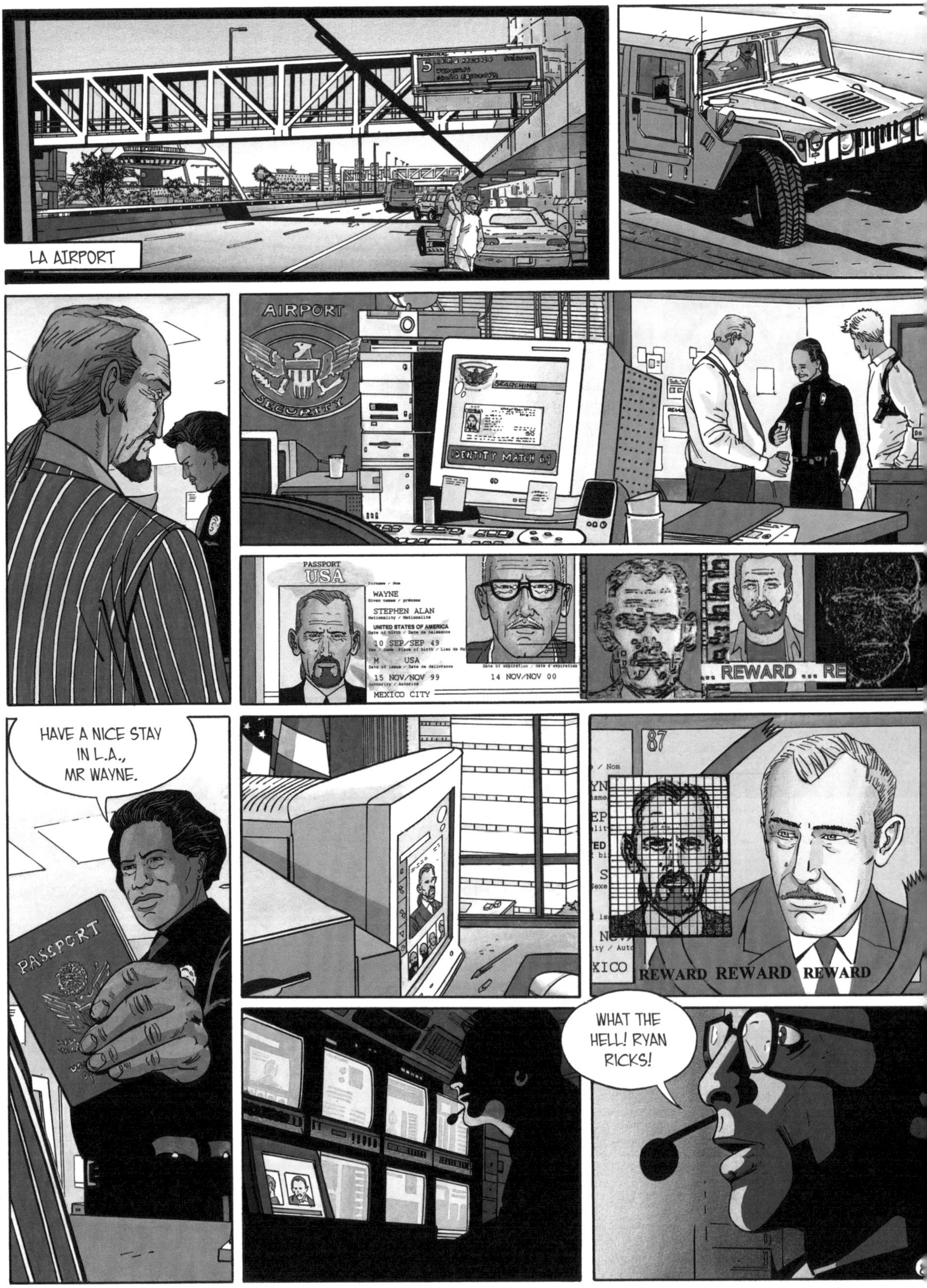
LA AIRPORT
AIRPORT SECURITY
SEARCHING
IDENTITY MATCH 6:1
PASSPORT USA
WAYNE
STEPHEN ALAN
UNITED STATES OF AMERICA
10 SEP/SEP 49
M USA
15 NOV/NOV 99
14 NOV/NOV 00
MEXICO CITY
... REWARD ... RE
HAVE A NICE STAY IN L.A., MR WAYNE.
PASSPORT
87
REWARD REWARD REWARD
WHAT THE HELL! RYAN RICKS!

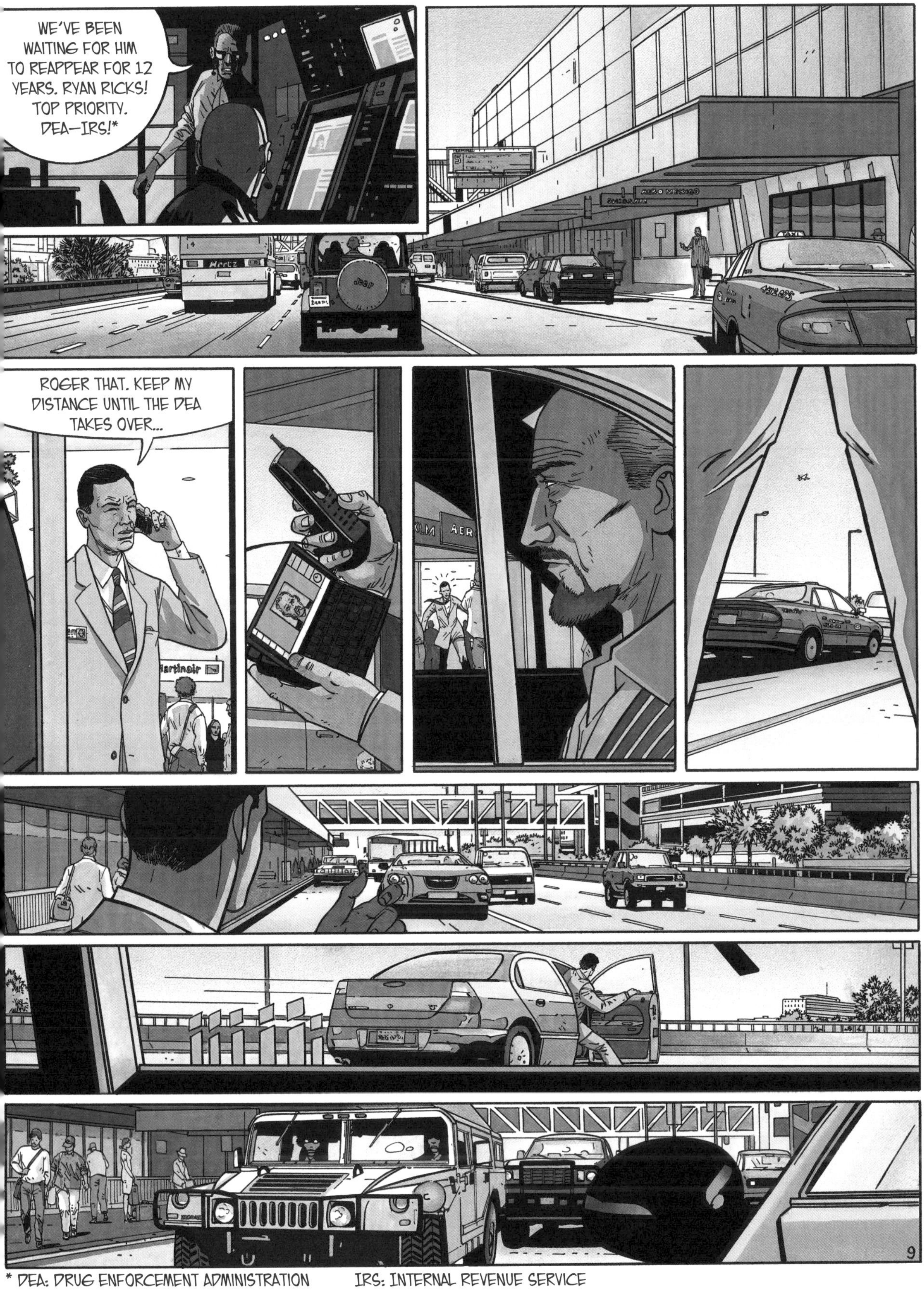
WE'VE BEEN WAITING FOR HIM TO REAPPEAR FOR 12 YEARS. RYAN RICKS! TOP PRIORITY. DEA–IRS!*
ROGER THAT. KEEP MY DISTANCE UNTIL THE DEA TAKES OVER...
9

* DEA: DRUG ENFORCEMENT ADMINISTRATION IRS: INTERNAL REVENUE SERVICE

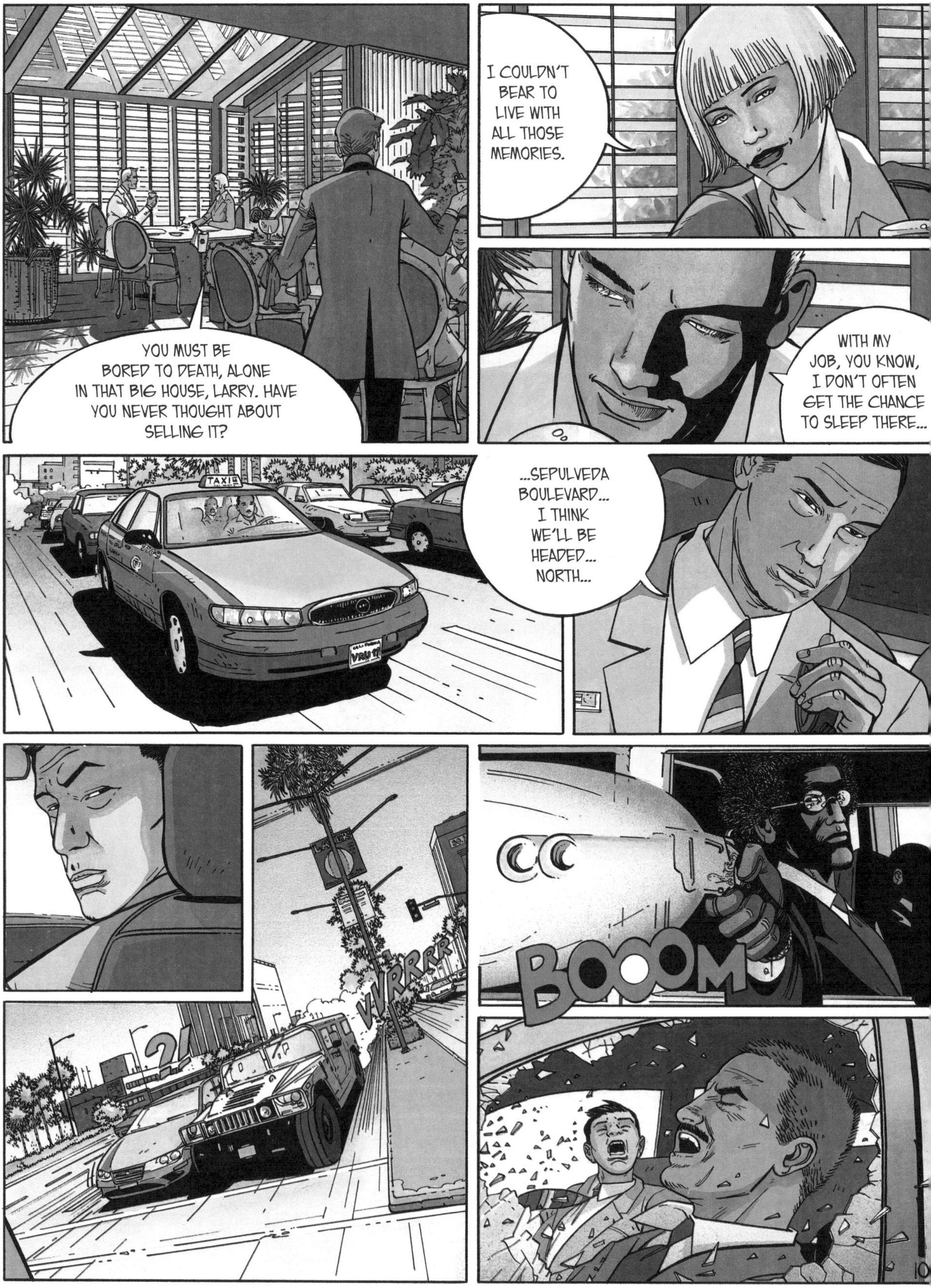
YOU MUST BE BORED TO DEATH, ALONE IN THAT BIG HOUSE, LARRY. HAVE YOU NEVER THOUGHT ABOUT SELLING IT?
I COULDN'T BEAR TO LIVE WITH ALL THOSE MEMORIES.
WITH MY JOB, YOU KNOW, I DON'T OFTEN GET THE CHANCE TO SLEEP THERE...
TAXI
...SEPULVEDA BOULEVARD... I THINK WE'LL BE HEADED... NORTH...
VVRRRR
BOOOM

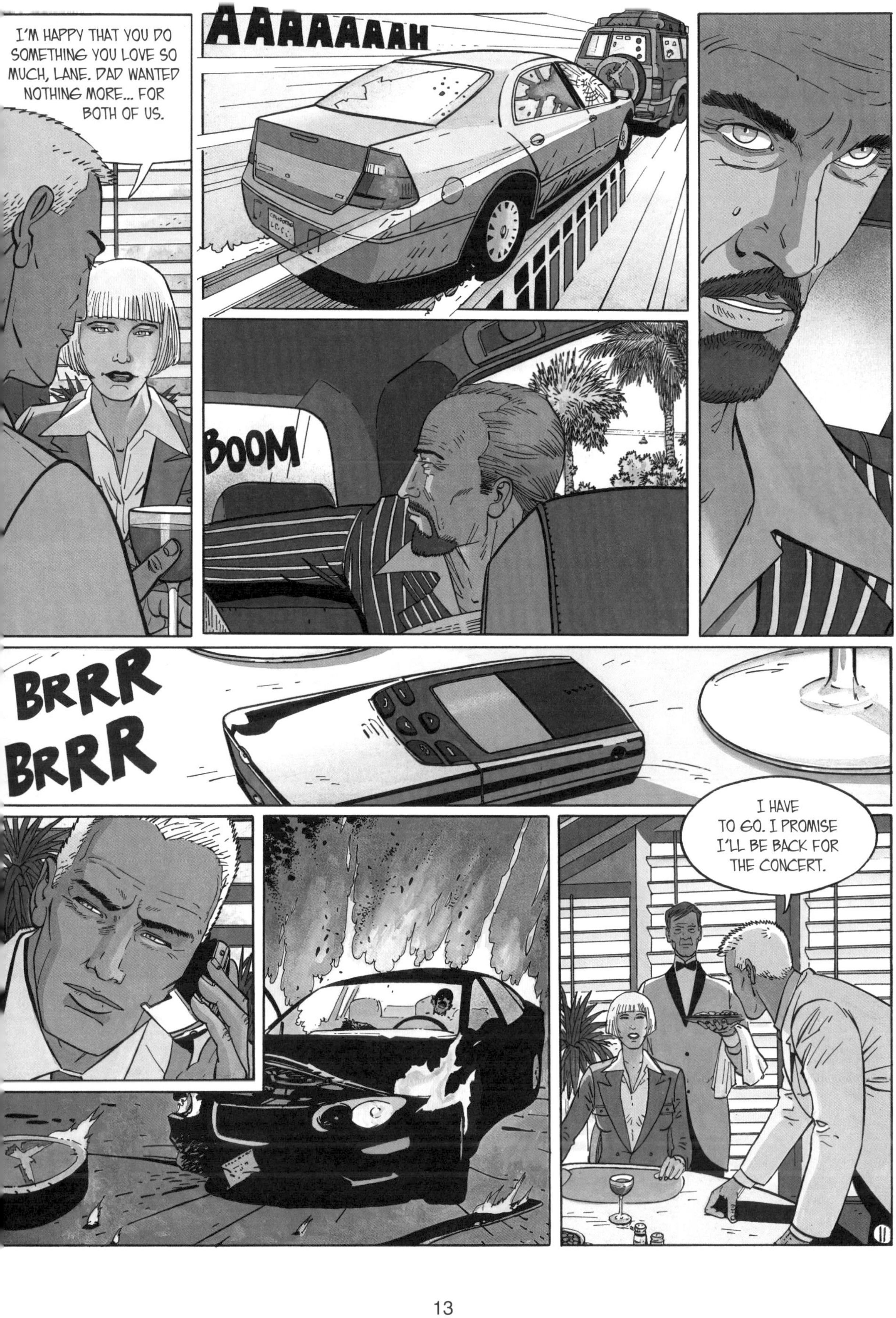
I'M HAPPY THAT YOU DO SOMETHING YOU LOVE SO MUCH, LANE. DAD WANTED NOTHING MORE... FOR BOTH OF US.
AAAAAAAH
BOOM
BRRR BRRR
I HAVE TO GO. I PROMISE I'LL BE BACK FOR THE CONCERT.

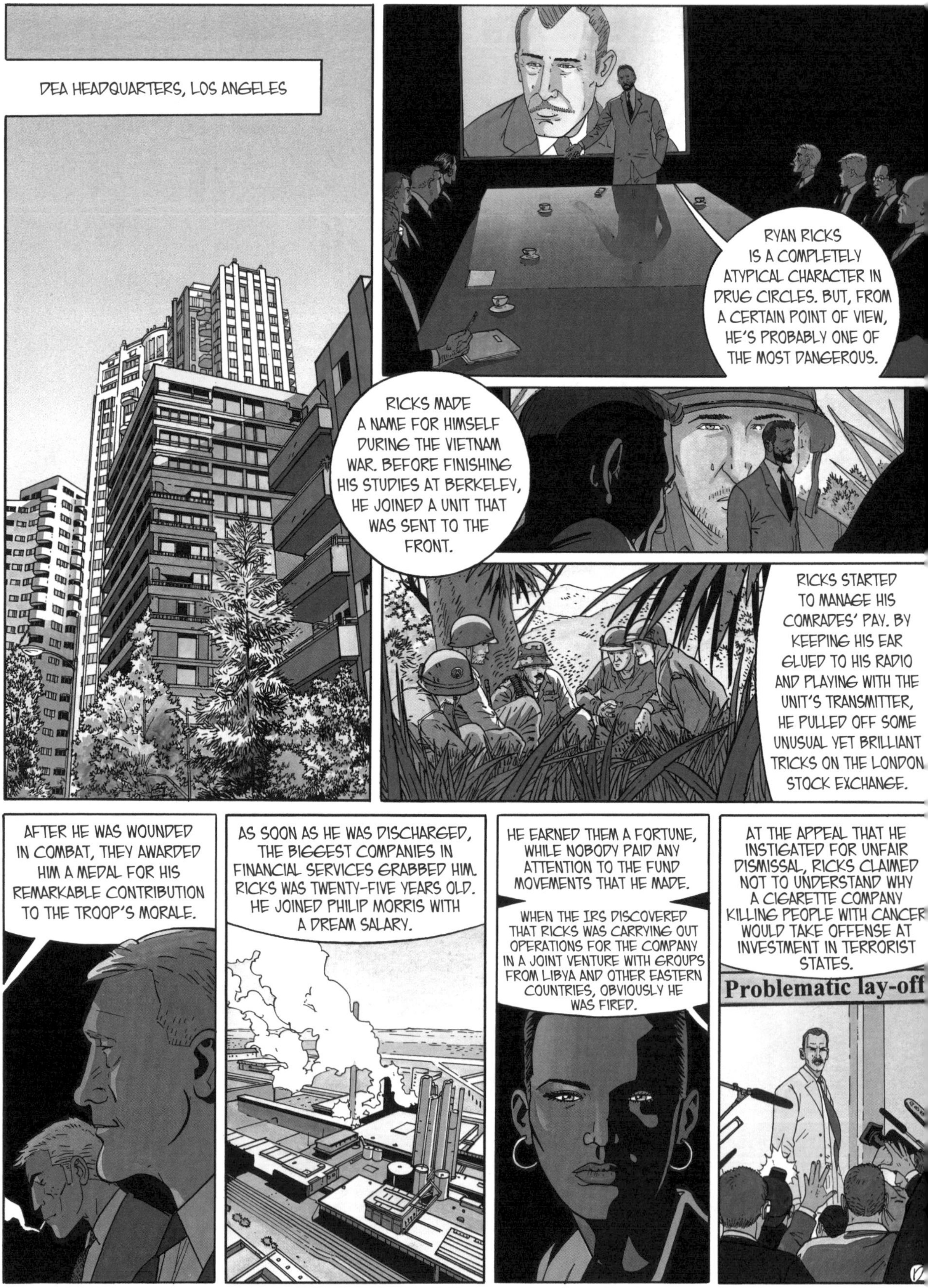
DEA HEADQUARTERS, LOS ANGELES
RYAN RICKS IS A COMPLETELY ATYPICAL CHARACTER IN DRUG CIRCLES. BUT, FROM A CERTAIN POINT OF VIEW, HE'S PROBABLY ONE OF THE MOST DANGEROUS.
RICKS MADE A NAME FOR HIMSELF DURING THE VIETNAM WAR. BEFORE FINISHING HIS STUDIES AT BERKELEY, HE JOINED A UNIT THAT WAS SENT TO THE FRONT.
RICKS STARTED TO MANAGE HIS COMRADES' PAY. BY KEEPING HIS EAR GLUED TO HIS RADIO AND PLAYING WITH THE UNIT'S TRANSMITTER, HE PULLED OFF SOME UNUSUAL YET BRILLIANT TRICKS ON THE LONDON STOCK EXCHANGE.
AFTER HE WAS WOUNDED IN COMBAT, THEY AWARDED HIM A MEDAL FOR HIS REMARKABLE CONTRIBUTION TO THE TROOP'S MORALE.
AS SOON AS HE WAS DISCHARGED, THE BIGGEST COMPANIES IN FINANCIAL SERVICES GRABBED HIM. RICKS WAS TWENTY-FIVE YEARS OLD. HE JOINED PHILIP MORRIS WITH A DREAM SALARY.
HE EARNED THEM A FORTUNE, WHILE NOBODY PAID ANY ATTENTION TO THE FUND MOVEMENTS THAT HE MADE.
WHEN THE IRS DISCOVERED THAT RICKS WAS CARRYING OUT OPERATIONS FOR THE COMPANY IN A JOINT VENTURE WITH GROUPS FROM LIBYA AND OTHER EASTERN COUNTRIES, OBVIOUSLY HE WAS FIRED.
AT THE APPEAL THAT HE INSTIGATED FOR UNFAIR DISMISSAL, RICKS CLAIMED NOT TO UNDERSTAND WHY A CIGARETTE COMPANY KILLING PEOPLE WITH CANCER WOULD TAKE OFFENSE AT INVESTMENT IN TERRORIST STATES.
Problematic lay-off

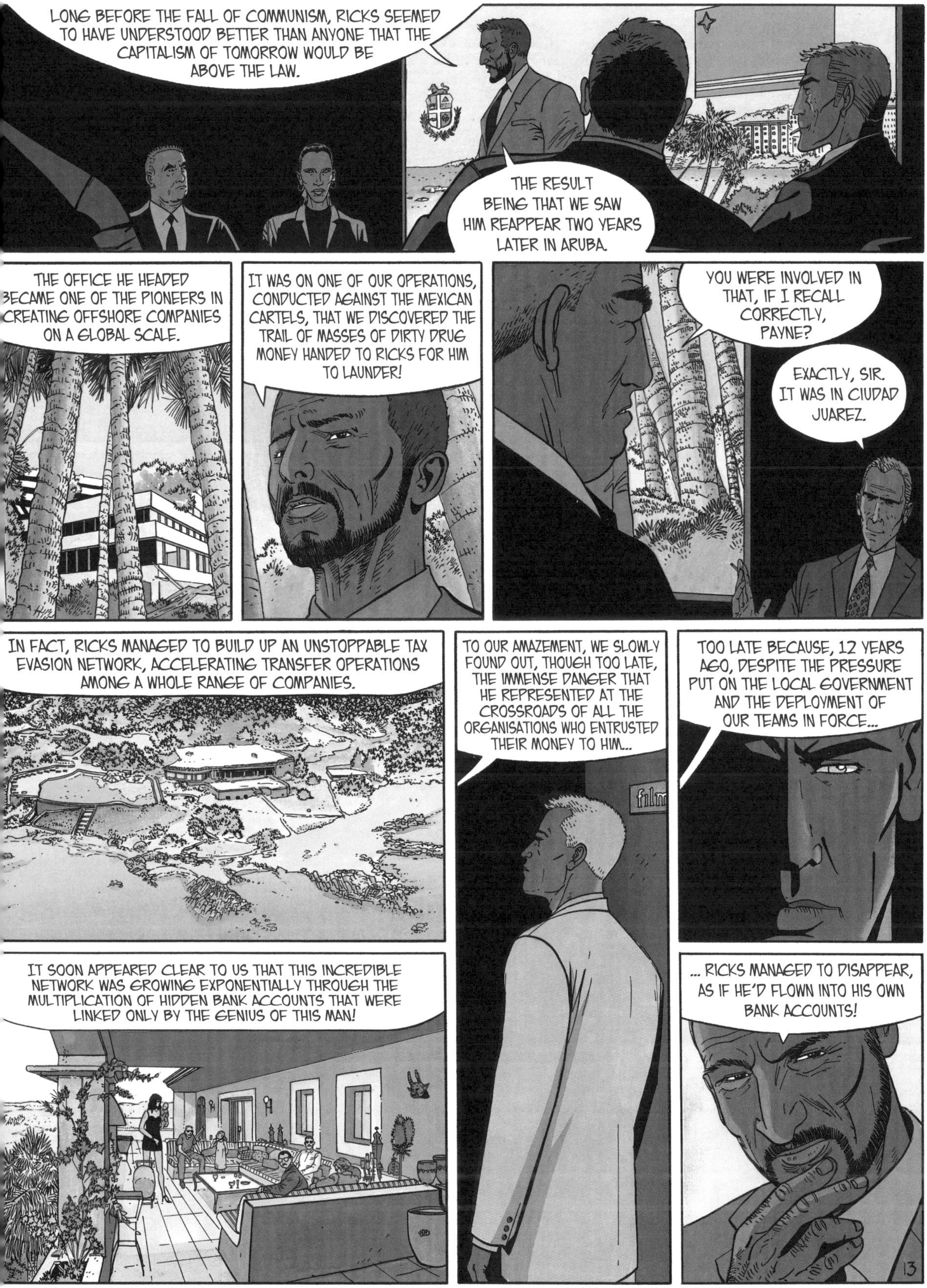
LONG BEFORE THE FALL OF COMMUNISM, RICKS SEEMED TO HAVE UNDERSTOOD BETTER THAN ANYONE THAT THE CAPITALISM OF TOMORROW WOULD BE ABOVE THE LAW.
THE RESULT BEING THAT WE SAW HIM REAPPEAR TWO YEARS LATER IN ARUBA.
THE OFFICE HE HEADED BECAME ONE OF THE PIONEERS IN CREATING OFFSHORE COMPANIES ON A GLOBAL SCALE.
IT WAS ON ONE OF OUR OPERATIONS, CONDUCTED AGAINST THE MEXICAN CARTELS, THAT WE DISCOVERED THE TRAIL OF MASSES OF DIRTY DRUG MONEY HANDED TO RICKS FOR HIM TO LAUNDER!
YOU WERE INVOLVED IN THAT, IF I RECALL CORRECTLY, PAYNE?
EXACTLY, SIR. IT WAS IN CIUDAD JUAREZ.
IN FACT, RICKS MANAGED TO BUILD UP AN UNSTOPPABLE TAX EVASION NETWORK, ACCELERATING TRANSFER OPERATIONS AMONG A WHOLE RANGE OF COMPANIES.
IT SOON APPEARED CLEAR TO US THAT THIS INCREDIBLE NETWORK WAS GROWING EXPONENTIALLY THROUGH THE MULTIPLICATION OF HIDDEN BANK ACCOUNTS THAT WERE LINKED ONLY BY THE GENIUS OF THIS MAN!
TO OUR AMAZEMENT, WE SLOWLY FOUND OUT, THOUGH TOO LATE, THE IMMENSE DANGER THAT HE REPRESENTED AT THE CROSSROADS OF ALL THE ORGANISATIONS WHO ENTRUSTED THEIR MONEY TO HIM...
film
TOO LATE BECAUSE, 12 YEARS AGO, DESPITE THE PRESSURE PUT ON THE LOCAL GOVERNMENT AND THE DEPLOYMENT OF OUR TEAMS IN FORCE...
... RICKS MANAGED TO DISAPPEAR, AS IF HE'D FLOWN INTO HIS OWN BANK ACCOUNTS!
13

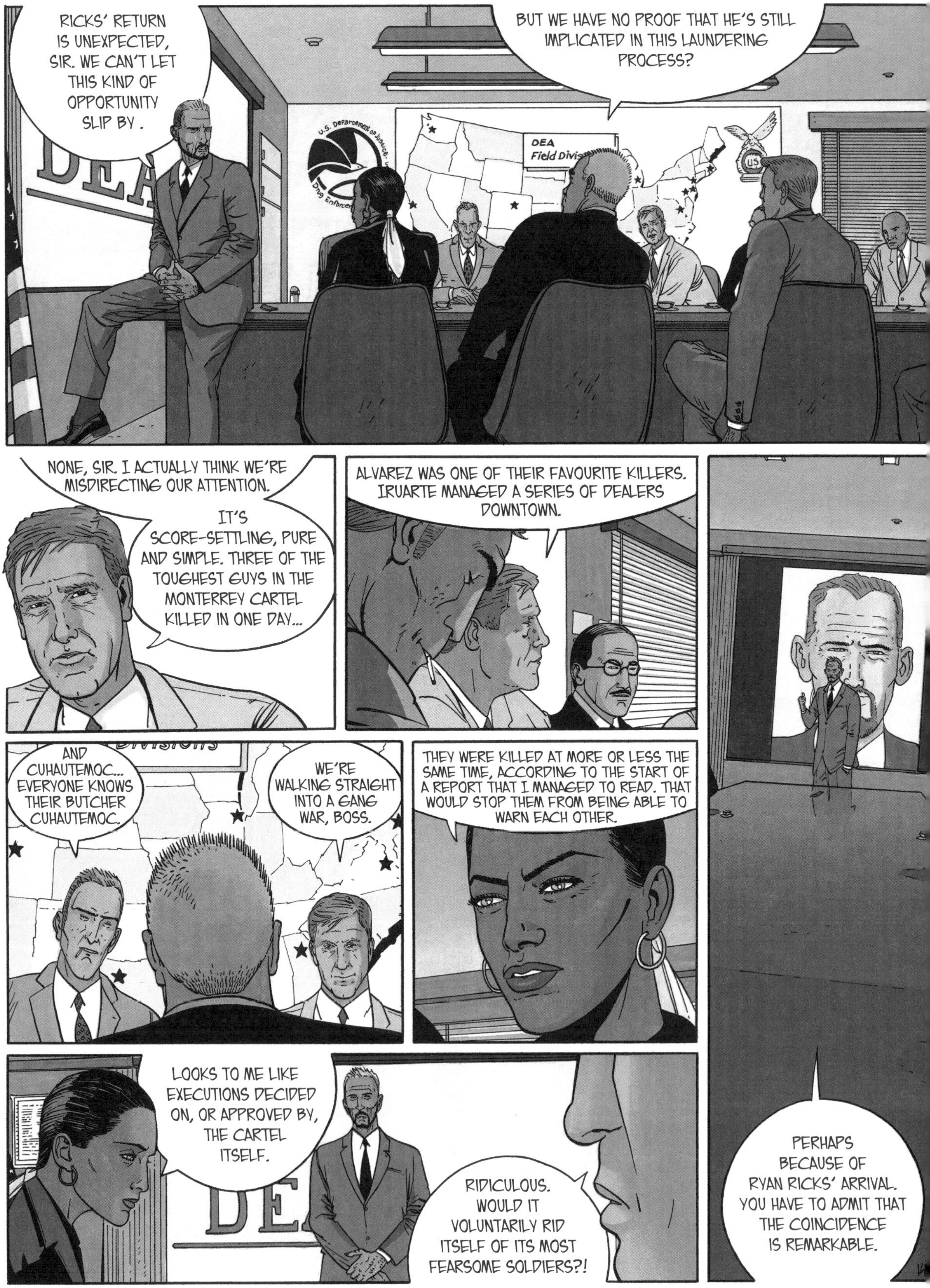
RICKS' RETURN IS UNEXPECTED, SIR. WE CAN'T LET THIS KIND OF OPPORTUNITY SLIP BY .
BUT WE HAVE NO PROOF THAT HE'S STILL IMPLICATED IN THIS LAUNDERING PROCESS?
DEA
DEA Field Divis
NONE, SIR. I ACTUALLY THINK WE'RE MISDIRECTING OUR ATTENTION.
IT'S SCORE-SETTLING, PURE AND SIMPLE. THREE OF THE TOUGHEST GUYS IN THE MONTERREY CARTEL KILLED IN ONE DAY...
ALVAREZ WAS ONE OF THEIR FAVOURITE KILLERS. IRUARTE MANAGED A SERIES OF DEALERS DOWNTOWN.
AND CUHAUTEMOC... EVERYONE KNOWS THEIR BUTCHER CUHAUTEMOC.
WE'RE WALKING STRAIGHT INTO A GANG WAR, BOSS.
THEY WERE KILLED AT MORE OR LESS THE SAME TIME, ACCORDING TO THE START OF A REPORT THAT I MANAGED TO READ. THAT WOULD STOP THEM FROM BEING ABLE TO WARN EACH OTHER.
LOOKS TO ME LIKE EXECUTIONS DECIDED ON, OR APPROVED BY, THE CARTEL ITSELF.
RIDICULOUS. WOULD IT VOLUNTARILY RID ITSELF OF ITS MOST FEARSOME SOLDIERS?!
PERHAPS BECAUSE OF RYAN RICKS' ARRIVAL. YOU HAVE TO ADMIT THAT THE COINCIDENCE IS REMARKABLE.

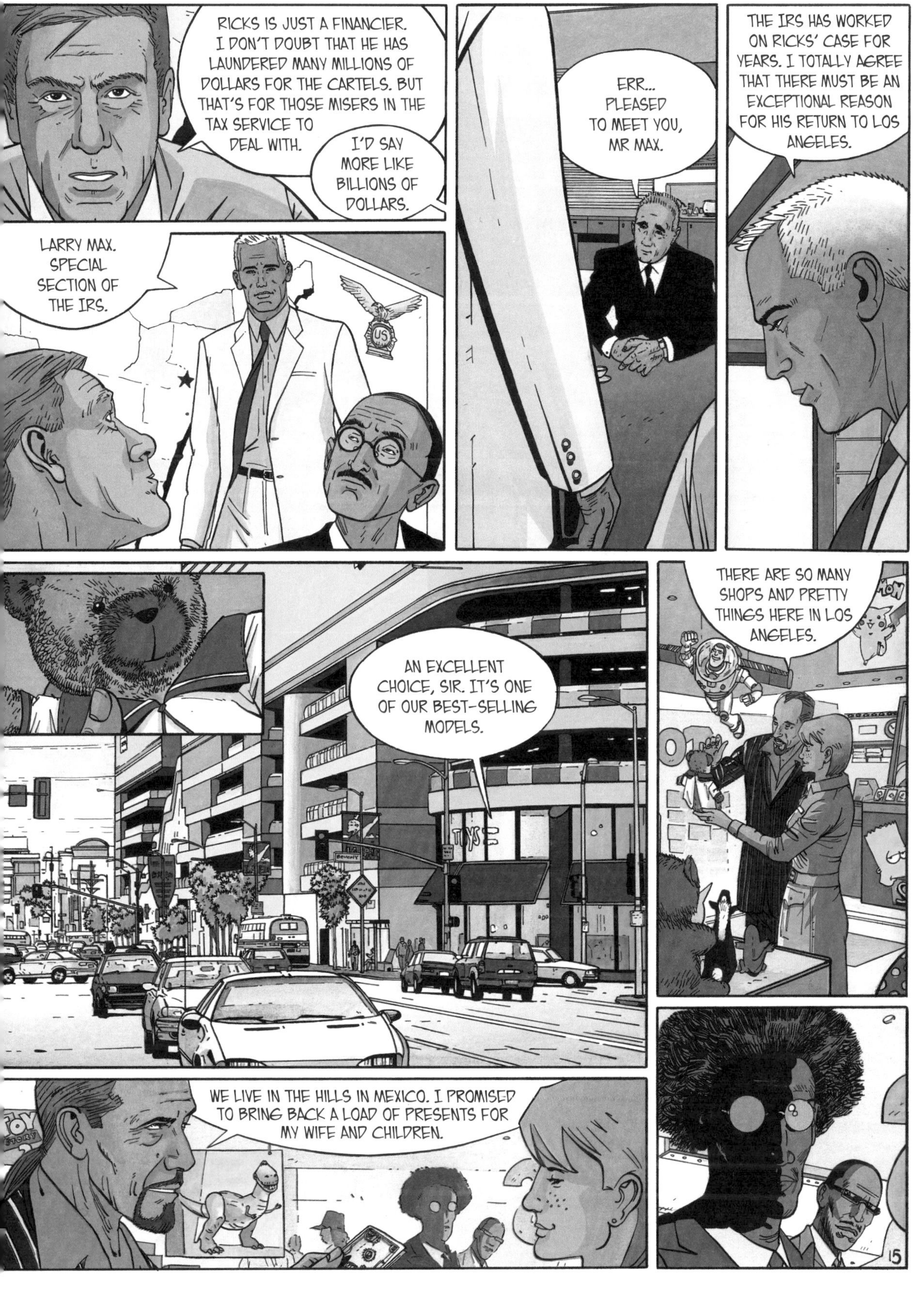
RICKS IS JUST A FINANCIER. I DON'T DOUBT THAT HE HAS LAUNDERED MANY MILLIONS OF DOLLARS FOR THE CARTELS. BUT THAT'S FOR THOSE MISERS IN THE TAX SERVICE TO DEAL WITH.
I'D SAY MORE LIKE BILLIONS OF DOLLARS.
LARRY MAX. SPECIAL SECTION OF THE IRS.
US
ERR... PLEASED TO MEET YOU, MR MAX.
THE IRS HAS WORKED ON RICKS' CASE FOR YEARS. I TOTALLY AGREE THAT THERE MUST BE AN EXCEPTIONAL REASON FOR HIS RETURN TO LOS ANGELES.
AN EXCELLENT CHOICE, SIR. IT'S ONE OF OUR BEST-SELLING MODELS.
TOYS
THERE ARE SO MANY SHOPS AND PRETTY THINGS HERE IN LOS ANGELES.
WE LIVE IN THE HILLS IN MEXICO. I PROMISED TO BRING BACK A LOAD OF PRESENTS FOR MY WIFE AND CHILDREN.
15

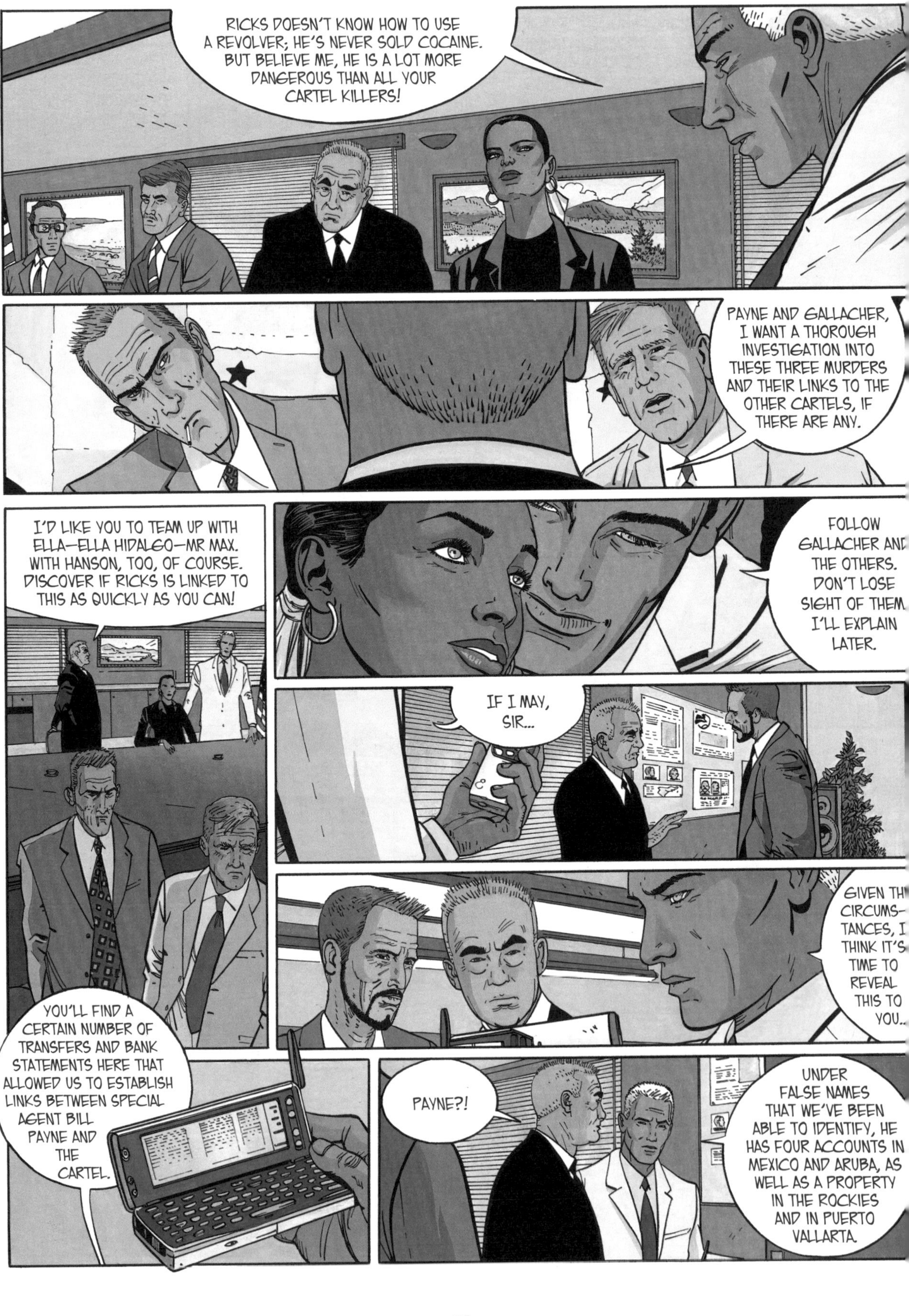
RICKS DOESN'T KNOW HOW TO USE A REVOLVER; HE'S NEVER SOLD COCAINE. BUT BELIEVE ME, HE IS A LOT MORE DANGEROUS THAN ALL YOUR CARTEL KILLERS!
PAYNE AND GALLACHER, I WANT A THOROUGH INVESTIGATION INTO THESE THREE MURDERS AND THEIR LINKS TO THE OTHER CARTELS, IF THERE ARE ANY.
I'D LIKE YOU TO TEAM UP WITH ELLA—ELLA HIDALGO—MR MAX. WITH HANSON, TOO, OF COURSE. DISCOVER IF RICKS IS LINKED TO THIS AS QUICKLY AS YOU CAN!
FOLLOW GALLACHER AND THE OTHERS. DON'T LOSE SIGHT OF THEM. I'LL EXPLAIN LATER.
IF I MAY, SIR...
GIVEN THE CIRCUMSTANCES, I THINK IT'S TIME TO REVEAL THIS TO YOU...
YOU'LL FIND A CERTAIN NUMBER OF TRANSFERS AND BANK STATEMENTS HERE THAT ALLOWED US TO ESTABLISH LINKS BETWEEN SPECIAL AGENT BILL PAYNE AND THE CARTEL.
PAYNE?!
UNDER FALSE NAMES THAT WE'VE BEEN ABLE TO IDENTIFY, HE HAS FOUR ACCOUNTS IN MEXICO AND ARUBA, AS WELL AS A PROPERTY IN THE ROCKIES AND IN PUERTO VALLARTA.

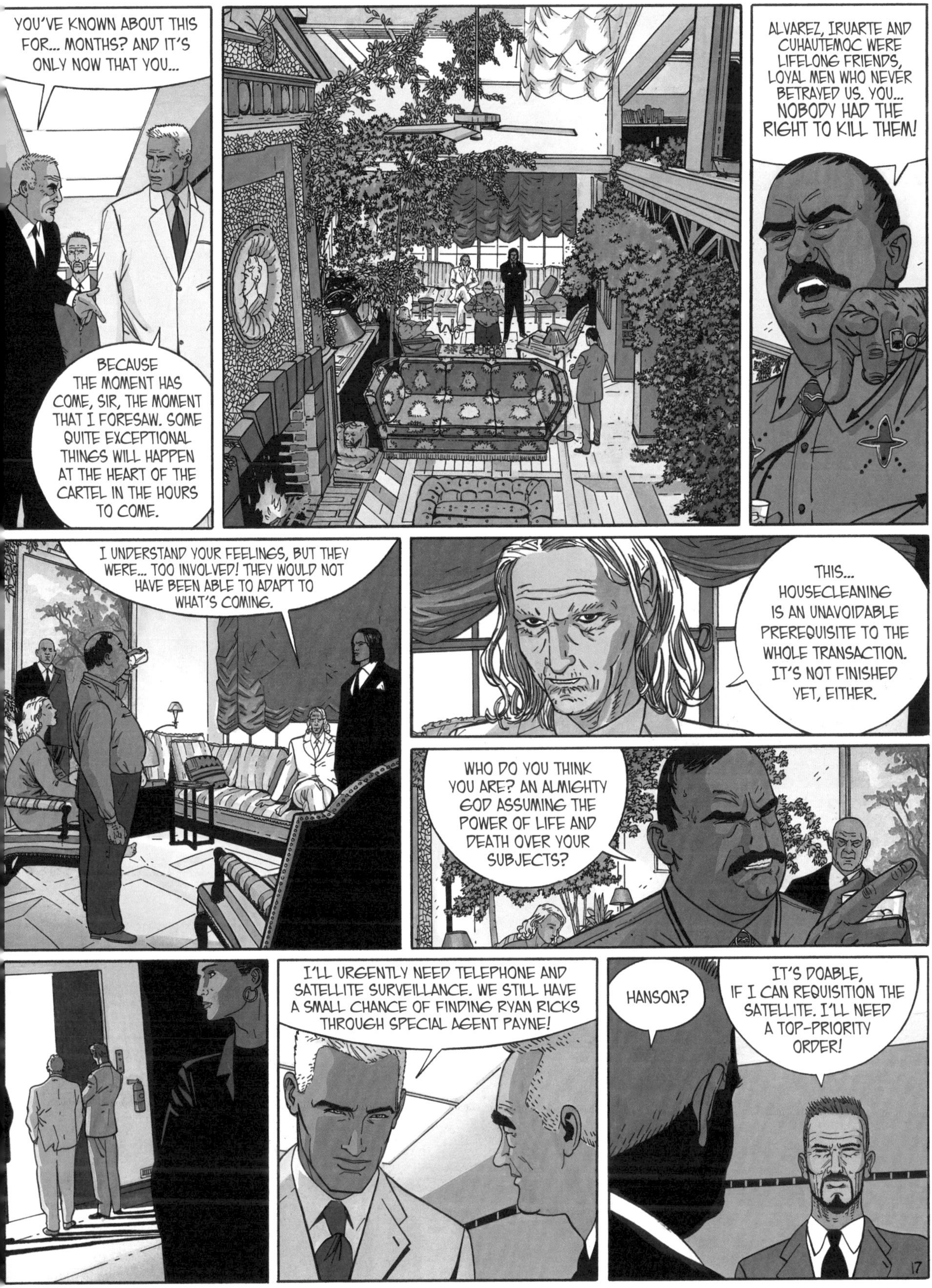
YOU'VE KNOWN ABOUT THIS FOR... MONTHS? AND IT'S ONLY NOW THAT YOU...
BECAUSE THE MOMENT HAS COME, SIR, THE MOMENT THAT I FORESAW. SOME QUITE EXCEPTIONAL THINGS WILL HAPPEN AT THE HEART OF THE CARTEL IN THE HOURS TO COME.
ALVAREZ, IRUARTE AND CUHAUTEMOC WERE LIFELONG FRIENDS, LOYAL MEN WHO NEVER BETRAYED US. YOU... NOBODY HAD THE RIGHT TO KILL THEM!
I UNDERSTAND YOUR FEELINGS, BUT THEY WERE... TOO INVOLVED! THEY WOULD NOT HAVE BEEN ABLE TO ADAPT TO WHAT'S COMING.
THIS... HOUSECLEANING IS AN UNAVOIDABLE PREREQUISITE TO THE WHOLE TRANSACTION. IT'S NOT FINISHED YET, EITHER.
WHO DO YOU THINK YOU ARE? AN ALMIGHTY GOD ASSUMING THE POWER OF LIFE AND DEATH OVER YOUR SUBJECTS?
I'LL URGENTLY NEED TELEPHONE AND SATELLITE SURVEILLANCE. WE STILL HAVE A SMALL CHANCE OF FINDING RYAN RICKS THROUGH SPECIAL AGENT PAYNE!
HANSON?
IT'S DOABLE, IF I CAN REQUISITION THE SATELLITE. I'LL NEED A TOP-PRIORITY ORDER!
17

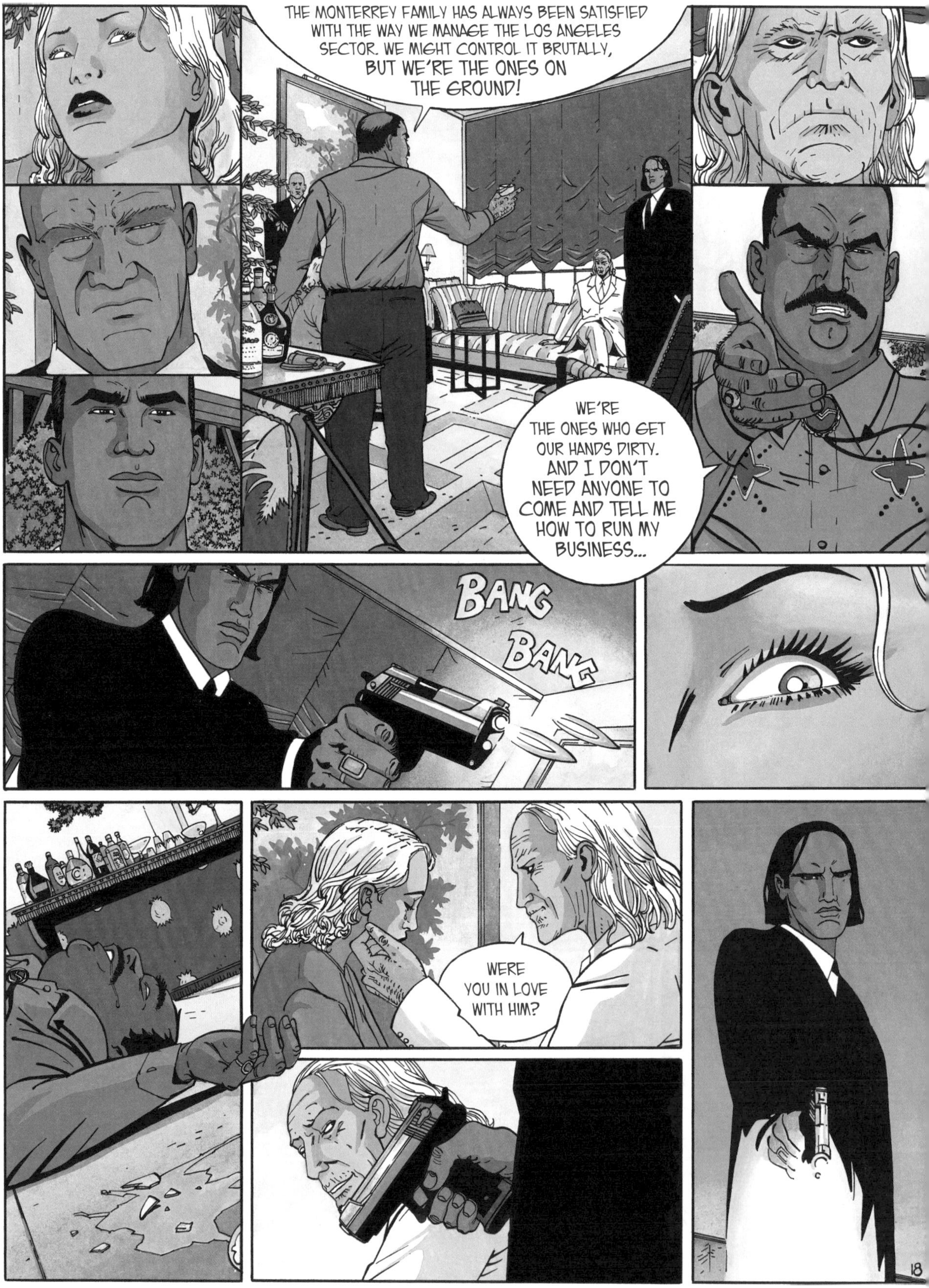
THE MONTERREY FAMILY HAS ALWAYS BEEN SATISFIED WITH THE WAY WE MANAGE THE LOS ANGELES SECTOR. WE MIGHT CONTROL IT BRUTALLY, BUT WE'RE THE ONES ON THE GROUND!
WE'RE THE ONES WHO GET OUR HANDS DIRTY. AND I DON'T NEED ANYONE TO COME AND TELL ME HOW TO RUN MY BUSINESS...
BANG
BANG
WERE YOU IN LOVE WITH HIM?
18

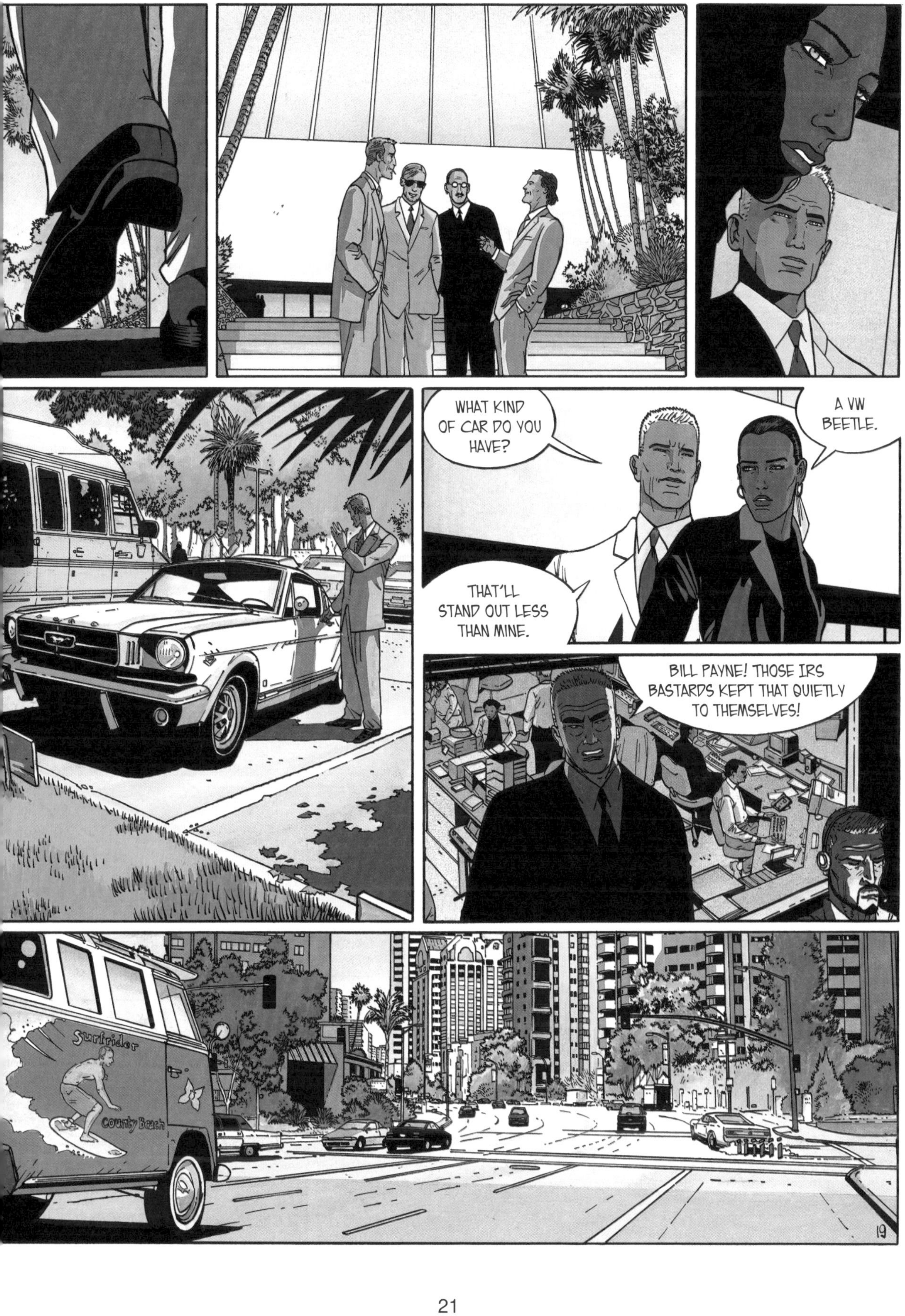
WHAT KIND OF CAR DO YOU HAVE?
A VW BEETLE.
THAT'LL STAND OUT LESS THAN MINE.
BILL PAYNE! THOSE IRS BASTARDS KEPT THAT QUIETLY TO THEMSELVES!
Surfrider
County Beach

SATELLITE LINK IN... TWO MINUTES, TWENTY-FOUR SECONDS!

HE'S SLOWING DOWN. I THINK WE CAN START.

OK. WILTSHIRE BOULEVARD AND HAMPTON AVENUE INTERSECTION. PUBLIC TELEPHONE.

WILTSHIRE-HAMPTON INTERSECTION. WE'RE ON IT...

... BLUE ICE, YES. WITH ONE OF THOSE IRS CROOKS...

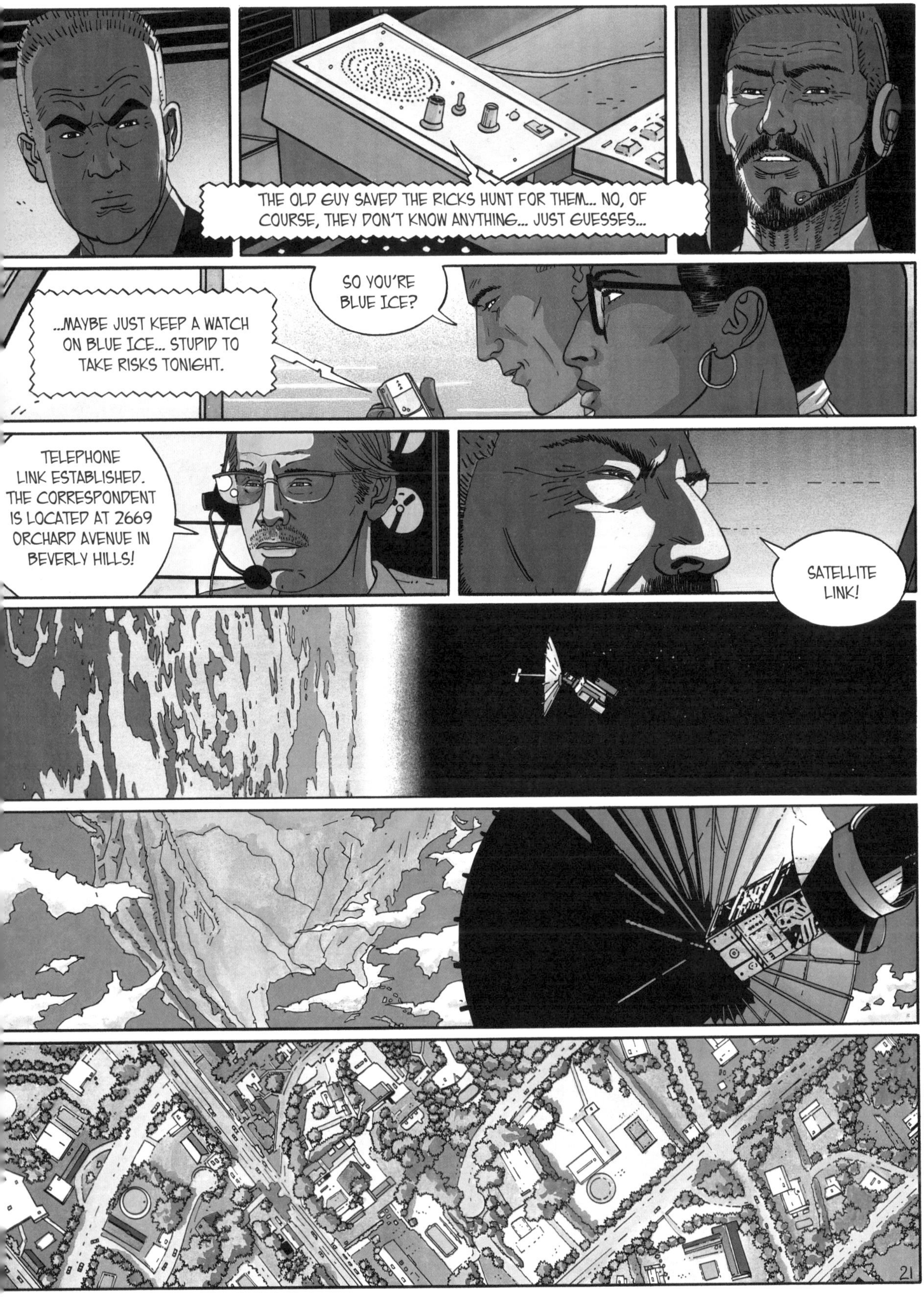
THE OLD GUY SAVED THE RICKS HUNT FOR THEM... NO, OF COURSE, THEY DON'T KNOW ANYTHING... JUST GUESSES...
...MAYBE JUST KEEP A WATCH ON BLUE ICE... STUPID TO TAKE RISKS TONIGHT.
SO YOU'RE BLUE ICE?
TELEPHONE LINK ESTABLISHED. THE CORRESPONDENT IS LOCATED AT 2669 ORCHARD AVENUE IN BEVERLY HILLS!
SATELLITE LINK!
21

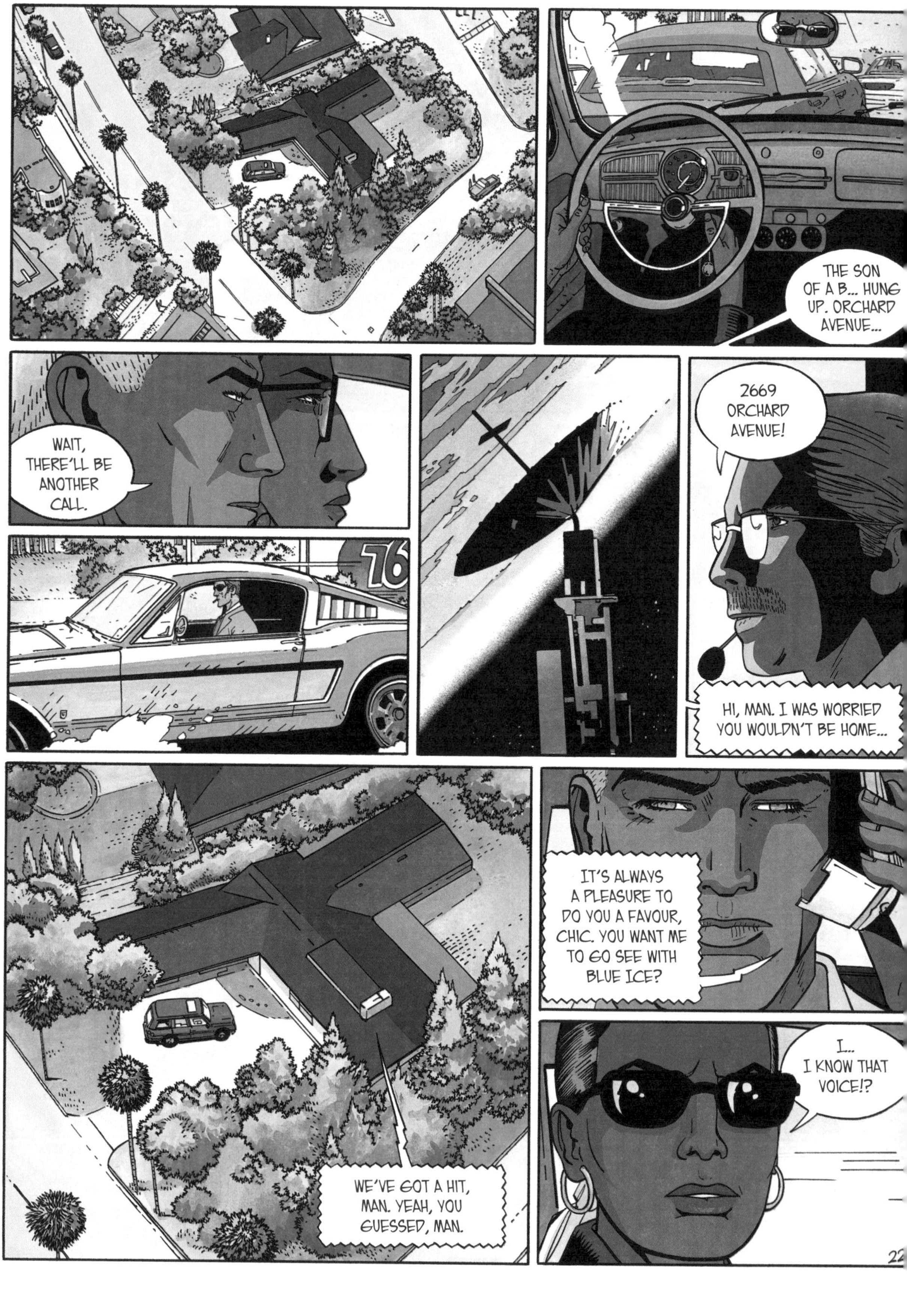
THE SON OF A B... HUNG UP. ORCHARD AVENUE...
WAIT, THERE'LL BE ANOTHER CALL.
76
2669 ORCHARD AVENUE!
HI, MAN. I WAS WORRIED YOU WOULDN'T BE HOME...
WE'VE GOT A HIT, MAN. YEAH, YOU GUESSED, MAN.
IT'S ALWAYS A PLEASURE TO DO YOU A FAVOUR, CHIC. YOU WANT ME TO GO SEE WITH BLUE ICE?
I... I KNOW THAT VOICE!?
22

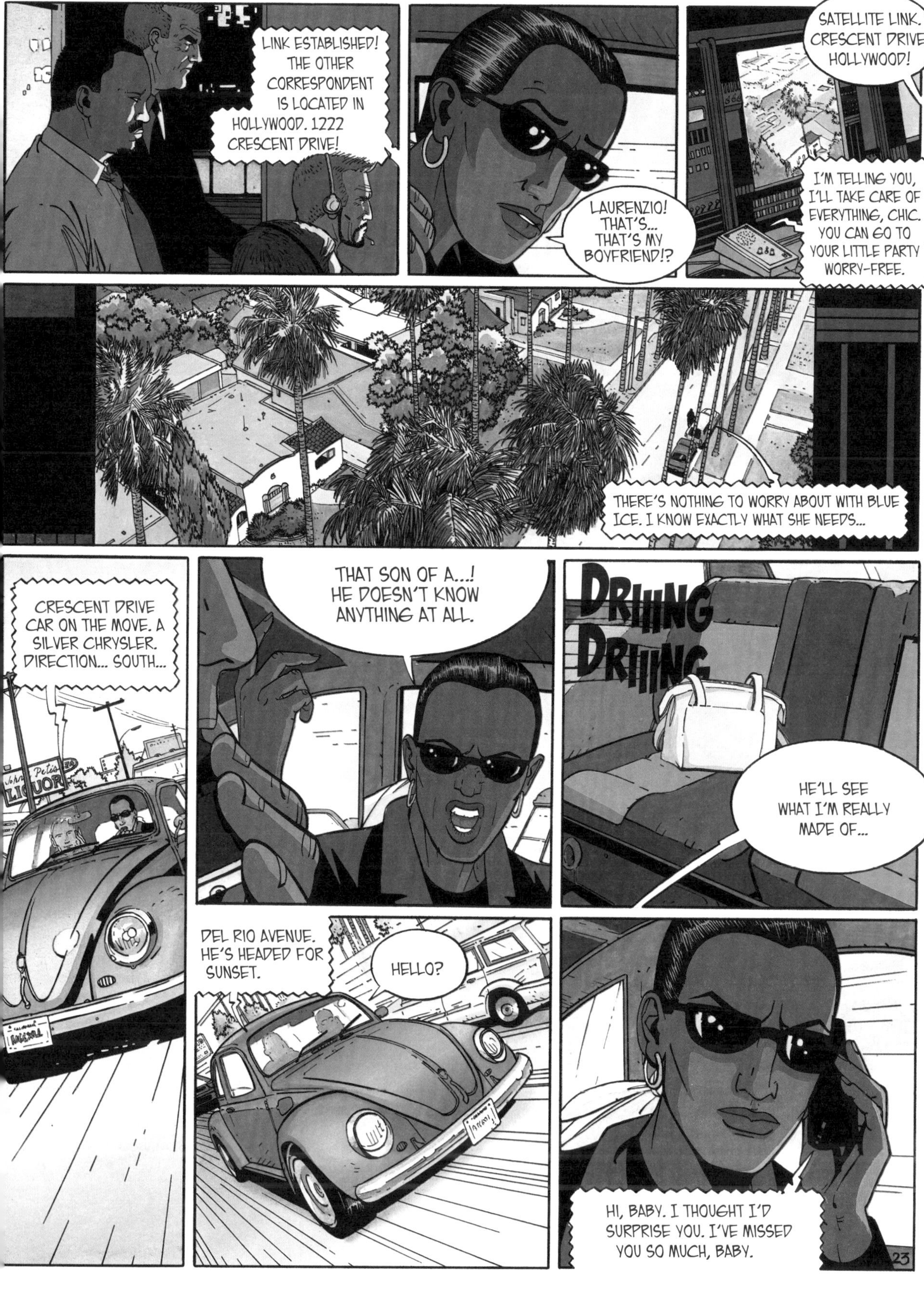
LINK ESTABLISHED! THE OTHER CORRESPONDENT IS LOCATED IN HOLLYWOOD. 1222 CRESCENT DRIVE!
LAURENZIO! THAT'S... THAT'S MY BOYFRIEND!?
SATELLITE LINK. CRESCENT DRIVE, HOLLYWOOD!
I'M TELLING YOU, I'LL TAKE CARE OF EVERYTHING, CHIC. YOU CAN GO TO YOUR LITTLE PARTY WORRY-FREE.
THERE'S NOTHING TO WORRY ABOUT WITH BLUE ICE. I KNOW EXACTLY WHAT SHE NEEDS...
CRESCENT DRIVE CAR ON THE MOVE. A SILVER CHRYSLER. DIRECTION... SOUTH...
LIQUOR
THAT SON OF A...! HE DOESN'T KNOW ANYTHING AT ALL.
DRIIING
DRIIING
HE'LL SEE WHAT I'M REALLY MADE OF...
DEL RIO AVENUE. HE'S HEADED FOR SUNSET.
HELLO?
HI, BABY. I THOUGHT I'D SURPRISE YOU. I'VE MISSED YOU SO MUCH, BABY.
23

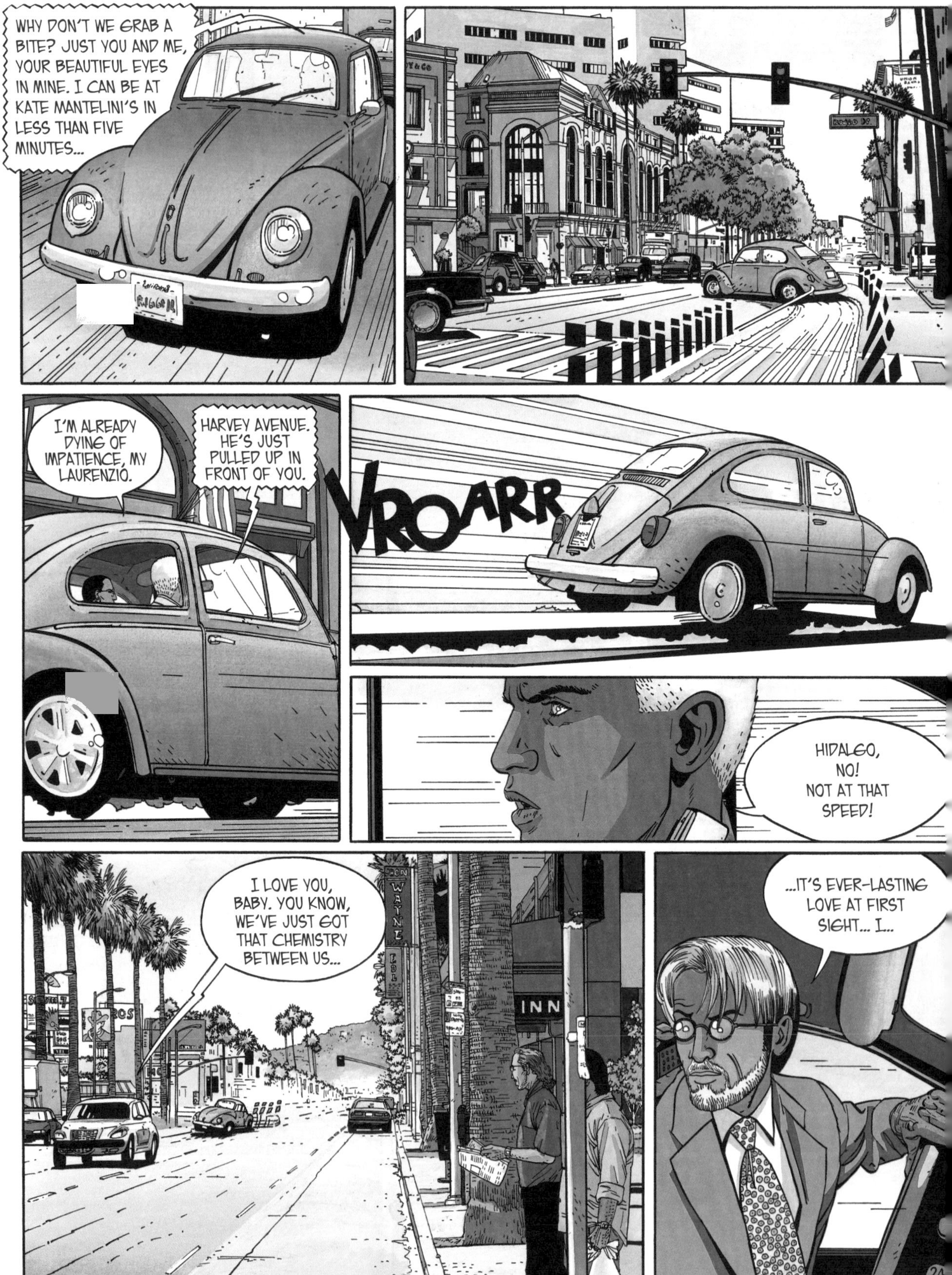
WHY DON'T WE GRAB A BITE? JUST YOU AND ME, YOUR BEAUTIFUL EYES IN MINE. I CAN BE AT KATE MANTELINI'S IN LESS THAN FIVE MINUTES...
I'M ALREADY DYING OF IMPATIENCE, MY LAURENZIO.
HARVEY AVENUE. HE'S JUST PULLED UP IN FRONT OF YOU.
VROARR
HIDALGO, NO! NOT AT THAT SPEED!
I LOVE YOU, BABY. YOU KNOW, WE'VE JUST GOT THAT CHEMISTRY BETWEEN US...
INN
...IT'S EVER-LASTING LOVE AT FIRST SIGHT... I...

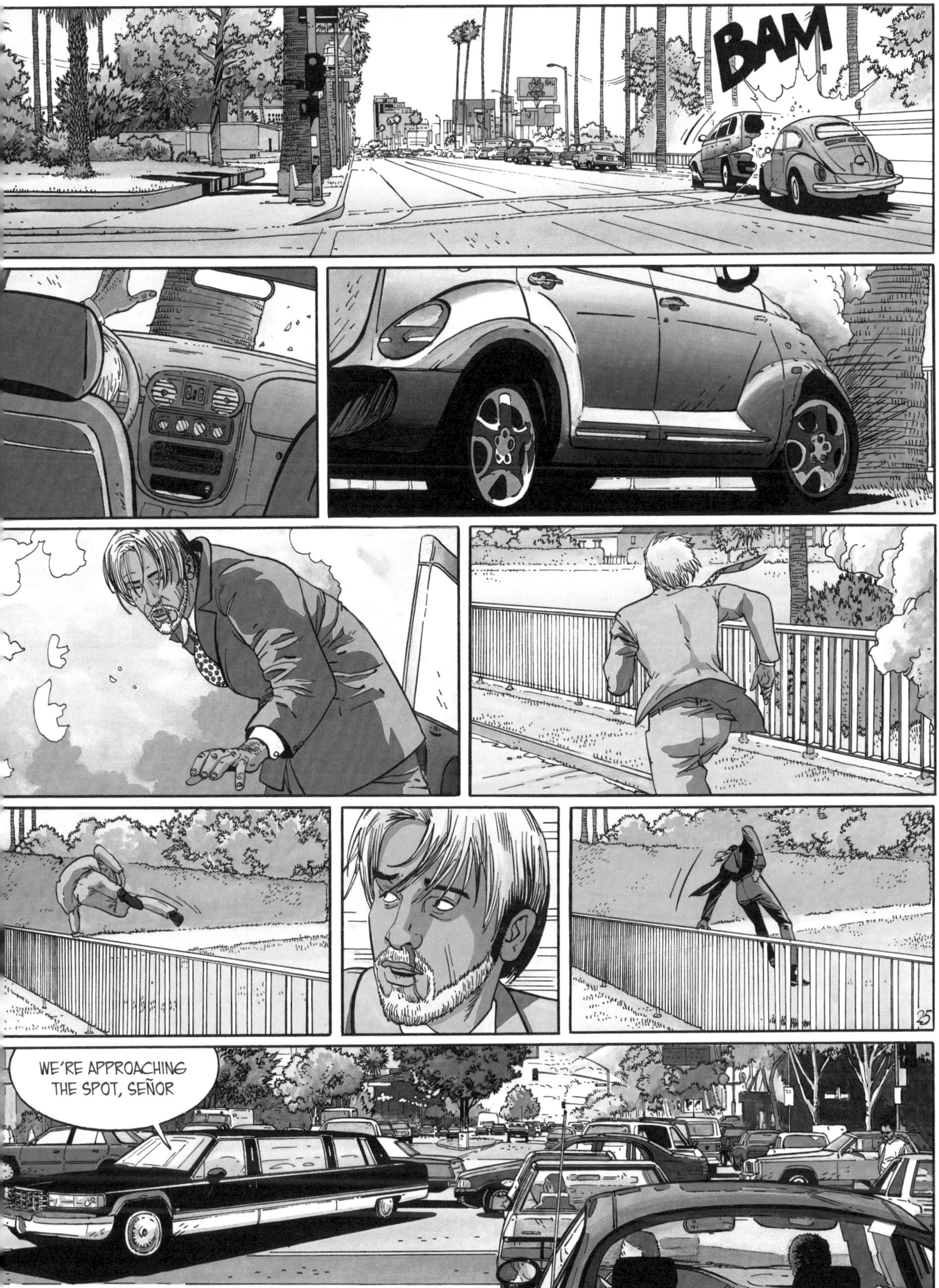
BAM
WE'RE APPROACHING THE SPOT, SEÑOR

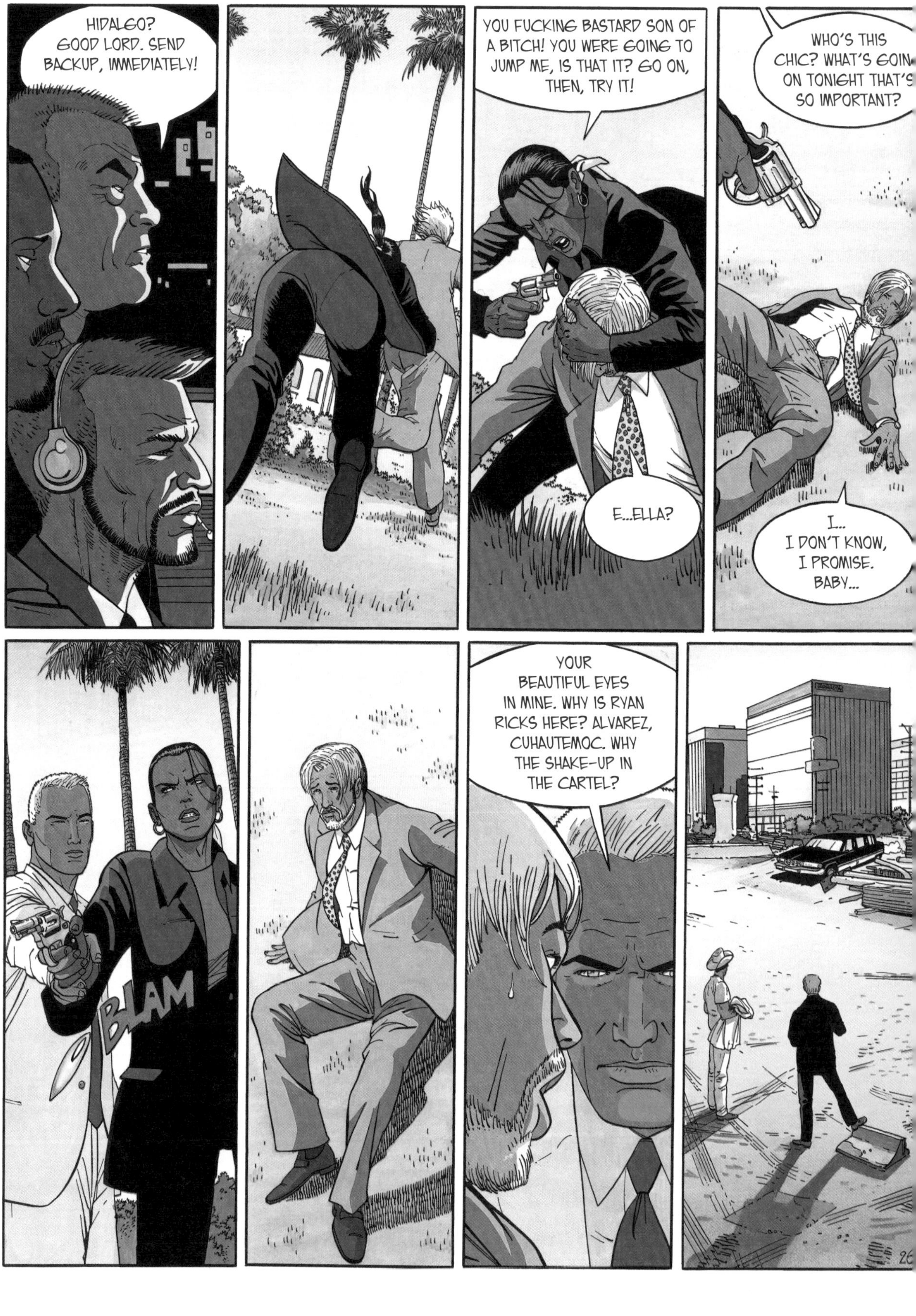
HIDALGO? GOOD LORD. SEND BACKUP, IMMEDIATELY!
YOU FUCKING BASTARD SON OF A BITCH! YOU WERE GOING TO JUMP ME, IS THAT IT? GO ON, THEN, TRY IT!
E...ELLA?
WHO'S THIS CHIC? WHAT'S GOIN ON TONIGHT THAT'S SO IMPORTANT?
I... I DON'T KNOW, I PROMISE. BABY...
BLAM
YOUR BEAUTIFUL EYES IN MINE. WHY IS RYAN RICKS HERE? ALVAREZ, CUHAUTEMOC. WHY THE SHAKE-UP IN THE CARTEL?
26

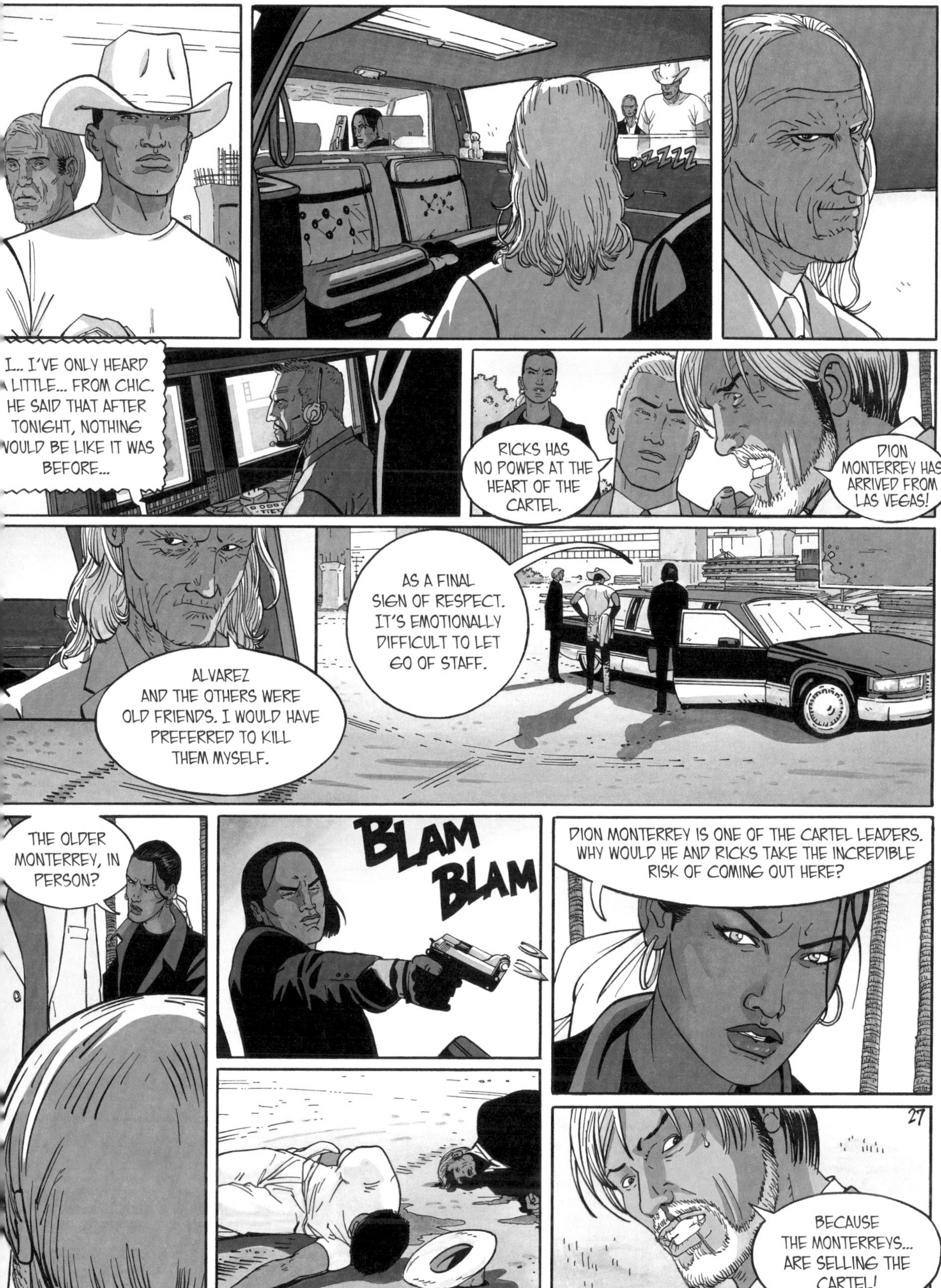
BZZZZ
I... I'VE ONLY HEARD A LITTLE... FROM CHIC. HE SAID THAT AFTER TONIGHT, NOTHING WOULD BE LIKE IT WAS BEFORE...
RICKS HAS NO POWER AT THE HEART OF THE CARTEL.
DION MONTERREY HAS ARRIVED FROM LAS VEGAS!
ALVAREZ AND THE OTHERS WERE OLD FRIENDS. I WOULD HAVE PREFERRED TO KILL THEM MYSELF.
AS A FINAL SIGN OF RESPECT. IT'S EMOTIONALLY DIFFICULT TO LET GO OF STAFF.
THE OLDER MONTERREY, IN PERSON?
BLAM BLAM
DION MONTERREY IS ONE OF THE CARTEL LEADERS. WHY WOULD HE AND RICKS TAKE THE INCREDIBLE RISK OF COMING OUT HERE?
27
BECAUSE THE MONTERREYS... ARE SELLING THE CARTEL!

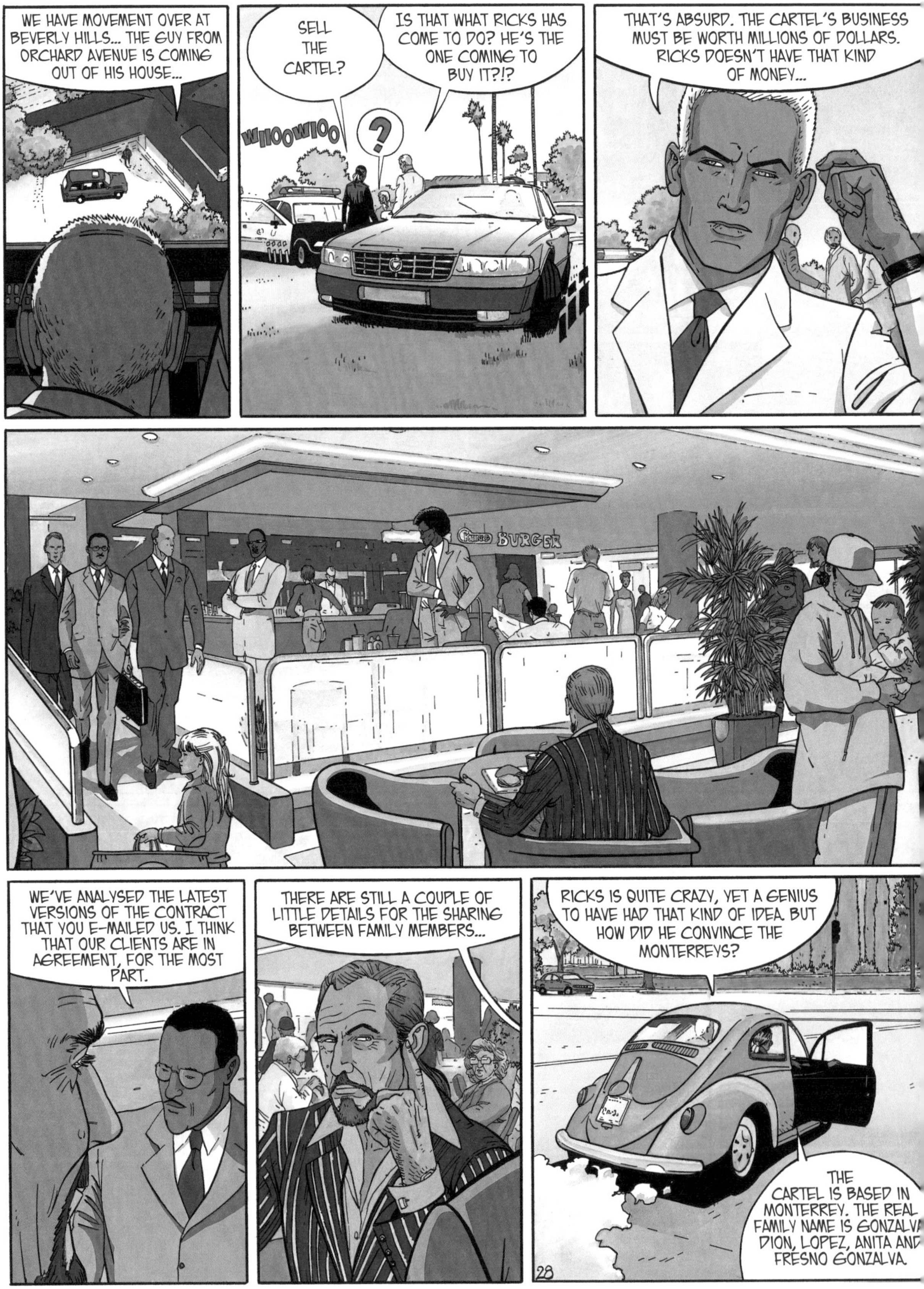
WE HAVE MOVEMENT OVER AT BEVERLY HILLS... THE GUY FROM ORCHARD AVENUE IS COMING OUT OF HIS HOUSE...
WIIOOWIOO
SELL THE CARTEL?
?
IS THAT WHAT RICKS HAS COME TO DO? HE'S THE ONE COMING TO BUY IT?!?
THAT'S ABSURD. THE CARTEL'S BUSINESS MUST BE WORTH MILLIONS OF DOLLARS. RICKS DOESN'T HAVE THAT KIND OF MONEY...
BURGER
WE'VE ANALYSED THE LATEST VERSIONS OF THE CONTRACT THAT YOU E-MAILED US. I THINK THAT OUR CLIENTS ARE IN AGREEMENT, FOR THE MOST PART.
THERE ARE STILL A COUPLE OF LITTLE DETAILS FOR THE SHARING BETWEEN FAMILY MEMBERS...
RICKS IS QUITE CRAZY, YET A GENIUS TO HAVE HAD THAT KIND OF IDEA. BUT HOW DID HE CONVINCE THE MONTERREYS?
THE CARTEL IS BASED IN MONTERREY. THE REAL FAMILY NAME IS GONZALVA DION, LOPEZ, ANITA AND FRESNO GONZALVA.
28

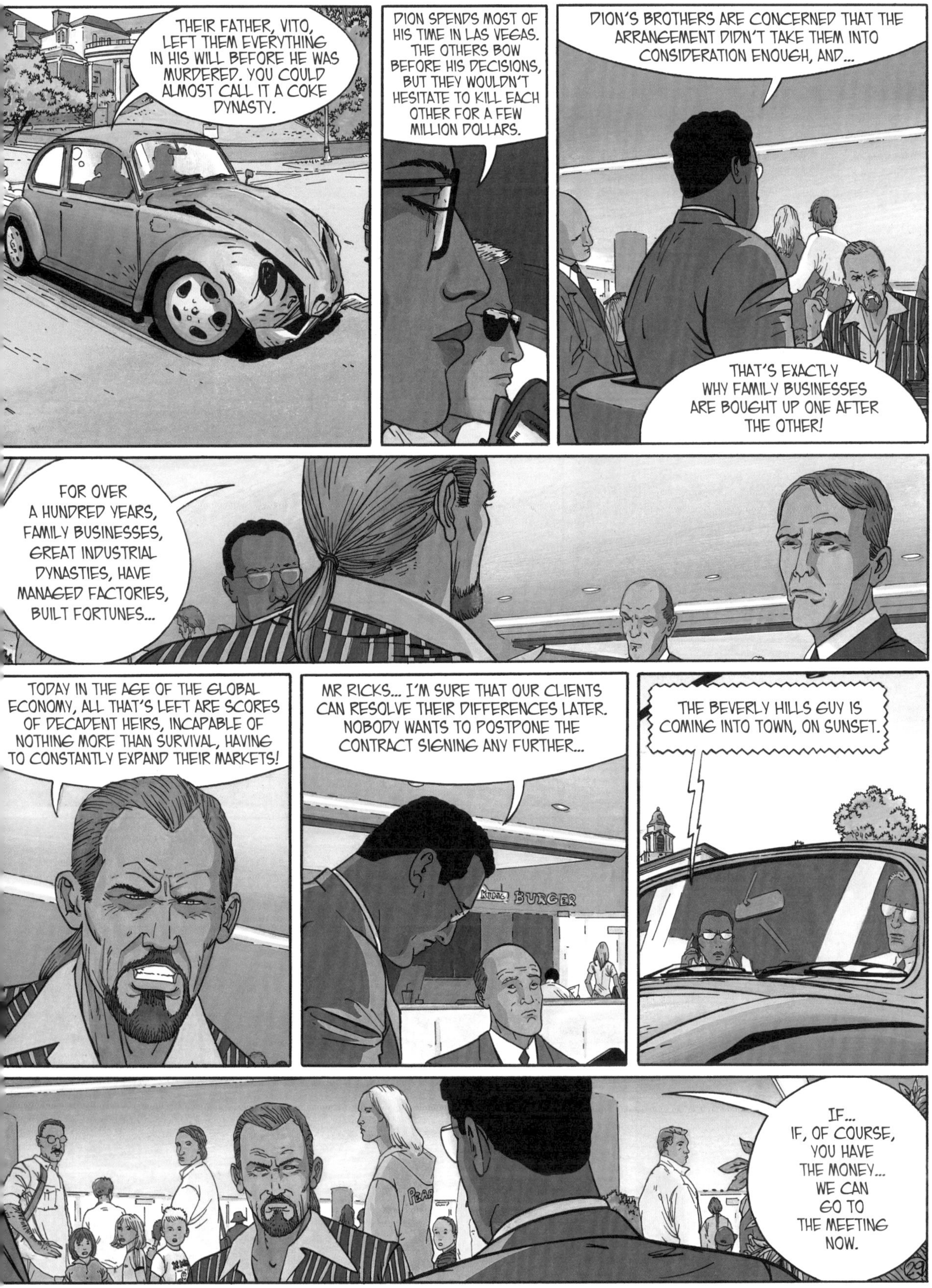
THEIR FATHER, VITO, LEFT THEM EVERYTHING IN HIS WILL BEFORE HE WAS MURDERED. YOU COULD ALMOST CALL IT A COKE DYNASTY.
DION SPENDS MOST OF HIS TIME IN LAS VEGAS. THE OTHERS BOW BEFORE HIS DECISIONS, BUT THEY WOULDN'T HESITATE TO KILL EACH OTHER FOR A FEW MILLION DOLLARS.
DION'S BROTHERS ARE CONCERNED THAT THE ARRANGEMENT DIDN'T TAKE THEM INTO CONSIDERATION ENOUGH, AND...
THAT'S EXACTLY WHY FAMILY BUSINESSES ARE BOUGHT UP ONE AFTER THE OTHER!
FOR OVER A HUNDRED YEARS, FAMILY BUSINESSES, GREAT INDUSTRIAL DYNASTIES, HAVE MANAGED FACTORIES, BUILT FORTUNES...
TODAY IN THE AGE OF THE GLOBAL ECONOMY, ALL THAT'S LEFT ARE SCORES OF DECADENT HEIRS, INCAPABLE OF NOTHING MORE THAN SURVIVAL, HAVING TO CONSTANTLY EXPAND THEIR MARKETS!
MR RICKS... I'M SURE THAT OUR CLIENTS CAN RESOLVE THEIR DIFFERENCES LATER. NOBODY WANTS TO POSTPONE THE CONTRACT SIGNING ANY FURTHER...
BURGER
THE BEVERLY HILLS GUY IS COMING INTO TOWN, ON SUNSET.
IF... IF, OF COURSE, YOU HAVE THE MONEY... WE CAN GO TO THE MEETING NOW.
29

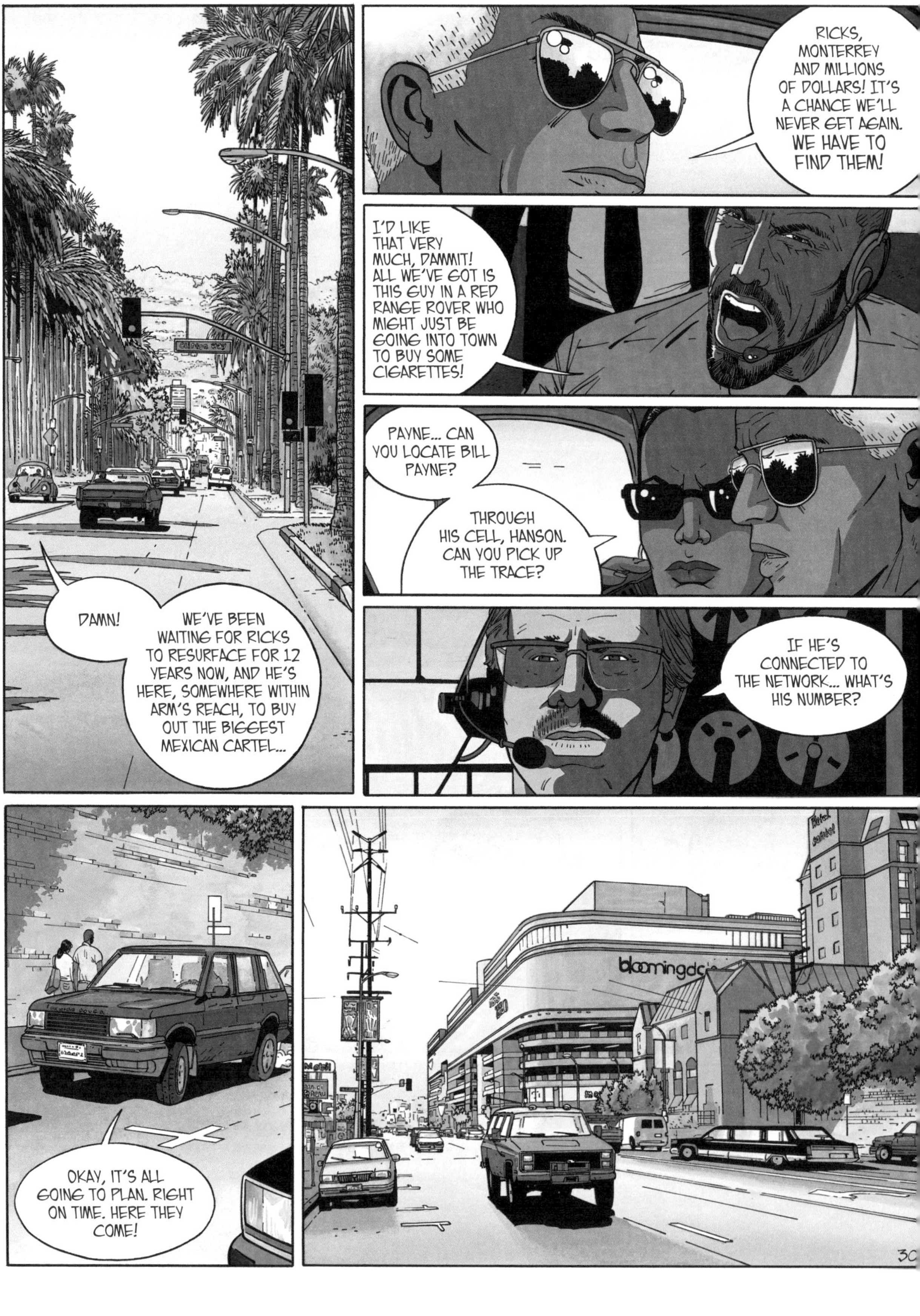
DAMN!
WE'VE BEEN WAITING FOR RICKS TO RESURFACE FOR 12 YEARS NOW, AND HE'S HERE, SOMEWHERE WITHIN ARM'S REACH, TO BUY OUT THE BIGGEST MEXICAN CARTEL...
RICKS, MONTERREY AND MILLIONS OF DOLLARS! IT'S A CHANCE WE'LL NEVER GET AGAIN. WE HAVE TO FIND THEM!
I'D LIKE THAT VERY MUCH, DAMMIT! ALL WE'VE GOT IS THIS GUY IN A RED RANGE ROVER WHO MIGHT JUST BE GOING INTO TOWN TO BUY SOME CIGARETTES!
PAYNE... CAN YOU LOCATE BILL PAYNE?
THROUGH HIS CELL, HANSON. CAN YOU PICK UP THE TRACE?
IF HE'S CONNECTED TO THE NETWORK... WHAT'S HIS NUMBER?
OKAY, IT'S ALL GOING TO PLAN. RIGHT ON TIME. HERE THEY COME!
bloomingda

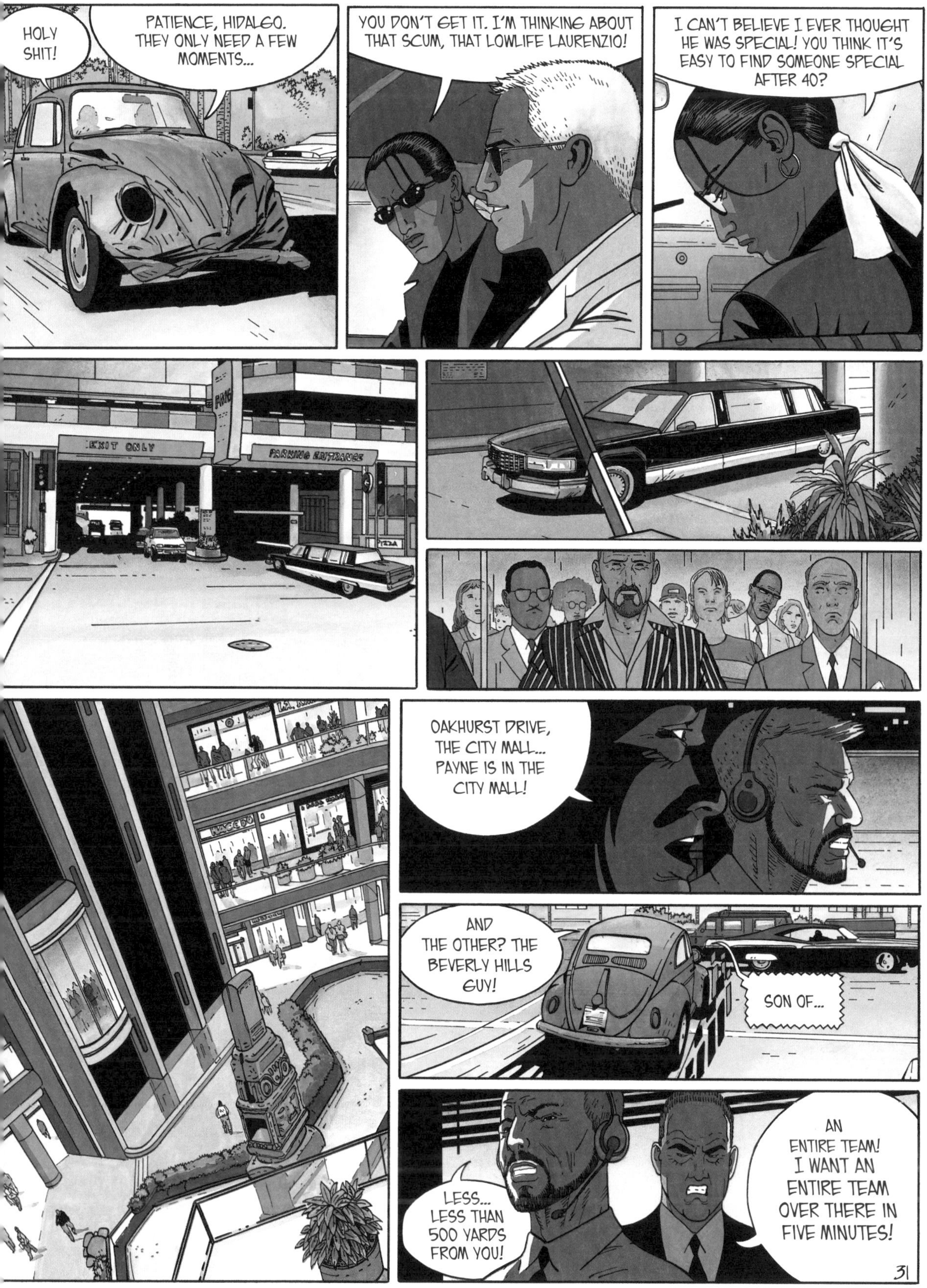
HOLY SHIT!
PATIENCE, HIDALGO. THEY ONLY NEED A FEW MOMENTS...
YOU DON'T GET IT. I'M THINKING ABOUT THAT SCUM, THAT LOWLIFE LAURENZIO!
I CAN'T BELIEVE I EVER THOUGHT HE WAS SPECIAL! YOU THINK IT'S EASY TO FIND SOMEONE SPECIAL AFTER 40?
EXIT ONLY
PARKING ENTRANCE
OAKHURST DRIVE, THE CITY MALL... PAYNE IS IN THE CITY MALL!
AND THE OTHER? THE BEVERLY HILLS GUY!
SON OF...
LESS... LESS THAN 500 YARDS FROM YOU!
AN ENTIRE TEAM! I WANT AN ENTIRE TEAM OVER THERE IN FIVE MINUTES!
31

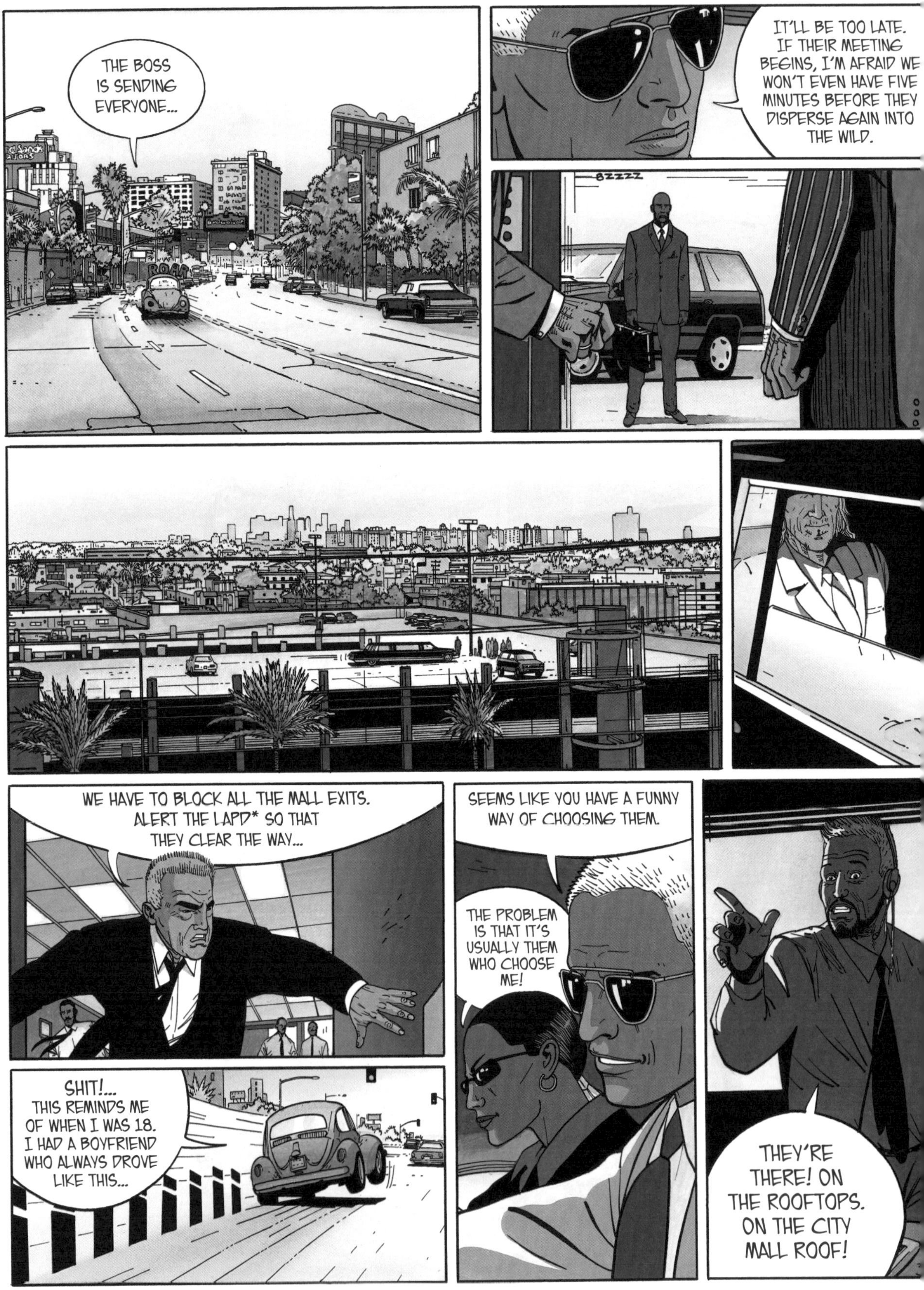
THE BOSS IS SENDING EVERYONE...
ROAR
IT'LL BE TOO LATE. IF THEIR MEETING BEGINS, I'M AFRAID WE WON'T EVEN HAVE FIVE MINUTES BEFORE THEY DISPERSE AGAIN INTO THE WILD.
BZZZZ
WE HAVE TO BLOCK ALL THE MALL EXITS. ALERT THE LAPD* SO THAT THEY CLEAR THE WAY...
SHIT!... THIS REMINDS ME OF WHEN I WAS 18. I HAD A BOYFRIEND WHO ALWAYS DROVE LIKE THIS...
SEEMS LIKE YOU HAVE A FUNNY WAY OF CHOOSING THEM.
THE PROBLEM IS THAT IT'S USUALLY THEM WHO CHOOSE ME!
THEY'RE THERE! ON THE ROOFTOPS. ON THE CITY MALL ROOF!

* LOS ANGELES POLICE DEPARTMENT

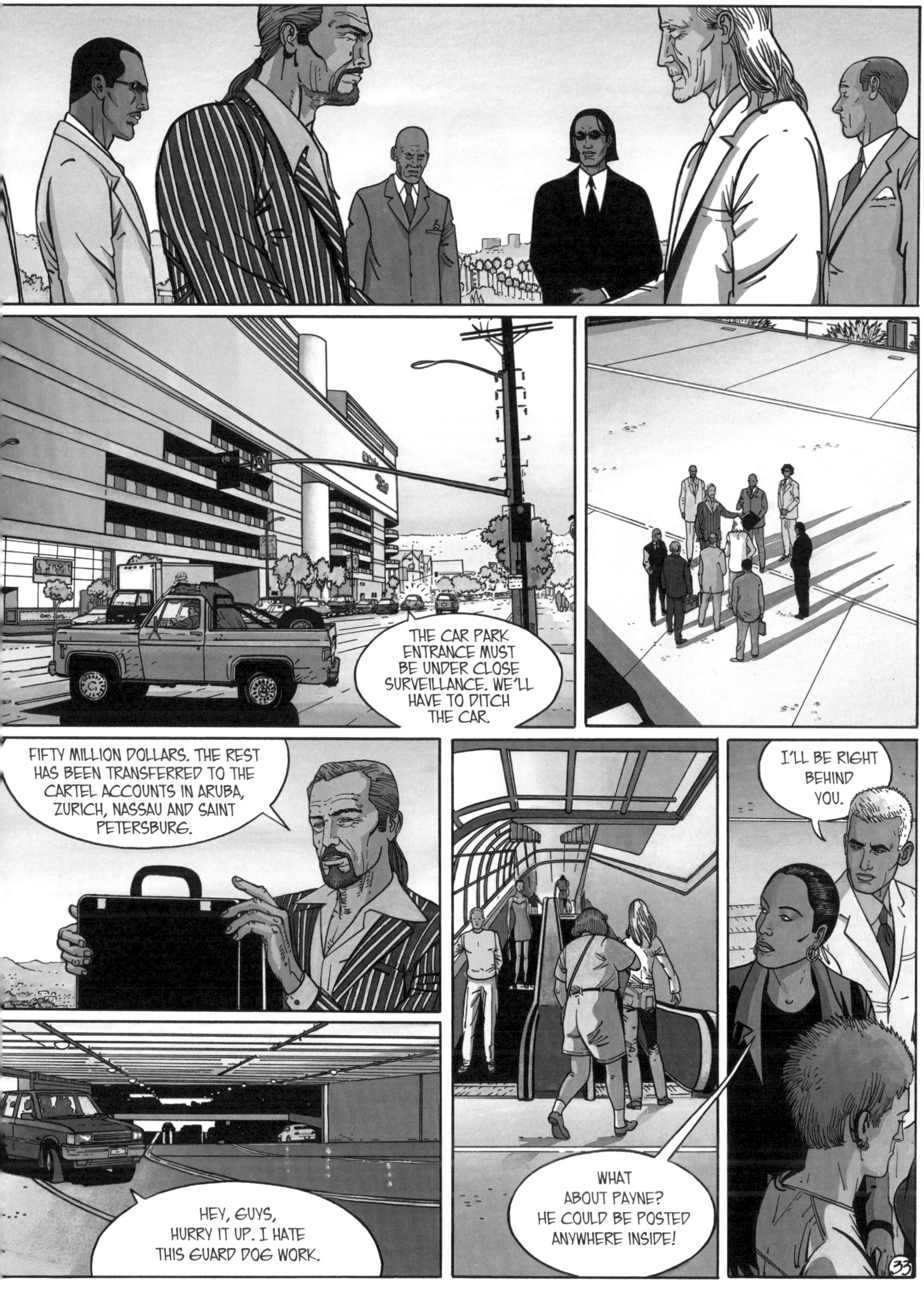
THE CAR PARK ENTRANCE MUST BE UNDER CLOSE SURVEILLANCE. WE'LL HAVE TO DITCH THE CAR.
FIFTY MILLION DOLLARS. THE REST HAS BEEN TRANSFERRED TO THE CARTEL ACCOUNTS IN ARUBA, ZURICH, NASSAU AND SAINT PETERSBURG.
HEY, GUYS, HURRY IT UP. I HATE THIS GUARD DOG WORK.
WHAT ABOUT PAYNE? HE COULD BE POSTED ANYWHERE INSIDE!
I'LL BE RIGHT BEHIND YOU.
33

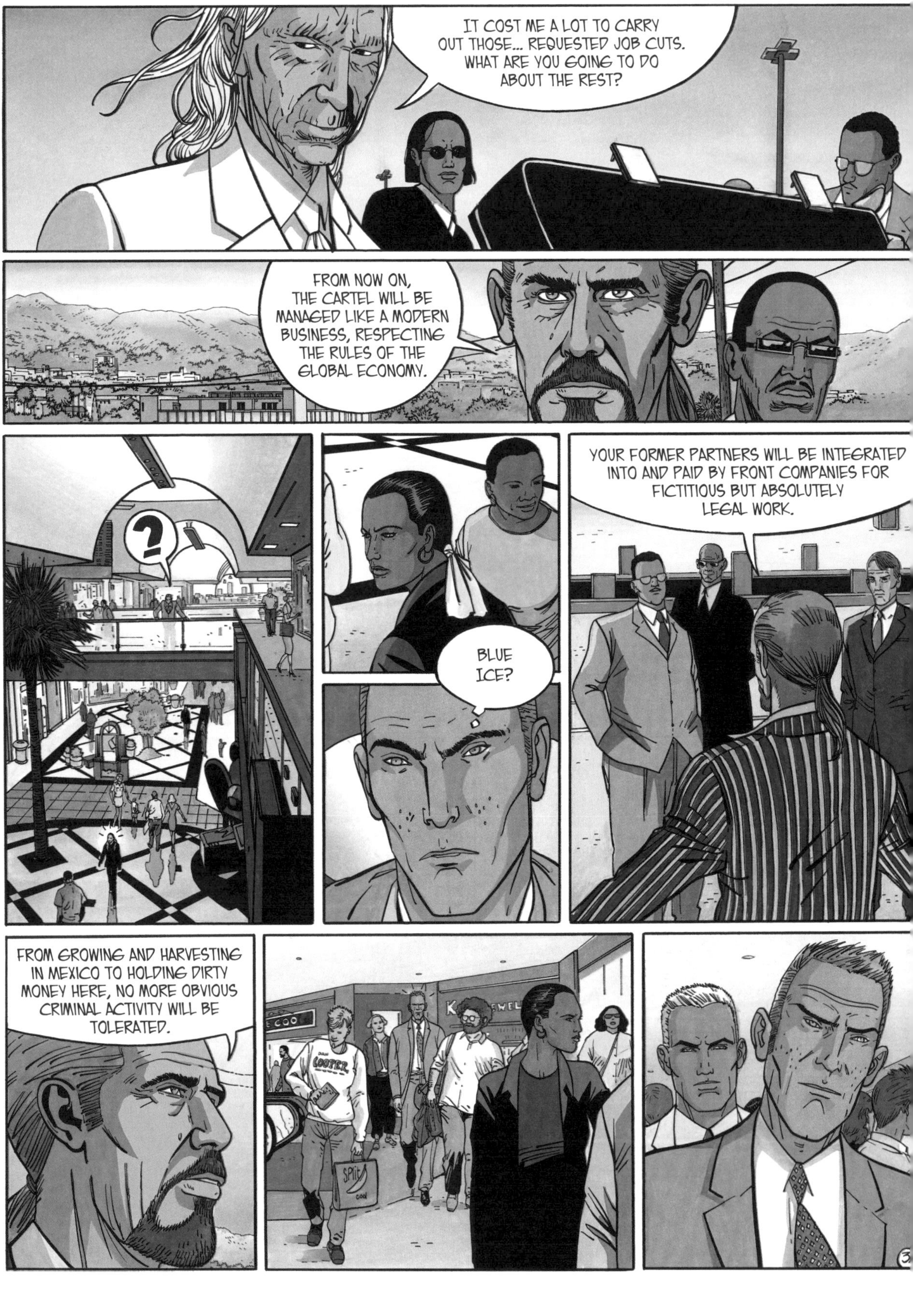
IT COST ME A LOT TO CARRY OUT THOSE... REQUESTED JOB CUTS. WHAT ARE YOU GOING TO DO ABOUT THE REST?
FROM NOW ON, THE CARTEL WILL BE MANAGED LIKE A MODERN BUSINESS, RESPECTING THE RULES OF THE GLOBAL ECONOMY.
?
YOUR FORMER PARTNERS WILL BE INTEGRATED INTO AND PAID BY FRONT COMPANIES FOR FICTITIOUS BUT ABSOLUTELY LEGAL WORK.
BLUE ICE?
FROM GROWING AND HARVESTING IN MEXICO TO HOLDING DIRTY MONEY HERE, NO MORE OBVIOUS CRIMINAL ACTIVITY WILL BE TOLERATED.

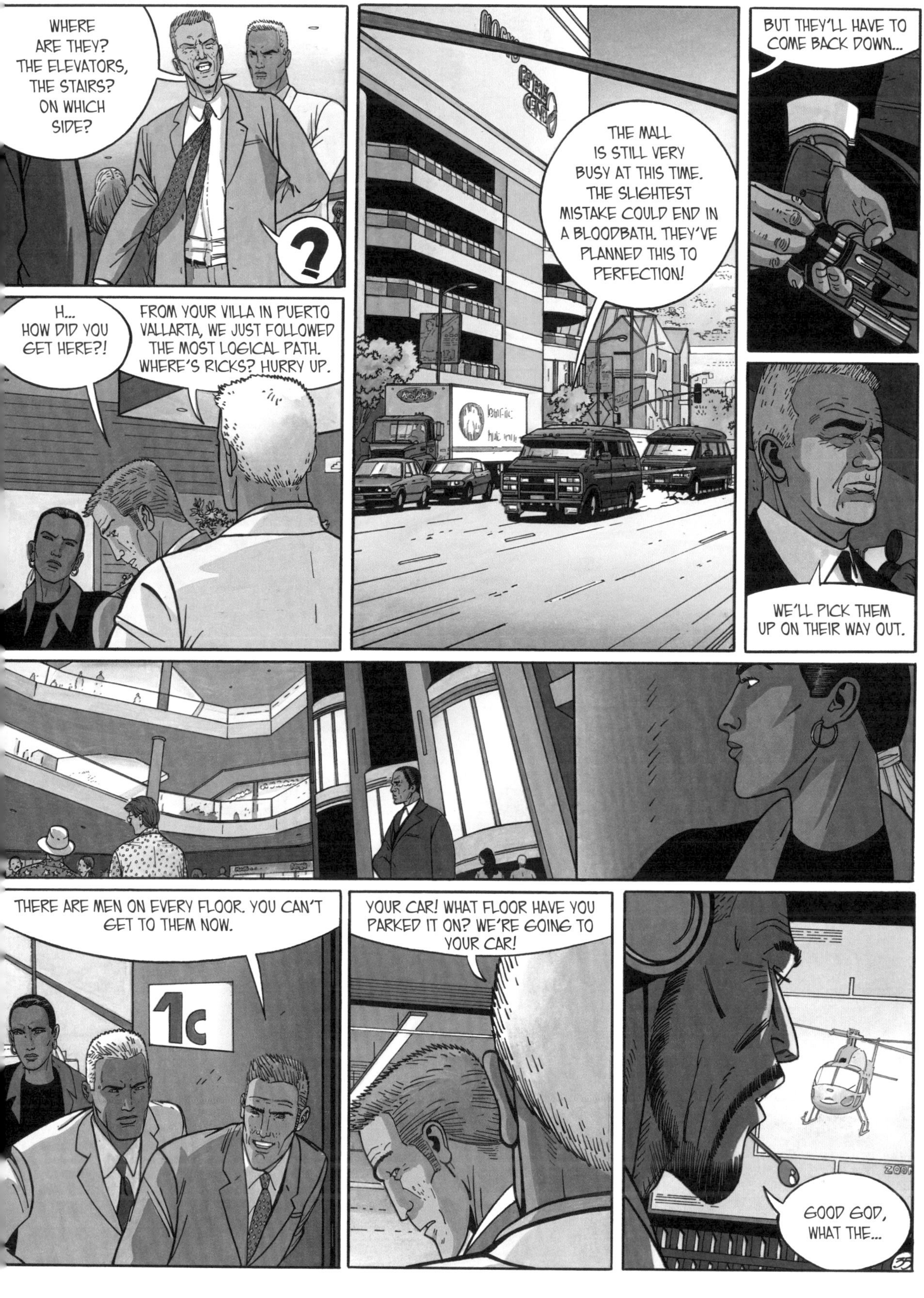
WHERE ARE THEY? THE ELEVATORS, THE STAIRS? ON WHICH SIDE?
?
THE MALL IS STILL VERY BUSY AT THIS TIME. THE SLIGHTEST MISTAKE COULD END IN A BLOODBATH. THEY'VE PLANNED THIS TO PERFECTION!
BUT THEY'LL HAVE TO COME BACK DOWN...
WE'LL PICK THEM UP ON THEIR WAY OUT.
H... HOW DID YOU GET HERE?!
FROM YOUR VILLA IN PUERTO VALLARTA, WE JUST FOLLOWED THE MOST LOGICAL PATH. WHERE'S RICKS? HURRY UP.
1c
THERE ARE MEN ON EVERY FLOOR. YOU CAN'T GET TO THEM NOW.
YOUR CAR! WHAT FLOOR HAVE YOU PARKED IT ON? WE'RE GOING TO YOUR CAR!
GOOD GOD, WHAT THE...

DRUG DEALING IN THE STREETS, SETTLING SCORES... IN THE FUTURE, ALL THAT WILL BE CARRIED OUT BY TEAMS OF SUBCONTRACTORS.

FRRFRRFRR

FRRFRRFR

WE'VE ALREADY STARTED THE BIDDING ON THAT.

PAYNE?

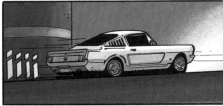

WHAT IS IT, PAYNE? YOU SEEN SOMETHING?

THE ONLY THING I CARE ABOUT... IS SUPPLYING THE DEMAND, DEVELOPING THE MARKETS.

AND BELIEVE ME, COKE IS AN ECONOMIC SECTOR THAT'S JUST WAITING TO EXPLODE!

IT'S ALREADY TOO LATE. THE CARTEL HAS COMPLETELY FOOLED YOU...

WHERE WAS IT? WAS IT IN "PULP FICTION" WHERE THAT SHOT WENT OFF ON ITS OWN?

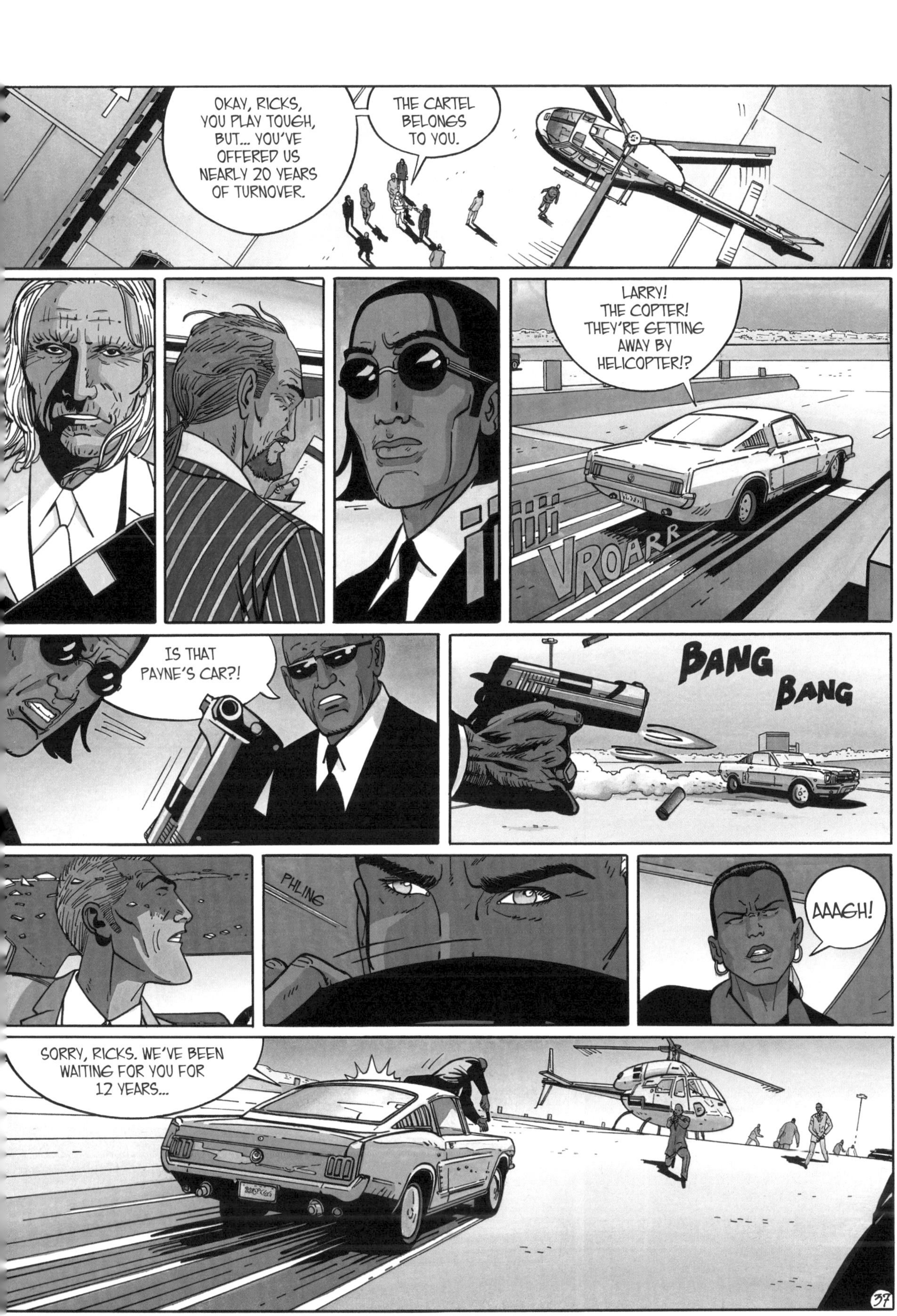
OKAY, RICKS, YOU PLAY TOUGH, BUT... YOU'VE OFFERED US NEARLY 20 YEARS OF TURNOVER.
THE CARTEL BELONGS TO YOU.
LARRY! THE COPTER! THEY'RE GETTING AWAY BY HELICOPTER!?
VROARR
IS THAT PAYNE'S CAR?!
BANG
BANG
PHLING
AAAGH!
SORRY, RICKS. WE'VE BEEN WAITING FOR YOU FOR 12 YEARS...
37

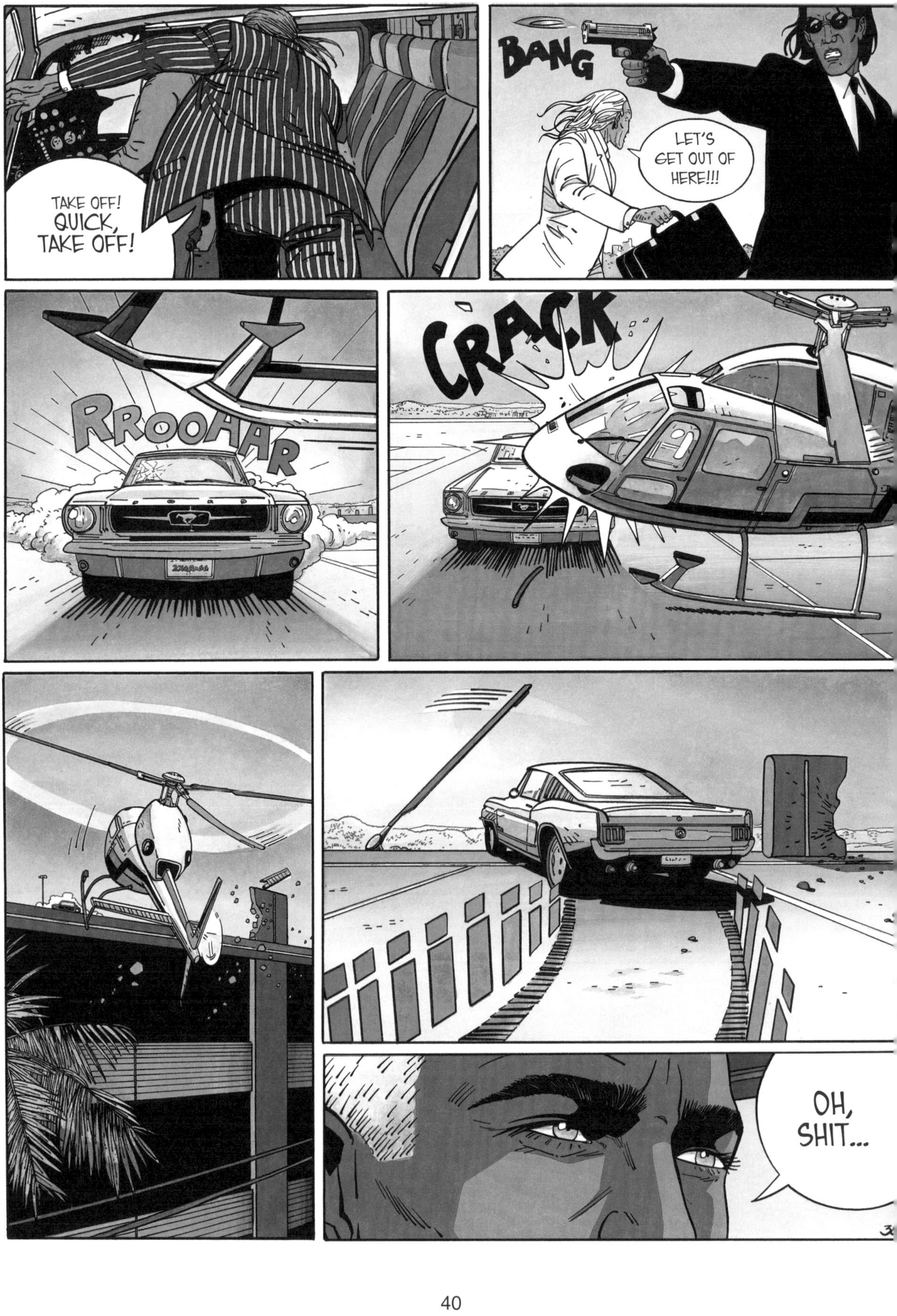
TAKE OFF! QUICK, TAKE OFF!
BANG
LET'S GET OUT OF HERE!!!
RROOAAR
CRACK
OH, SHIT...

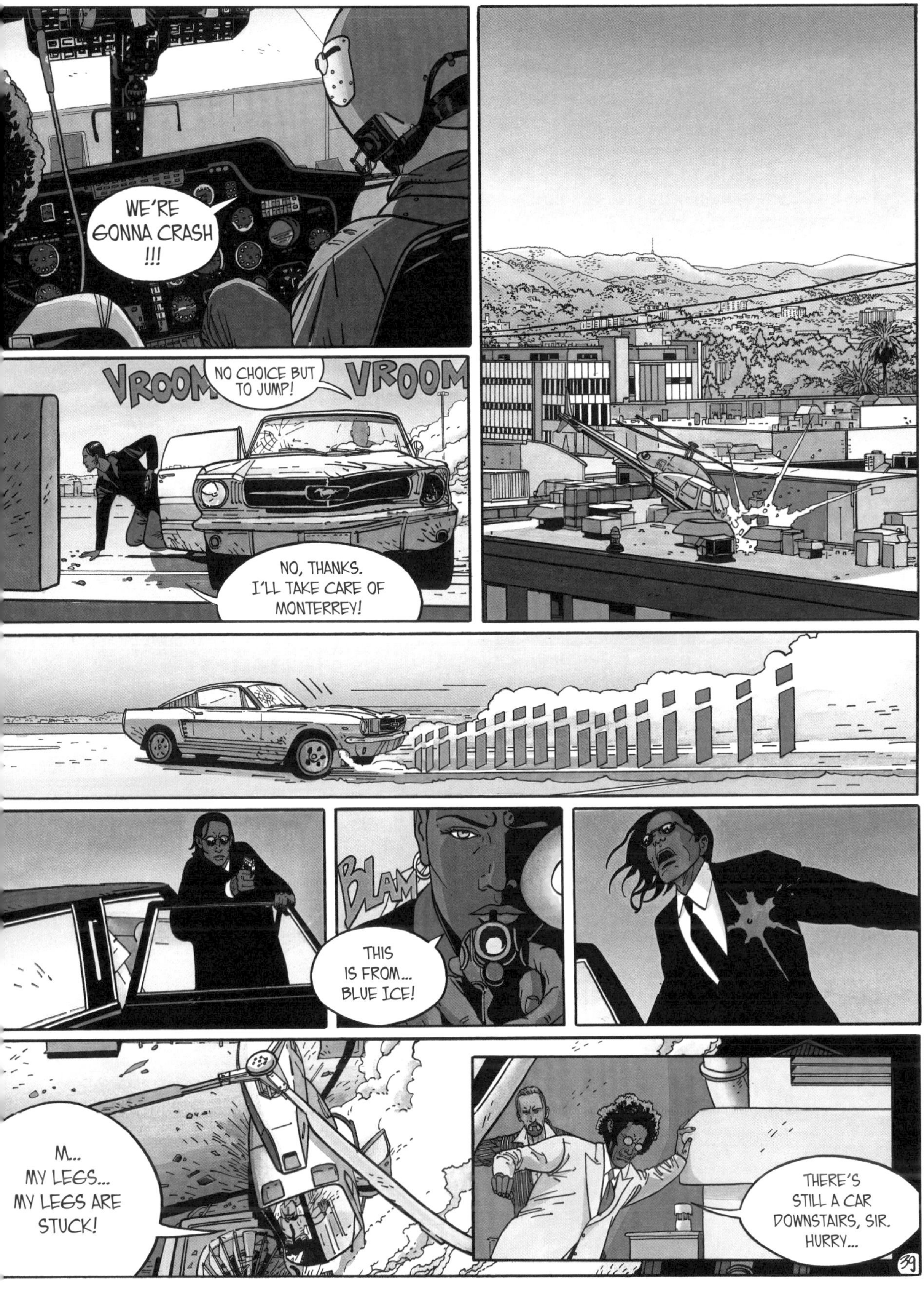
WE'RE GONNA CRASH !!!
VROOM
NO CHOICE BUT TO JUMP!
VROOM
NO, THANKS. I'LL TAKE CARE OF MONTERREY!
BLAM
THIS IS FROM... BLUE ICE!
M... MY LEGS... MY LEGS ARE STUCK!
THERE'S STILL A CAR DOWNSTAIRS, SIR. HURRY...
39

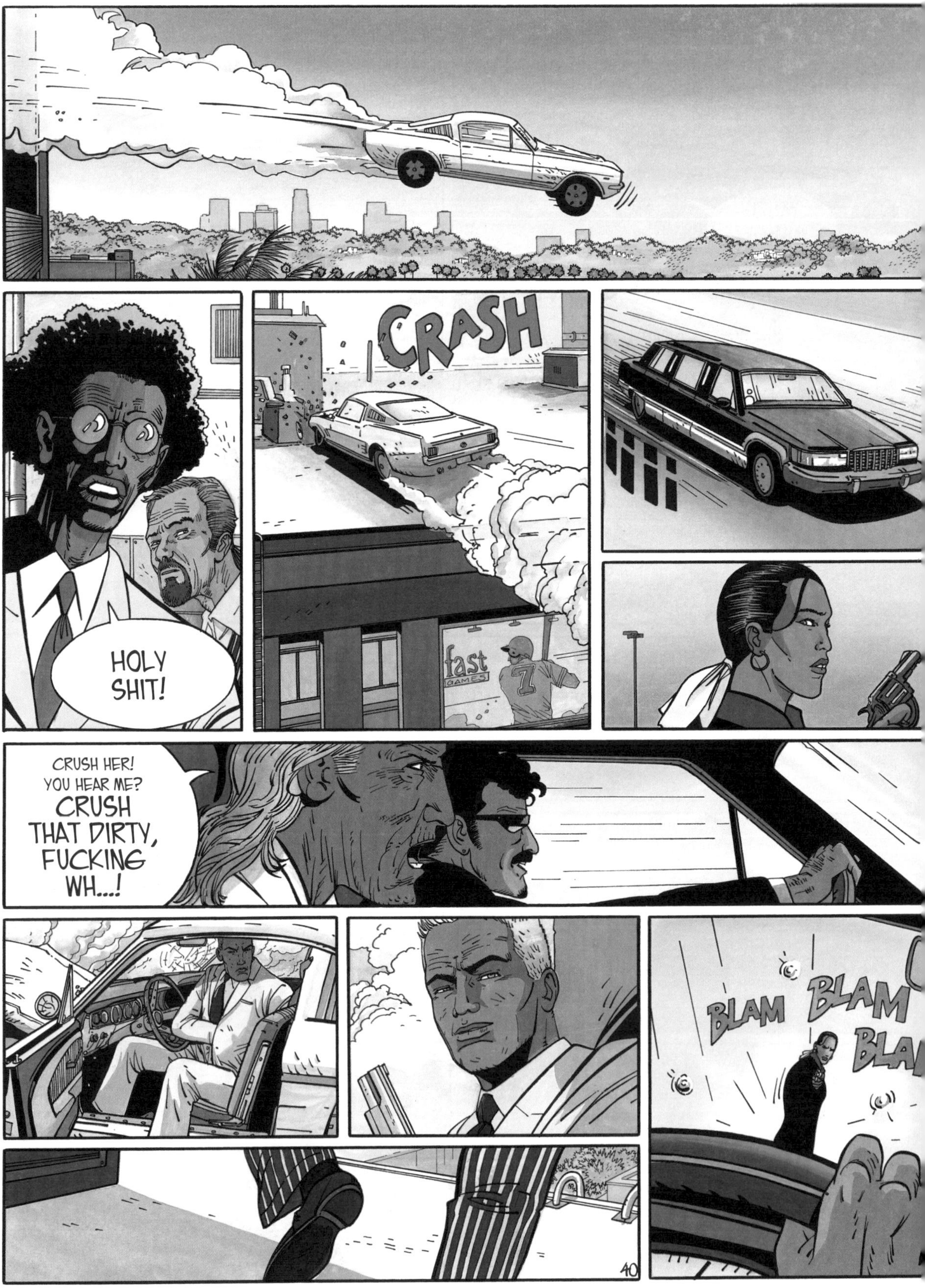

CRASH
HOLY SHIT!
CRUSH HER! YOU HEAR ME? CRUSH THAT DIRTY, FUCKING WH...!
BLAM BLAM
40

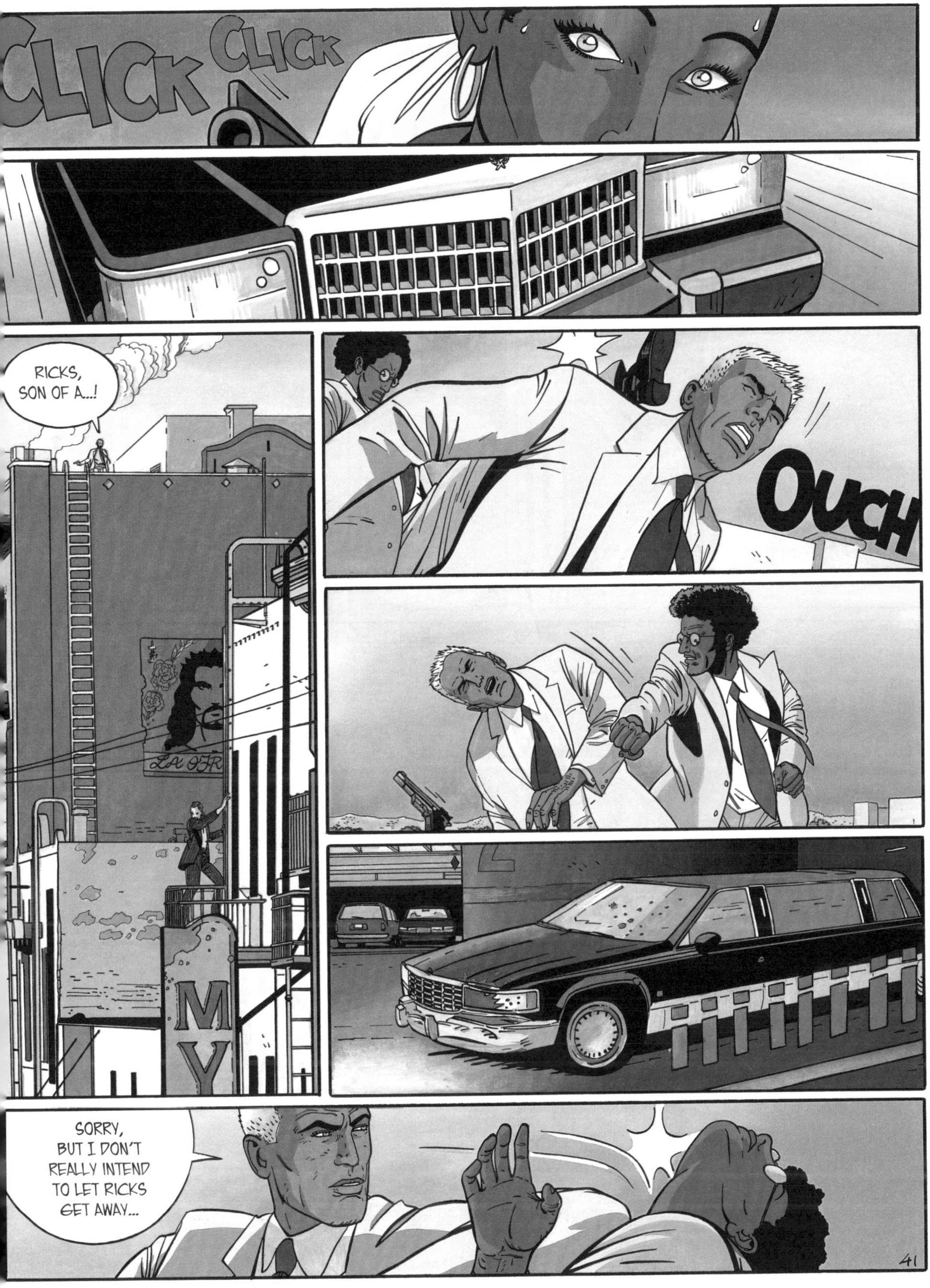
CLICK CLICK
RICKS, SON OF A...!
OUCH
SORRY, BUT I DON'T REALLY INTEND TO LET RICKS GET AWAY...
41

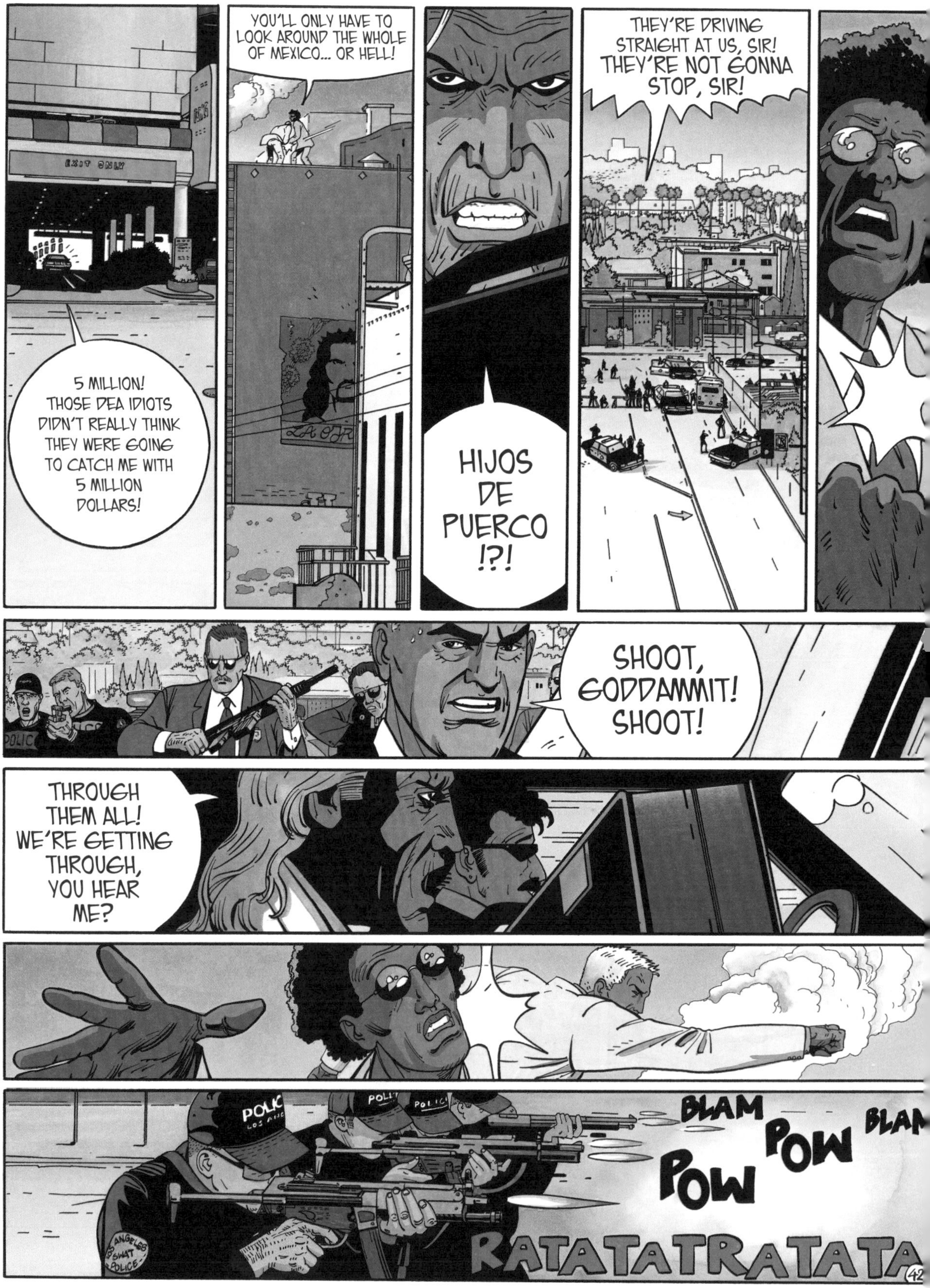
EXIT ONLY
5 MILLION! THOSE DEA IDIOTS DIDN'T REALLY THINK THEY WERE GOING TO CATCH ME WITH 5 MILLION DOLLARS!
YOU'LL ONLY HAVE TO LOOK AROUND THE WHOLE OF MEXICO... OR HELL!
HIJOS DE PUERCO !?!
THEY'RE DRIVING STRAIGHT AT US, SIR! THEY'RE NOT GONNA STOP, SIR!
SHOOT, GODDAMMIT! SHOOT!
THROUGH THEM ALL! WE'RE GETTING THROUGH, YOU HEAR ME?
BLAM
POW
BLAM
POW
RATATATRATATA
42

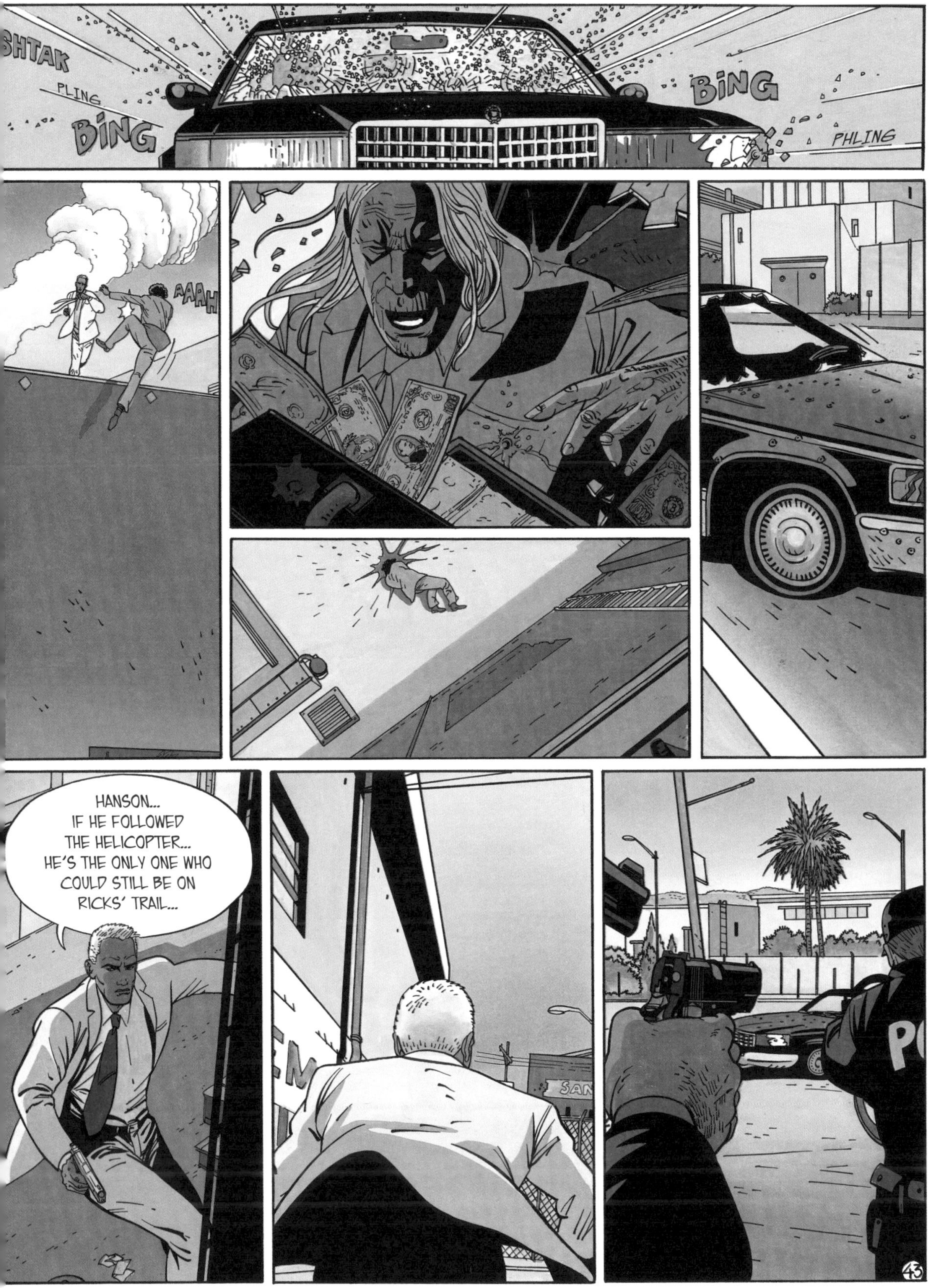

SHTAK
PLING
BING
BING
PHLING
AAAH
HANSON... IF HE FOLLOWED THE HELICOPTER... HE'S THE ONLY ONE WHO COULD STILL BE ON RICKS' TRAIL...
43

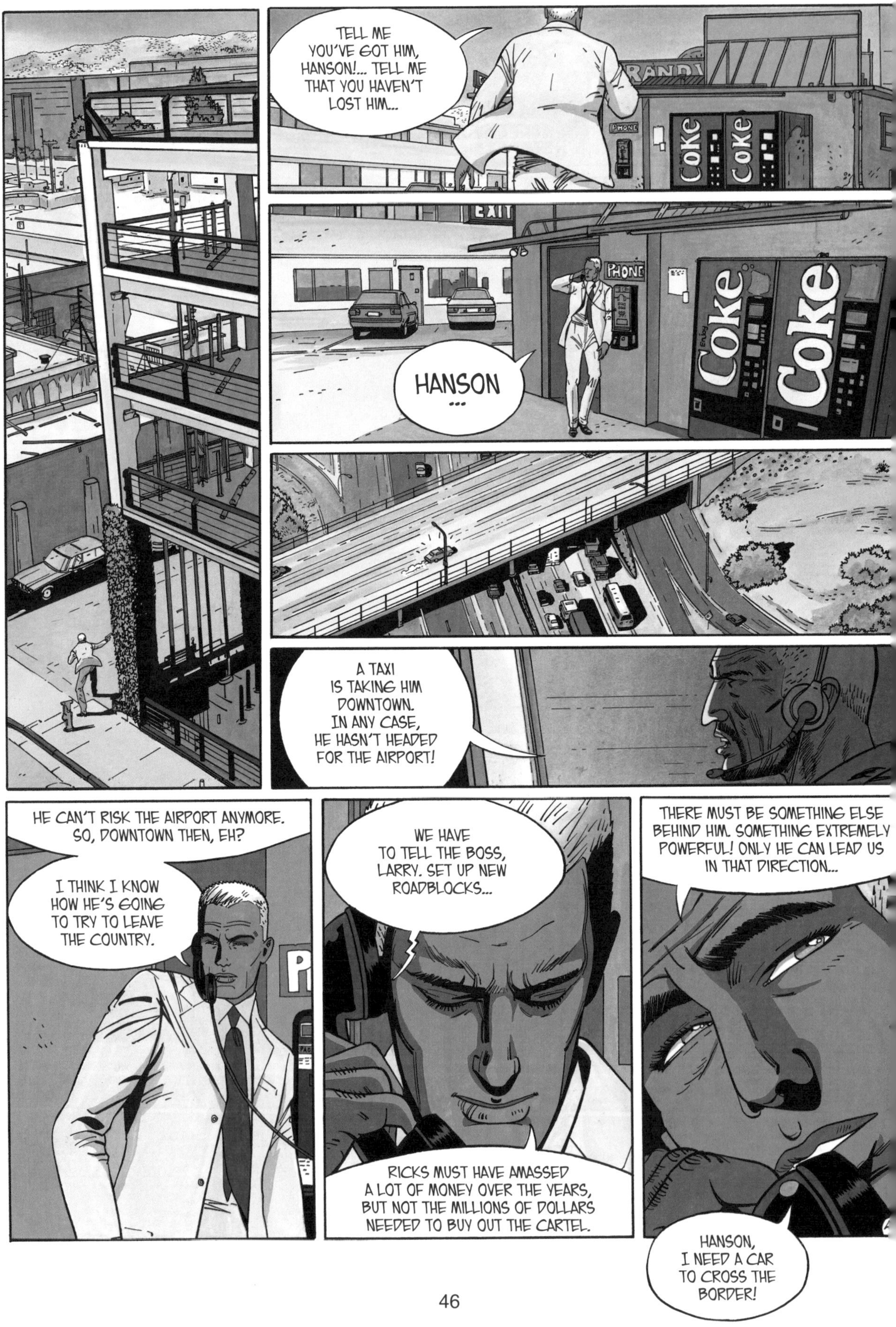
TELL ME YOU'VE GOT HIM, HANSON!... TELL ME THAT YOU HAVEN'T LOST HIM...
PHONE
COKE
EXIT
PHONE
HANSON ...
Enjoy Coke
Coke
A TAXI IS TAKING HIM DOWNTOWN. IN ANY CASE, HE HASN'T HEADED FOR THE AIRPORT!
HE CAN'T RISK THE AIRPORT ANYMORE. SO, DOWNTOWN THEN, EH?
I THINK I KNOW HOW HE'S GOING TO TRY TO LEAVE THE COUNTRY.
WE HAVE TO TELL THE BOSS, LARRY. SET UP NEW ROADBLOCKS...
RICKS MUST HAVE AMASSED A LOT OF MONEY OVER THE YEARS, BUT NOT THE MILLIONS OF DOLLARS NEEDED TO BUY OUT THE CARTEL.
THERE MUST BE SOMETHING ELSE BEHIND HIM. SOMETHING EXTREMELY POWERFUL! ONLY HE CAN LEAD US IN THAT DIRECTION...
HANSON, I NEED A CAR TO CROSS THE BORDER!

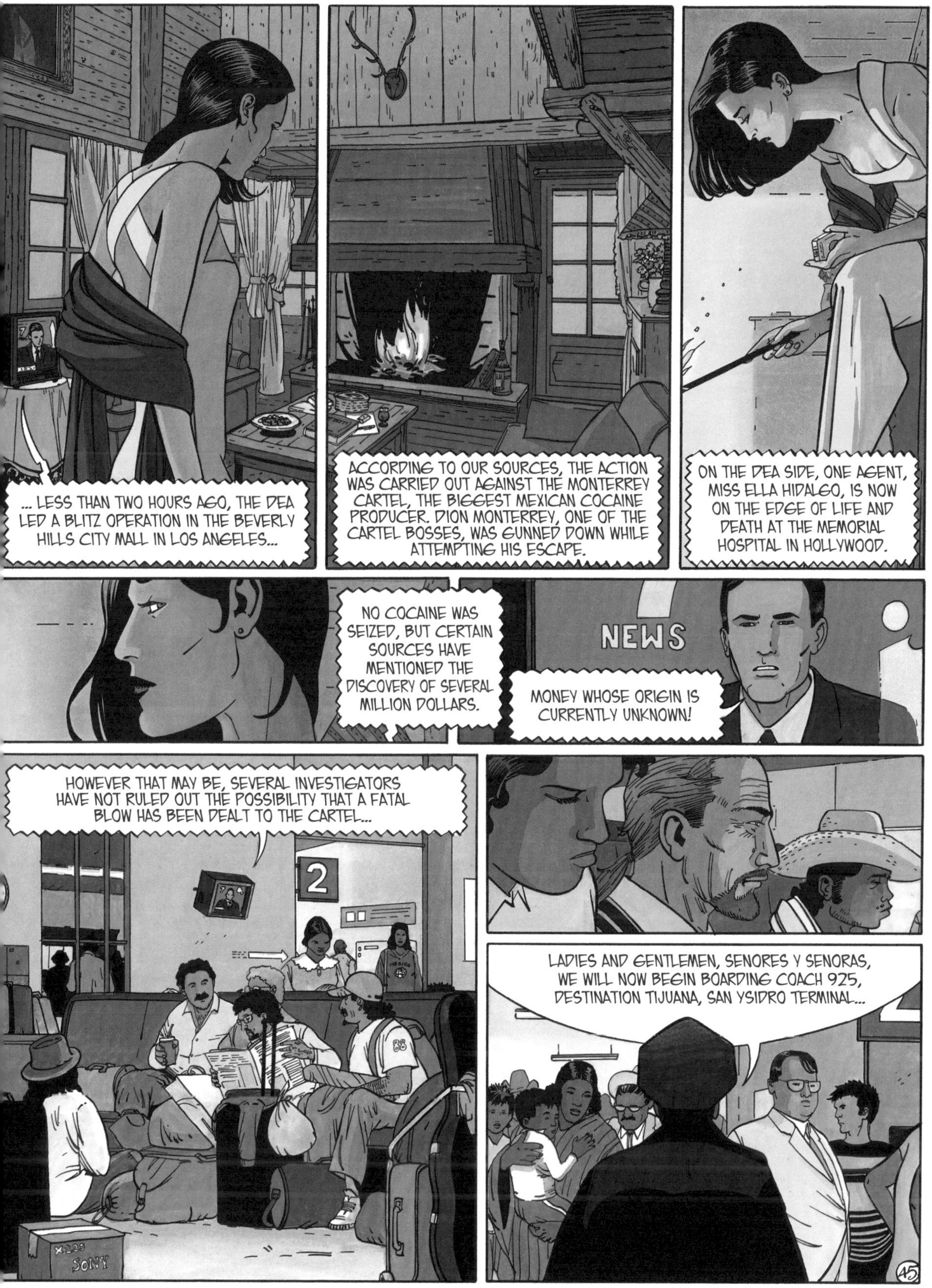
... LESS THAN TWO HOURS AGO, THE DEA LED A BLITZ OPERATION IN THE BEVERLY HILLS CITY MALL IN LOS ANGELES...
ACCORDING TO OUR SOURCES, THE ACTION WAS CARRIED OUT AGAINST THE MONTERREY CARTEL, THE BIGGEST MEXICAN COCAINE PRODUCER. DION MONTERREY, ONE OF THE CARTEL BOSSES, WAS GUNNED DOWN WHILE ATTEMPTING HIS ESCAPE.
ON THE DEA SIDE, ONE AGENT, MISS ELLA HIDALGO, IS NOW ON THE EDGE OF LIFE AND DEATH AT THE MEMORIAL HOSPITAL IN HOLLYWOOD.
NO COCAINE WAS SEIZED, BUT CERTAIN SOURCES HAVE MENTIONED THE DISCOVERY OF SEVERAL MILLION DOLLARS.
NEWS
MONEY WHOSE ORIGIN IS CURRENTLY UNKNOWN!
HOWEVER THAT MAY BE, SEVERAL INVESTIGATORS HAVE NOT RULED OUT THE POSSIBILITY THAT A FATAL BLOW HAS BEEN DEALT TO THE CARTEL...
2
SONY
LADIES AND GENTLEMEN, SENORES Y SENORAS, WE WILL NOW BEGIN BOARDING COACH 925, DESTINATION TIJUANA, SAN YSIDRO TERMINAL...
45

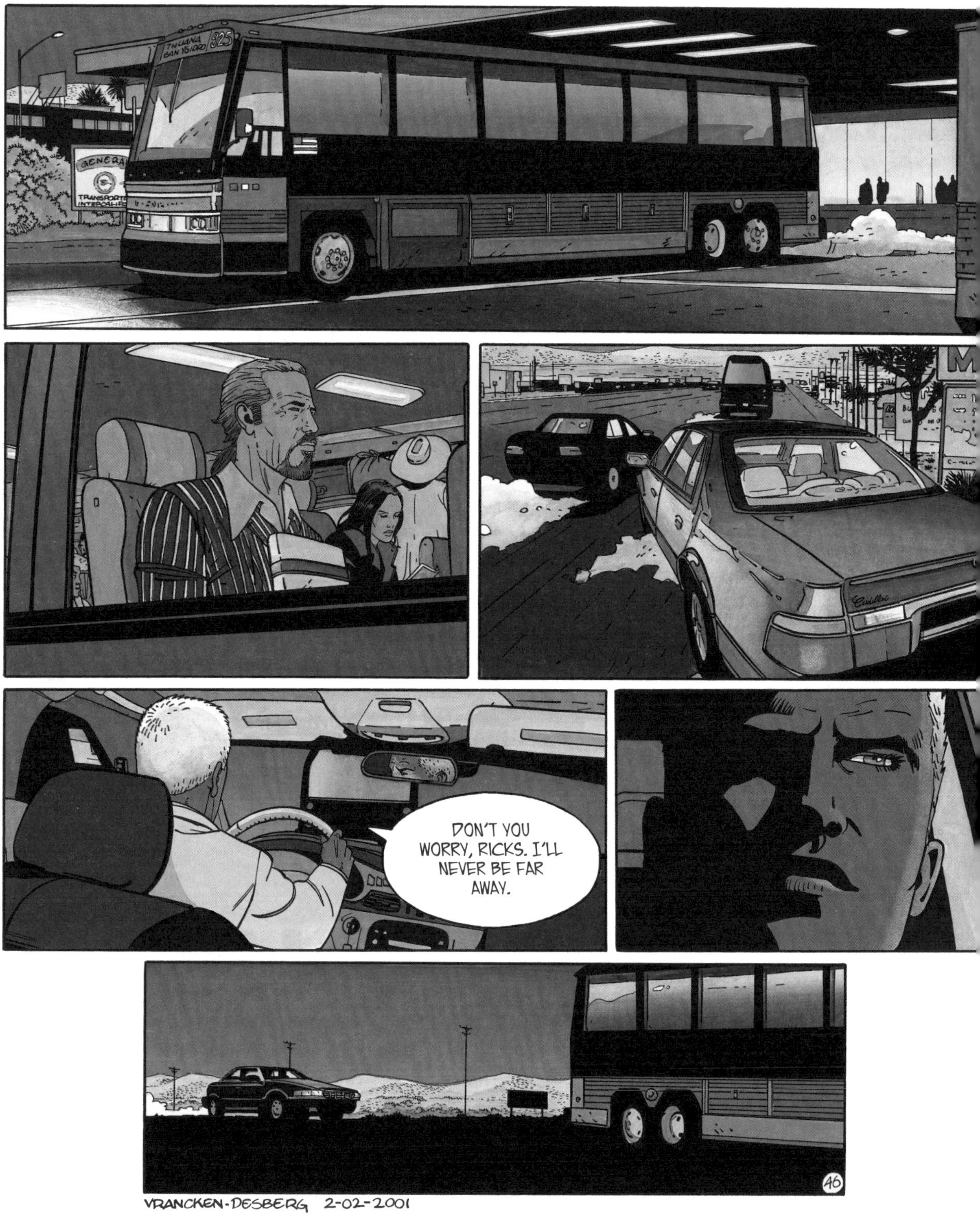
DON'T YOU WORRY, RICKS. I'LL NEVER BE FAR AWAY.
46

VRANCKEN-DESBERG 2-02-2001

VRANCKEN DESBERG

I.R.$.

NARCOCRACY

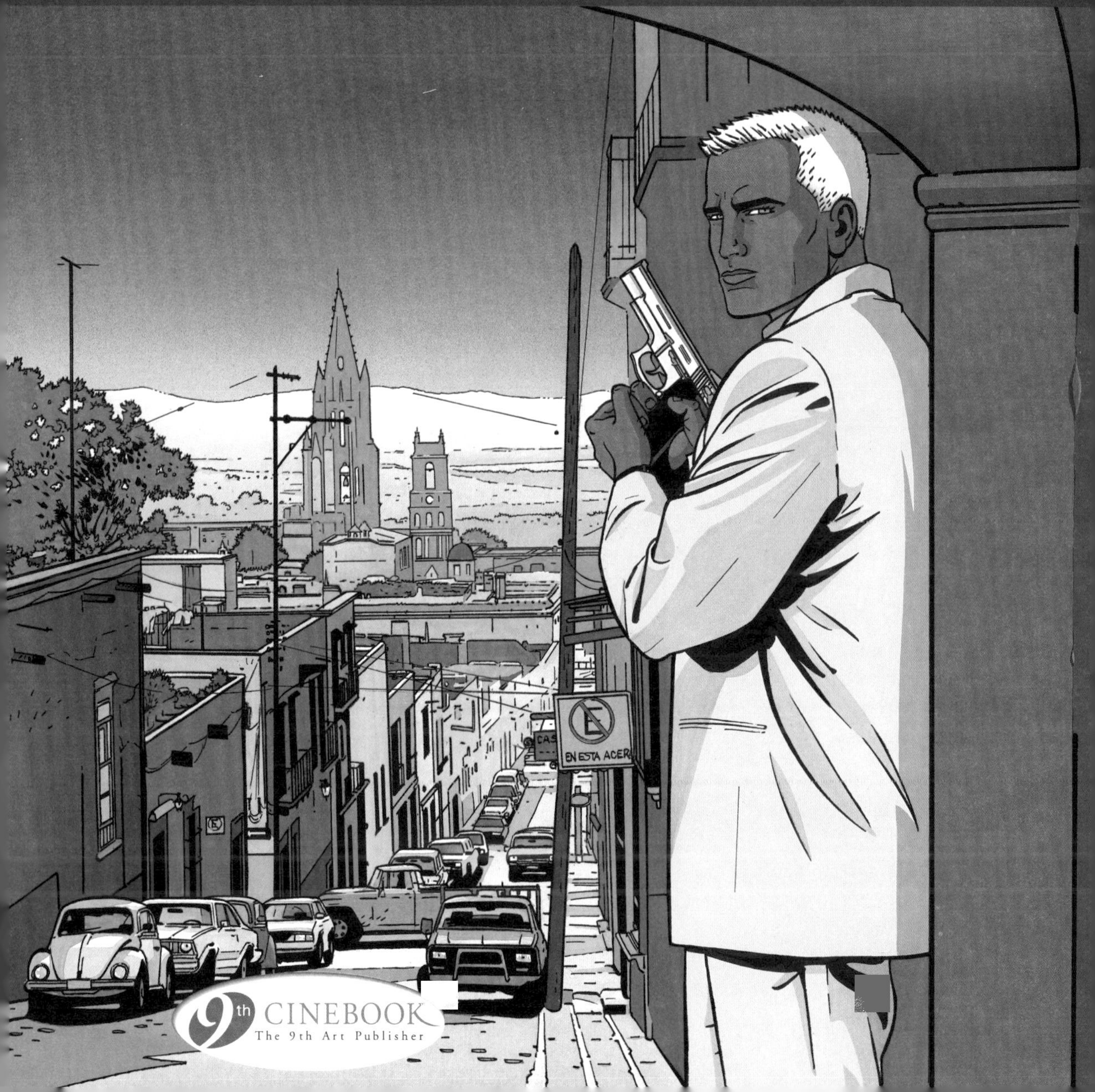
EN ESTA ACER

CINEBOOK
The 9th Art Publisher

VRANCKEN   DESBERG

I.R.$.

NARCOCRACY

COLOUR WORK: COQUELICOT

9th CINEBOOK
The 9th Art Publisher

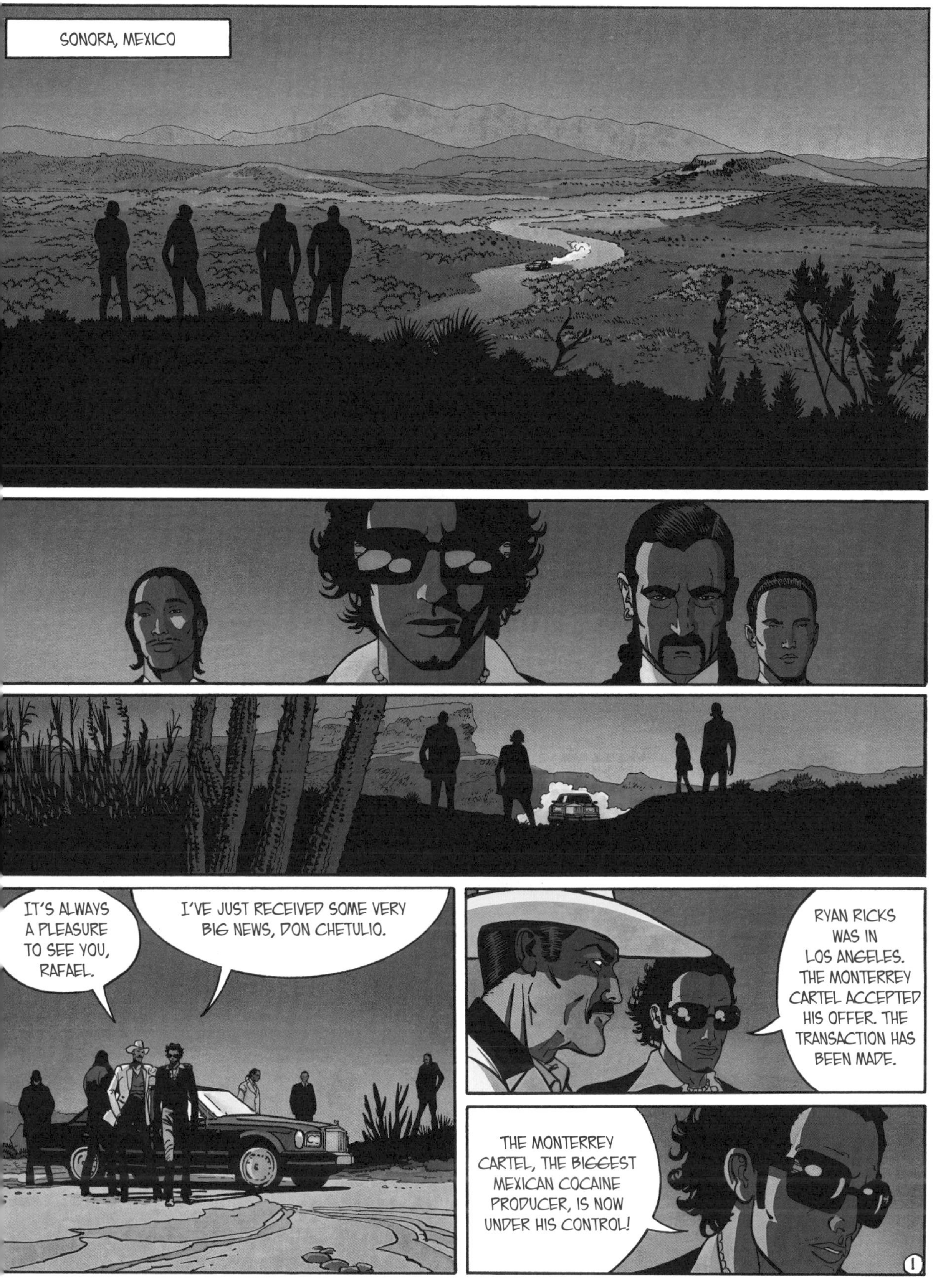
SONORA, MEXICO
IT'S ALWAYS A PLEASURE TO SEE YOU, RAFAEL.
I'VE JUST RECEIVED SOME VERY BIG NEWS, DON CHETULIO.
RYAN RICKS WAS IN LOS ANGELES. THE MONTERREY CARTEL ACCEPTED HIS OFFER. THE TRANSACTION HAS BEEN MADE.
THE MONTERREY CARTEL, THE BIGGEST MEXICAN COCAINE PRODUCER, IS NOW UNDER HIS CONTROL!
1

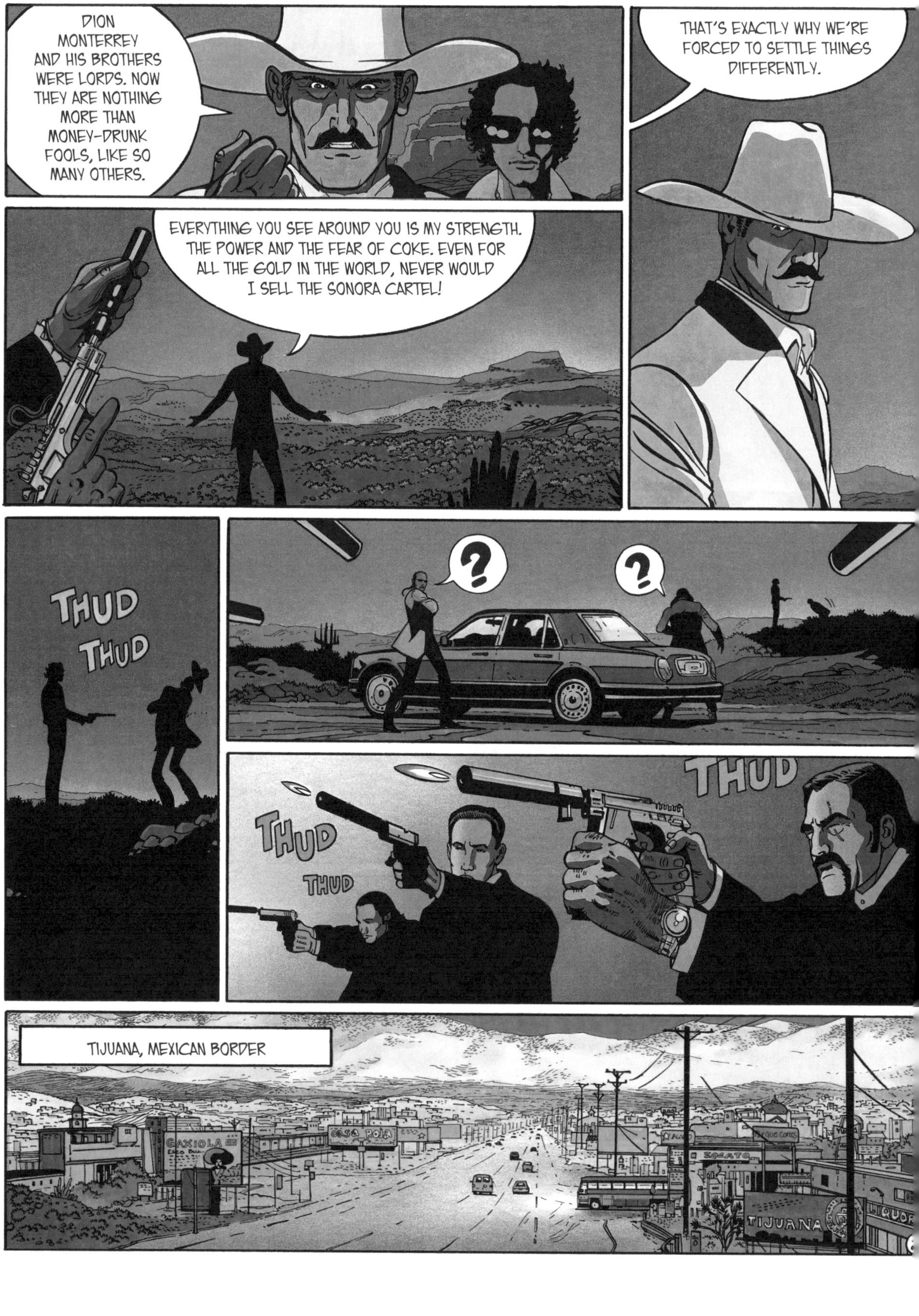
DION MONTERREY AND HIS BROTHERS WERE LORDS. NOW THEY ARE NOTHING MORE THAN MONEY-DRUNK FOOLS, LIKE SO MANY OTHERS.
THAT'S EXACTLY WHY WE'RE FORCED TO SETTLE THINGS DIFFERENTLY.
EVERYTHING YOU SEE AROUND YOU IS MY STRENGTH. THE POWER AND THE FEAR OF COKE. EVEN FOR ALL THE GOLD IN THE WORLD, NEVER WOULD I SELL THE SONORA CARTEL!
THUD
THUD
?
?
THUD
THUD
THUD
TIJUANA, MEXICAN BORDER
GAXIOLA
CASA ROJA
ZOCALO
TIJUANA
LIQUOR

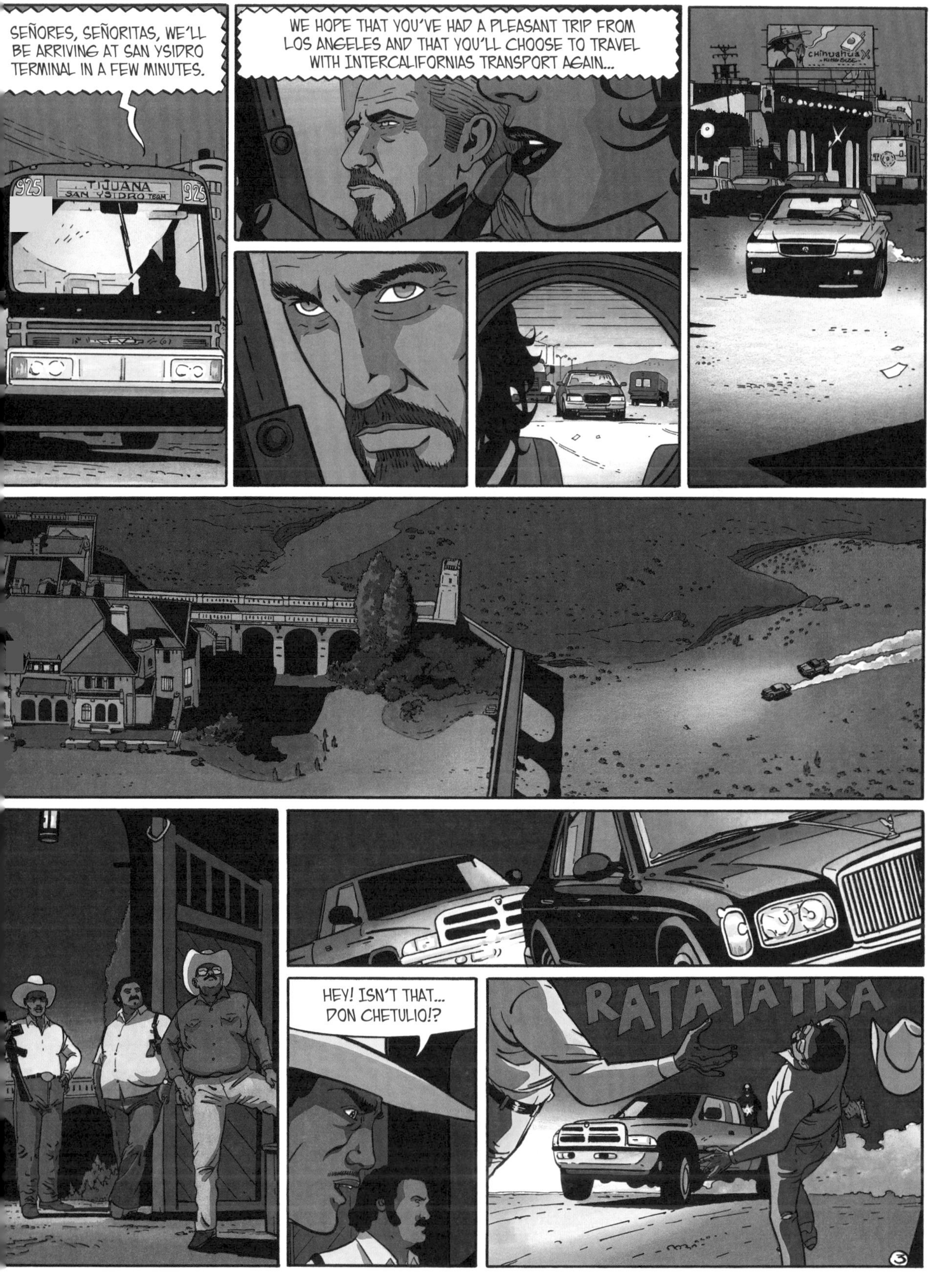
SEÑORES, SEÑORITAS, WE'LL BE ARRIVING AT SAN YSIDRO TERMINAL IN A FEW MINUTES.
925 TIJUANA SAN YSIDRO TERM 925
WE HOPE THAT YOU'VE HAD A PLEASANT TRIP FROM LOS ANGELES AND THAT YOU'LL CHOOSE TO TRAVEL WITH INTERCALIFORNIAS TRANSPORT AGAIN...
HEY! ISN'T THAT... DON CHETULIO!?
RATATATRA

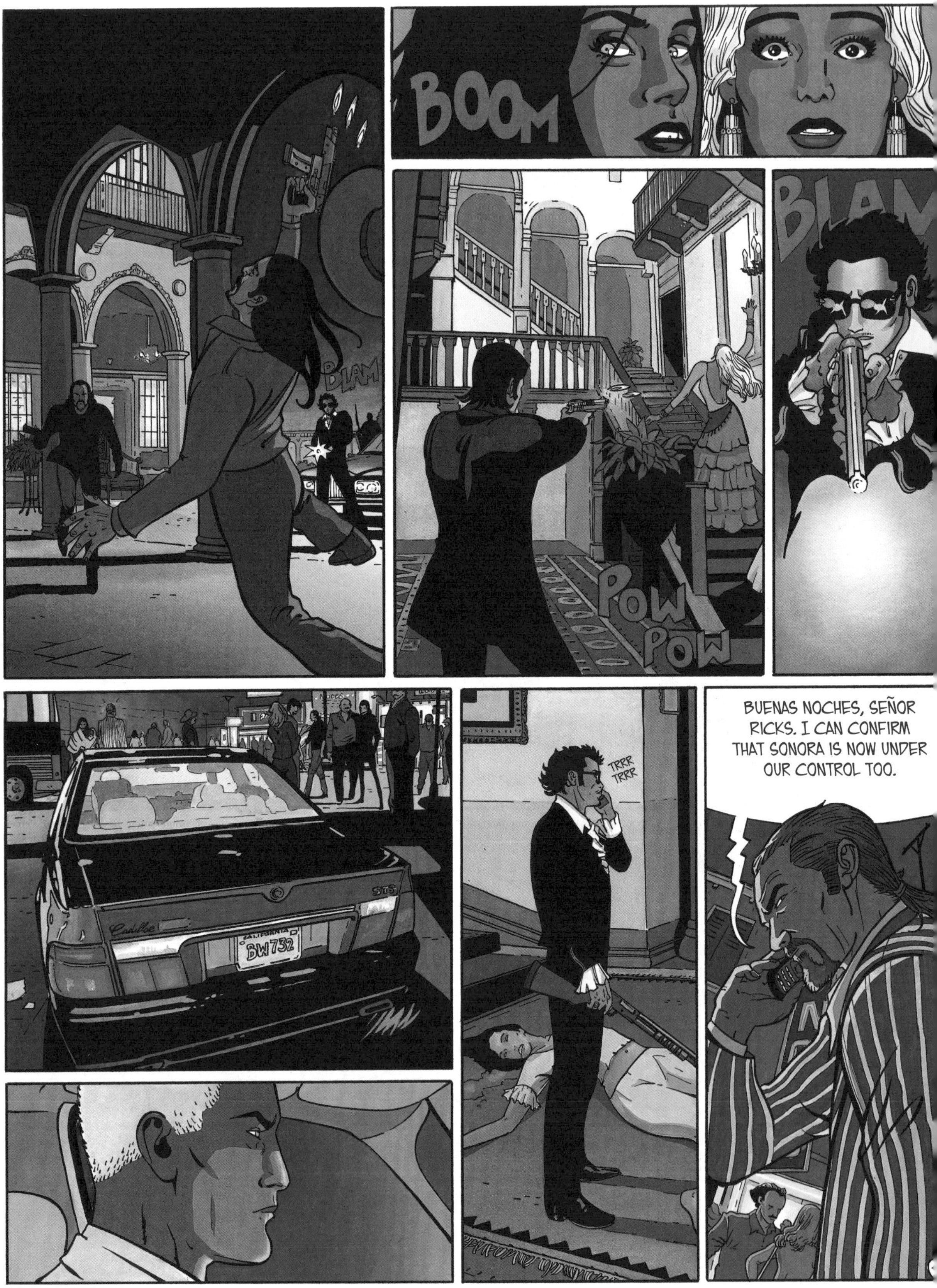
BIAM
BOOM
BLAM
POW
POW
TRRR
TRRR
BUENAS NOCHES, SEÑOR RICKS. I CAN CONFIRM THAT SONORA IS NOW UNDER OUR CONTROL TOO.

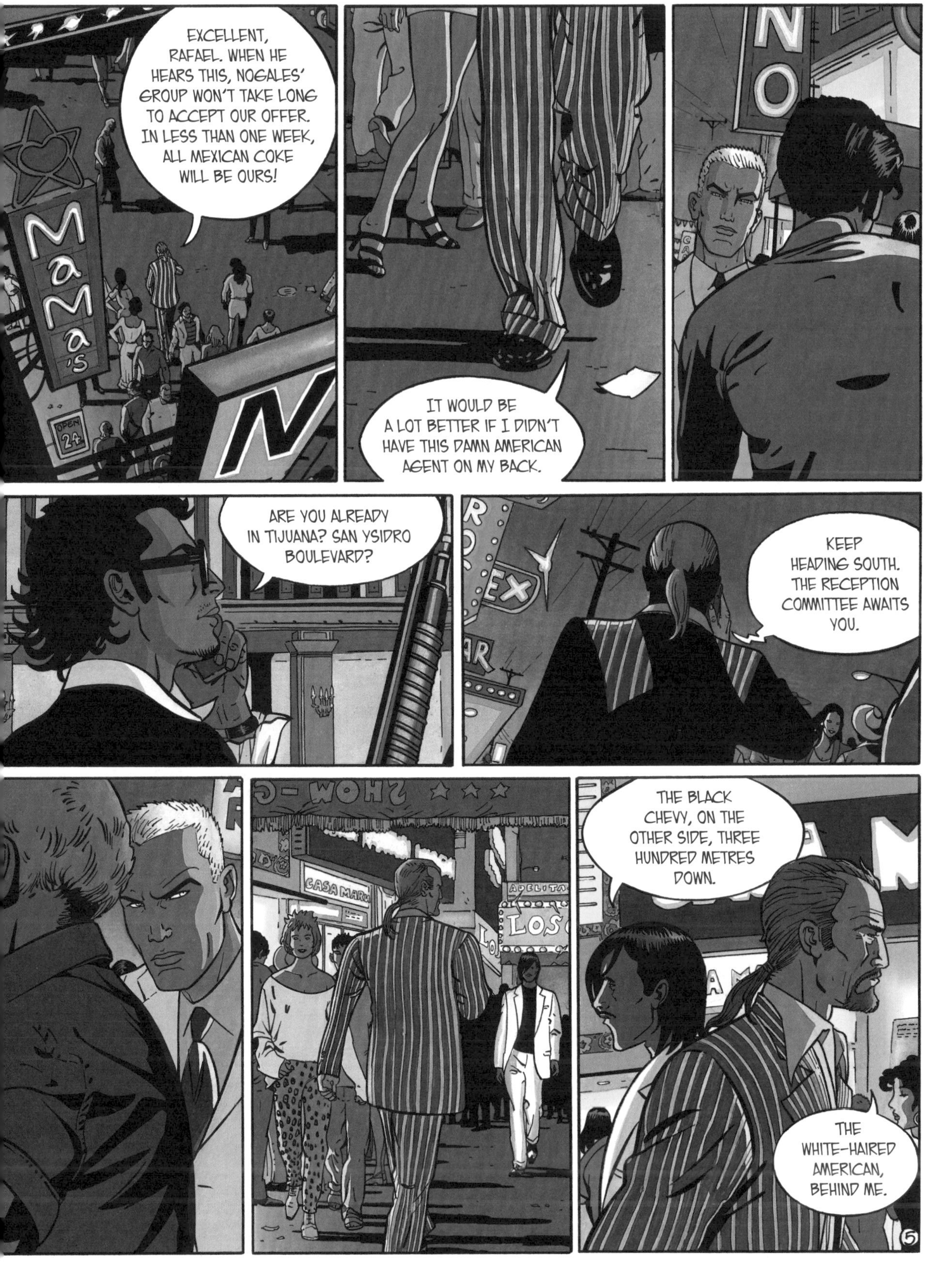
EXCELLENT, RAFAEL. WHEN HE HEARS THIS, NOGALES' GROUP WON'T TAKE LONG TO ACCEPT OUR OFFER. IN LESS THAN ONE WEEK, ALL MEXICAN COKE WILL BE OURS!
MaMa's
OPEN 24
IT WOULD BE A LOT BETTER IF I DIDN'T HAVE THIS DAMN AMERICAN AGENT ON MY BACK.
ARE YOU ALREADY IN TIJUANA? SAN YSIDRO BOULEVARD?
KEEP HEADING SOUTH. THE RECEPTION COMMITTEE AWAITS YOU.
CASA MARU
LOS
THE BLACK CHEVY, ON THE OTHER SIDE, THREE HUNDRED METRES DOWN.
THE WHITE-HAIRED AMERICAN, BEHIND ME.

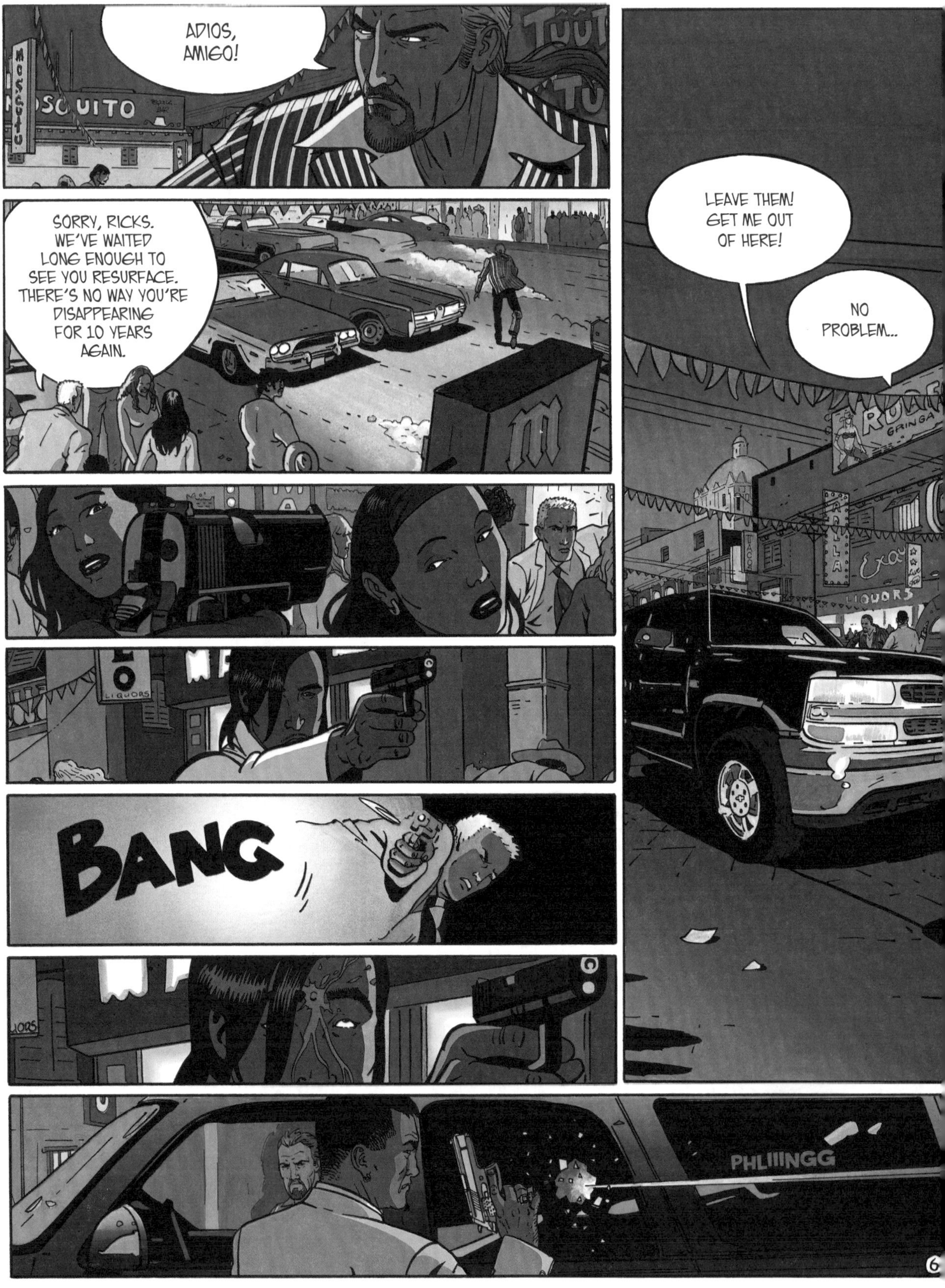
ADIOS, AMIGO!
SORRY, RICKS. WE'VE WAITED LONG ENOUGH TO SEE YOU RESURFACE. THERE'S NO WAY YOU'RE DISAPPEARING FOR 10 YEARS AGAIN.
LEAVE THEM! GET ME OUT OF HERE!
NO PROBLEM...
BANG
PHLIIINGG

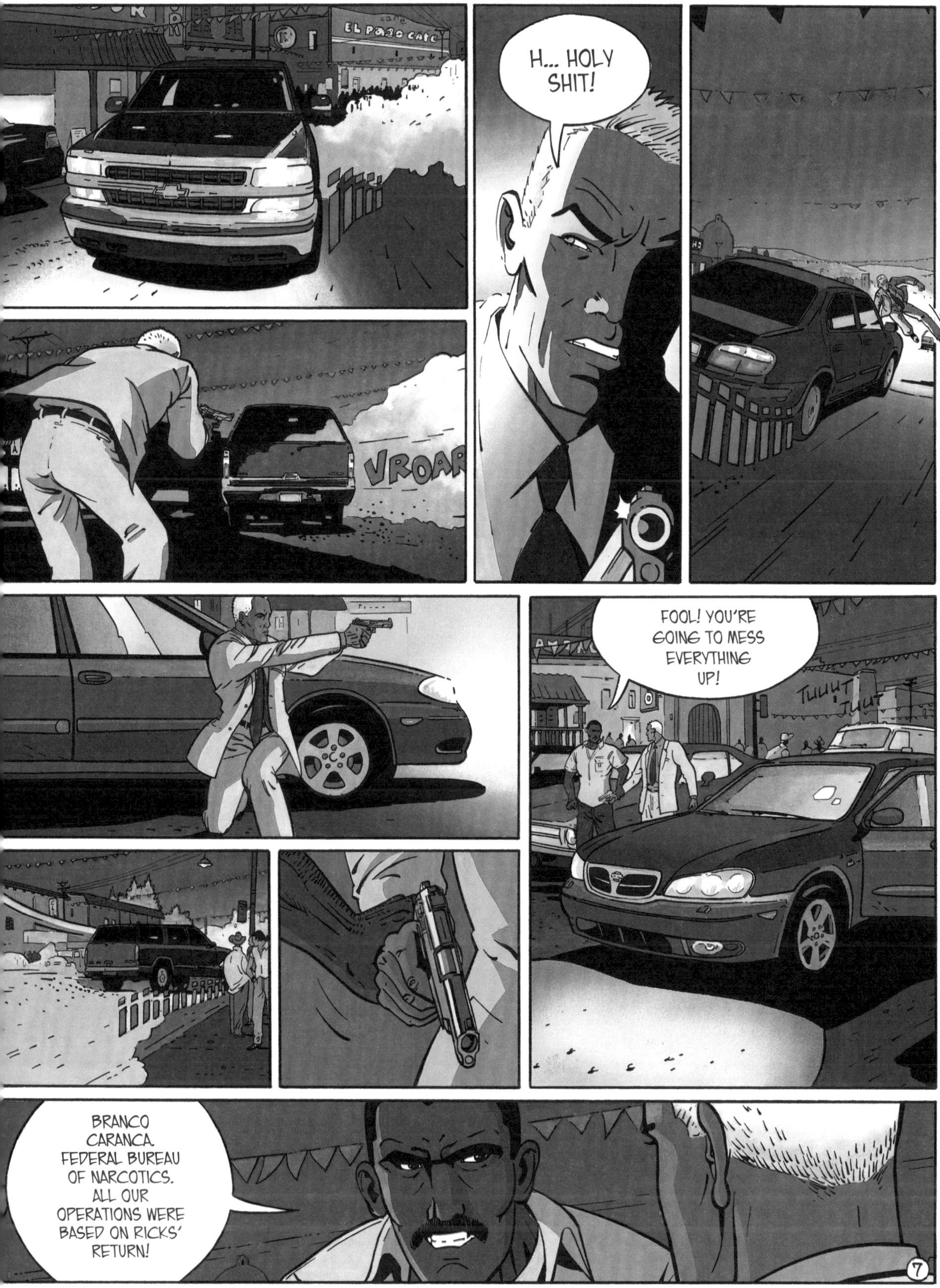
EL PASO CAFE
H... HOLY
SHIT!
VROAR
FOOL! YOU'RE
GOING TO MESS
EVERYTHING
UP!
TUUUT
TUUT
BRANCO
CARANCA.
FEDERAL BUREAU
OF NARCOTICS.
ALL OUR
OPERATIONS WERE
BASED ON RICKS'
RETURN!
7

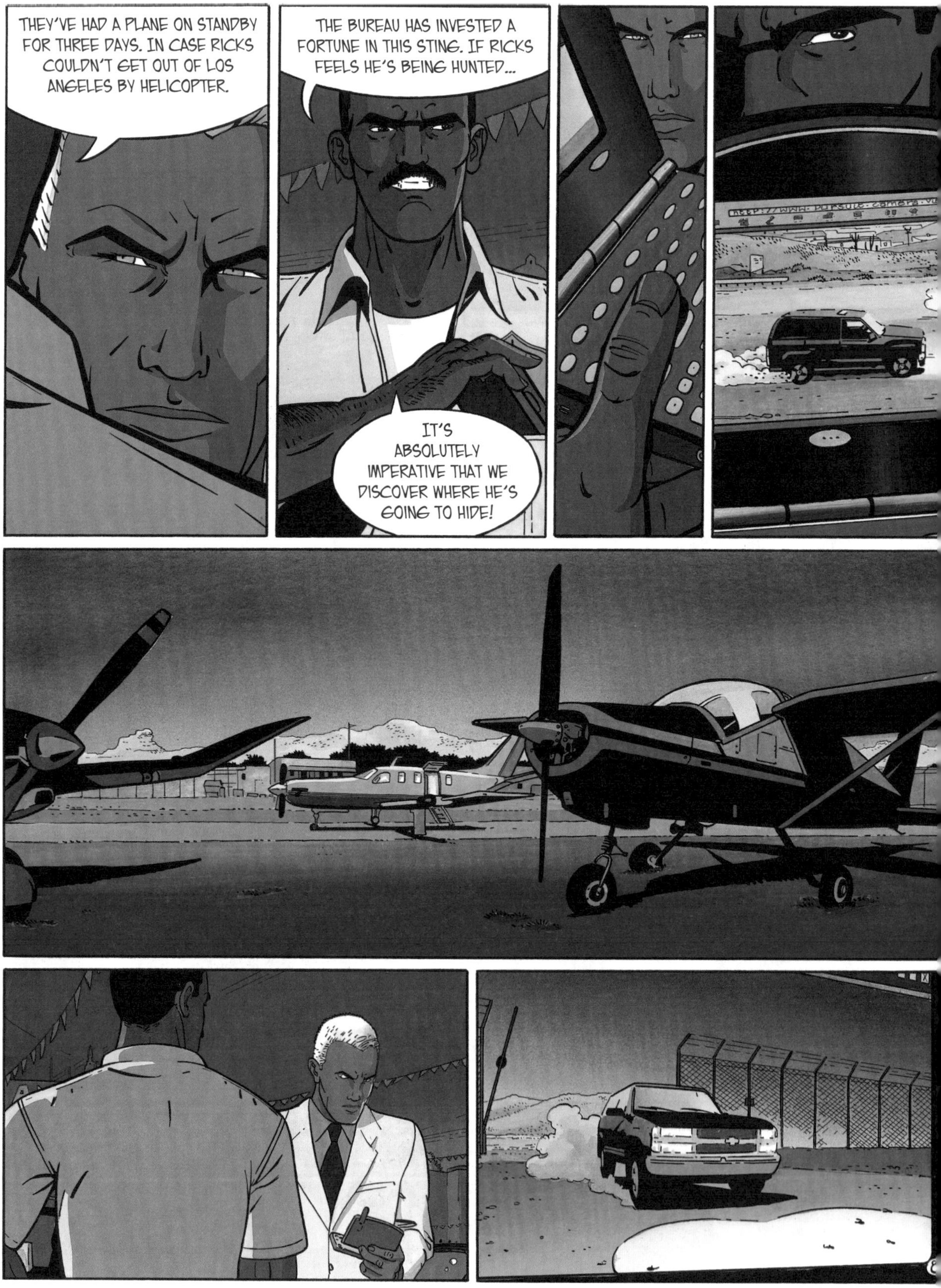
THEY'VE HAD A PLANE ON STANDBY FOR THREE DAYS. IN CASE RICKS COULDN'T GET OUT OF LOS ANGELES BY HELICOPTER.
THE BUREAU HAS INVESTED A FORTUNE IN THIS STING. IF RICKS FEELS HE'S BEING HUNTED...
IT'S ABSOLUTELY IMPERATIVE THAT WE DISCOVER WHERE HE'S GOING TO HIDE!

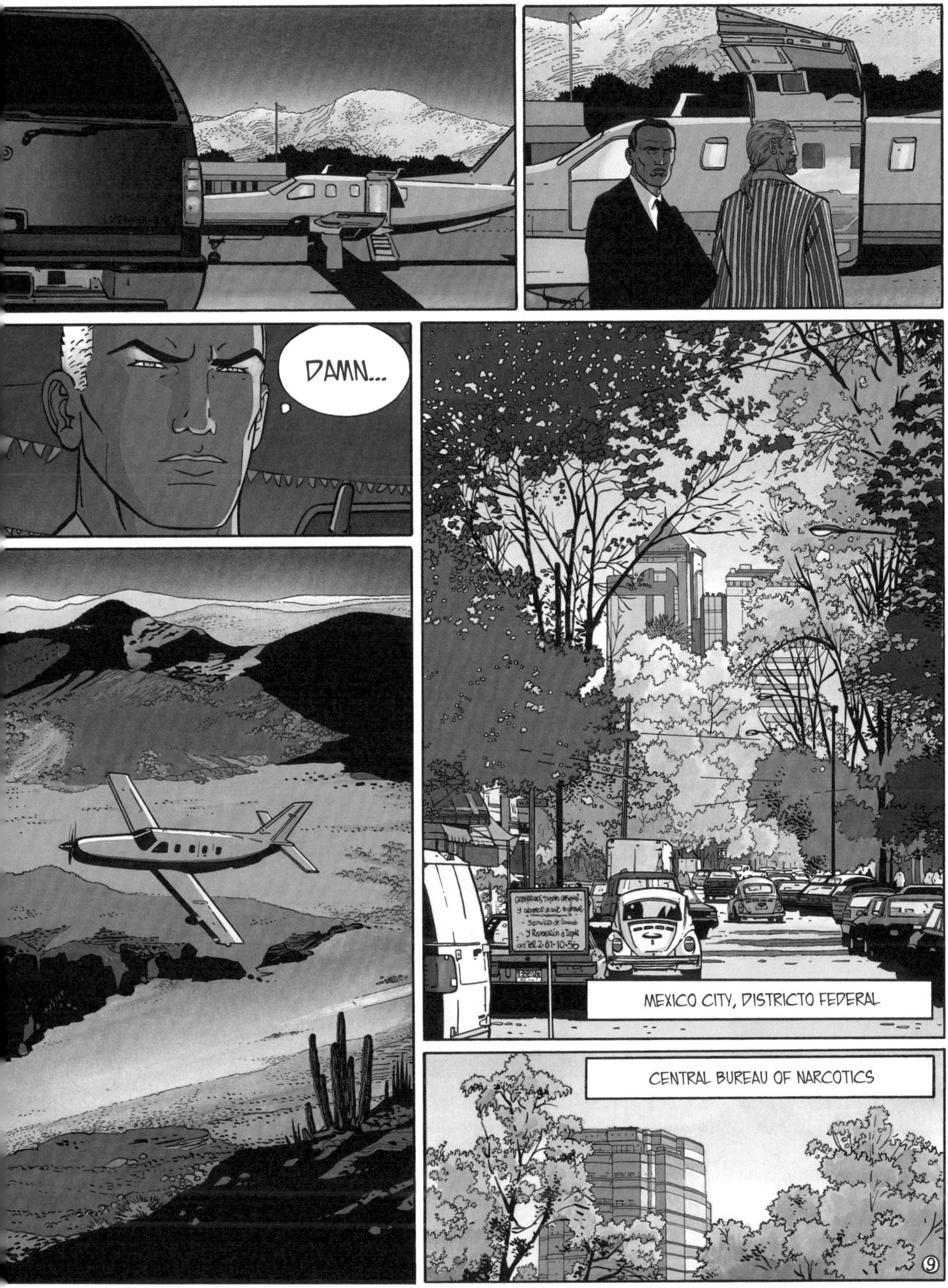
DAMN...
MEXICO CITY, DISTRICTO FEDERAL
CENTRAL BUREAU OF NARCOTICS

I'VE ALREADY TOLD YOU. I'M AN IRS AGENT. AMERICAN LAW DEMANDS THAT EACH CITIZEN FILE HIS TAXES, EVEN IF HE RESIDES ABROAD.

THE AMERICAN EMBASSY HAS CONFIRMED YOUR IDENTITY. AN IDENTITY THAT GIVES YOU NOT EVEN THE SLIGHTEST AUTHORITY TO INTERVENE ON MEXICAN SOIL, IN TOTAL VIOLATION OF OUR SOVEREIGN LAWS.

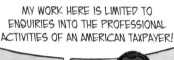
MY WORK HERE IS LIMITED TO ENQUIRIES INTO THE PROFESSIONAL ACTIVITIES OF AN AMERICAN TAXPAYER!

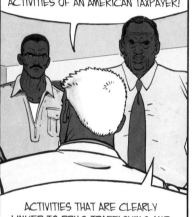
ACTIVITIES THAT ARE CLEARLY LINKED TO DRUG TRAFFICKING AND MONEY LAUNDERING, IN WHICH DOMAIN YOU HAVE NO MANDATE.

NOT TO MENTION THE LACK OF CONTACT WITH OUR BUREAU, WHICH SHOULD HAVE BEEN THE FIRST THING IN YOUR INVESTIGATIONS!

YOU ARE ON THE TERRITORY OF THE FEDERAL REPUBLIC OF MEXICO!

I SEE YOU'VE ALREADY BEEN WELCOMED HERE, MR MAX. ALLOW ME TO INTRODUCE MYSELF.

DIEGO AMATO PERALTA.

OUR COUNTRY EXPERIENCED AN EXEMPLARY FINANCIAL CRISIS AT THE END OF 1994, START OF '95.

THE PESO FOUNDERED, THE GOVERNMENT FOUND ITSELF ON THE BRINK OF BANKRUPTCY. NOT TO MENTION THE THOUSANDS OF BUSINESSES GONE BUST. DO YOU KNOW WHY, MR MAX?

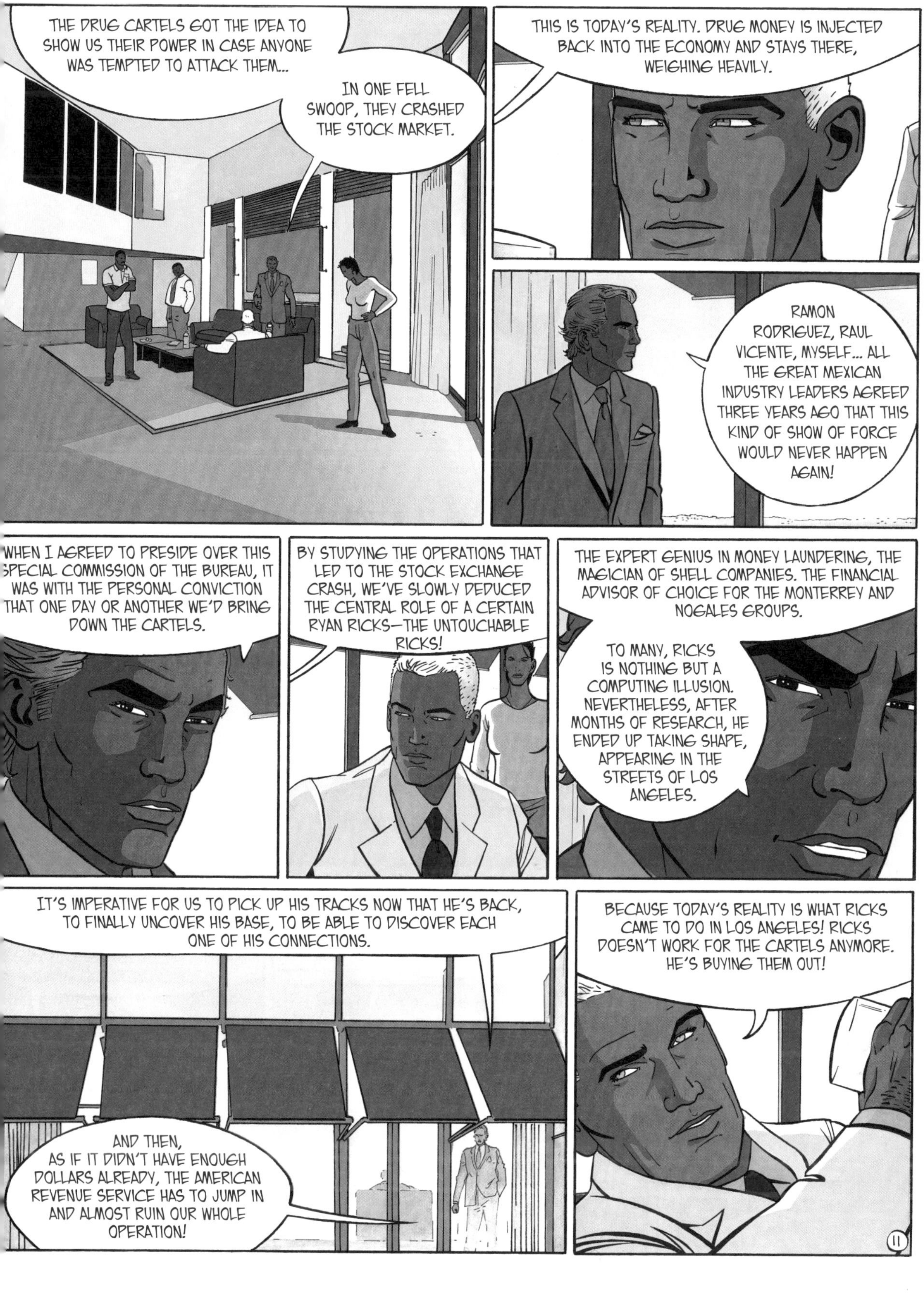
THE DRUG CARTELS GOT THE IDEA TO SHOW US THEIR POWER IN CASE ANYONE WAS TEMPTED TO ATTACK THEM...
IN ONE FELL SWOOP, THEY CRASHED THE STOCK MARKET.
THIS IS TODAY'S REALITY. DRUG MONEY IS INJECTED BACK INTO THE ECONOMY AND STAYS THERE, WEIGHING HEAVILY.
RAMON RODRIGUEZ, RAUL VICENTE, MYSELF... ALL THE GREAT MEXICAN INDUSTRY LEADERS AGREED THREE YEARS AGO THAT THIS KIND OF SHOW OF FORCE WOULD NEVER HAPPEN AGAIN!
WHEN I AGREED TO PRESIDE OVER THIS SPECIAL COMMISSION OF THE BUREAU, IT WAS WITH THE PERSONAL CONVICTION THAT ONE DAY OR ANOTHER WE'D BRING DOWN THE CARTELS.
BY STUDYING THE OPERATIONS THAT LED TO THE STOCK EXCHANGE CRASH, WE'VE SLOWLY DEDUCED THE CENTRAL ROLE OF A CERTAIN RYAN RICKS—THE UNTOUCHABLE RICKS!
THE EXPERT GENIUS IN MONEY LAUNDERING, THE MAGICIAN OF SHELL COMPANIES. THE FINANCIAL ADVISOR OF CHOICE FOR THE MONTERREY AND NOGALES GROUPS.
TO MANY, RICKS IS NOTHING BUT A COMPUTING ILLUSION. NEVERTHELESS, AFTER MONTHS OF RESEARCH, HE ENDED UP TAKING SHAPE, APPEARING IN THE STREETS OF LOS ANGELES.
IT'S IMPERATIVE FOR US TO PICK UP HIS TRACKS NOW THAT HE'S BACK, TO FINALLY UNCOVER HIS BASE, TO BE ABLE TO DISCOVER EACH ONE OF HIS CONNECTIONS.
AND THEN, AS IF IT DIDN'T HAVE ENOUGH DOLLARS ALREADY, THE AMERICAN REVENUE SERVICE HAS TO JUMP IN AND ALMOST RUIN OUR WHOLE OPERATION!
BECAUSE TODAY'S REALITY IS WHAT RICKS CAME TO DO IN LOS ANGELES! RICKS DOESN'T WORK FOR THE CARTELS ANYMORE. HE'S BUYING THEM OUT!
11

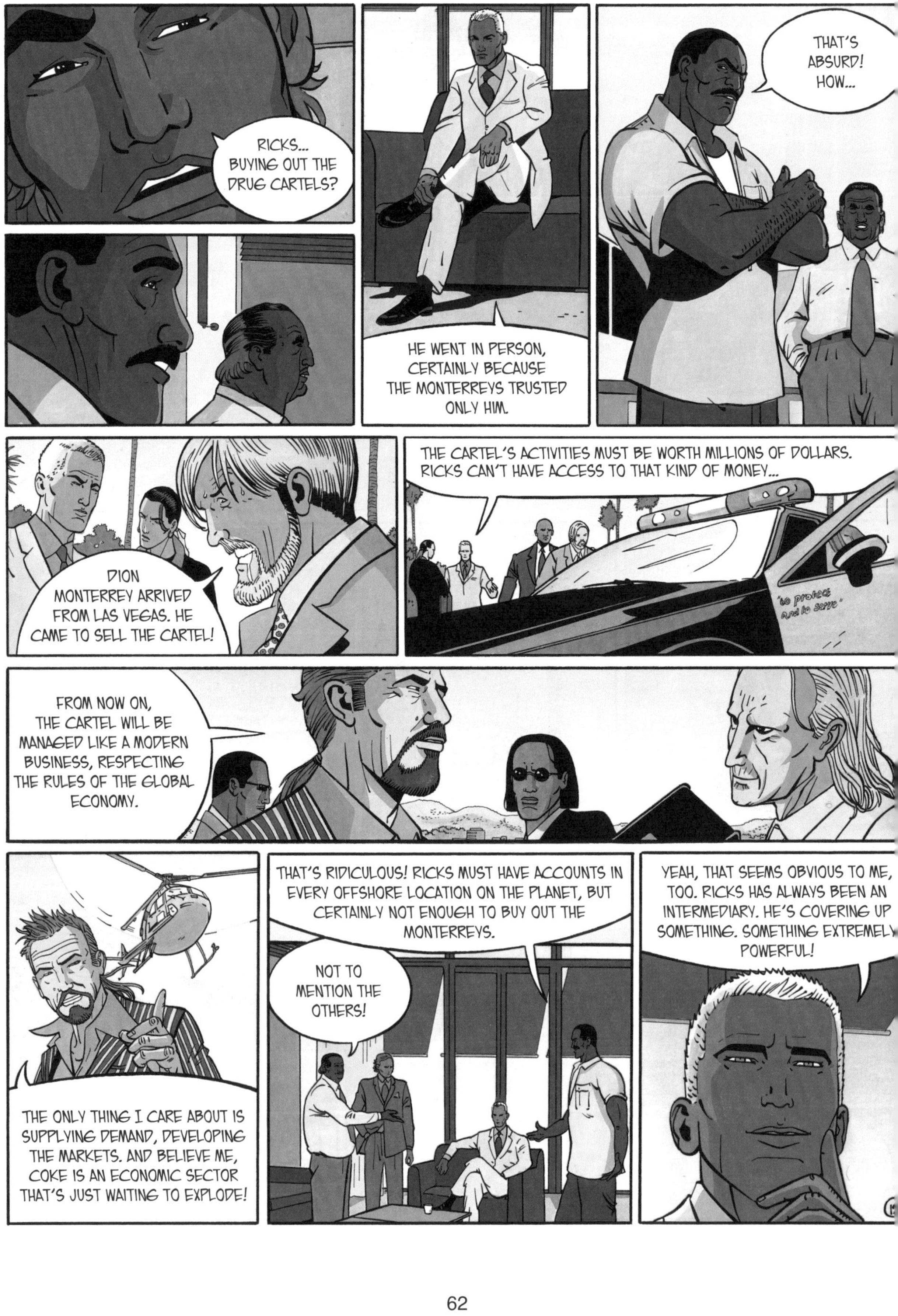
RICKS... BUYING OUT THE DRUG CARTELS?
HE WENT IN PERSON, CERTAINLY BECAUSE THE MONTERREYS TRUSTED ONLY HIM.
THAT'S ABSURD! HOW...
DION MONTERREY ARRIVED FROM LAS VEGAS. HE CAME TO SELL THE CARTEL!
THE CARTEL'S ACTIVITIES MUST BE WORTH MILLIONS OF DOLLARS. RICKS CAN'T HAVE ACCESS TO THAT KIND OF MONEY...
"to protect and to serve"
FROM NOW ON, THE CARTEL WILL BE MANAGED LIKE A MODERN BUSINESS, RESPECTING THE RULES OF THE GLOBAL ECONOMY.
THE ONLY THING I CARE ABOUT IS SUPPLYING DEMAND, DEVELOPING THE MARKETS. AND BELIEVE ME, COKE IS AN ECONOMIC SECTOR THAT'S JUST WAITING TO EXPLODE!
THAT'S RIDICULOUS! RICKS MUST HAVE ACCOUNTS IN EVERY OFFSHORE LOCATION ON THE PLANET, BUT CERTAINLY NOT ENOUGH TO BUY OUT THE MONTERREYS.
NOT TO MENTION THE OTHERS!
YEAH, THAT SEEMS OBVIOUS TO ME, TOO. RICKS HAS ALWAYS BEEN AN INTERMEDIARY. HE'S COVERING UP SOMETHING. SOMETHING EXTREMELY POWERFUL!

RICKS HAS LAUNDERED MONEY FOR THE COLOMBIANS, FOR LA COSA NOSTRA. IT COULD BE ANY MAFIA.

UNLESS THEY WERE ALL IN IT TOGETHER!

RYAN RICKS IS OUR ONLY LEAD. WE'VE AGREED ON THAT FROM THE START.

LET ME FOLLOW HIM. SOONER OR LATER HE'LL END UP TAKING US TO HIS LEADERS!

GIVE HIM THE PHOTOS.

SEÑOR PERALTA...

GIVE HIM THE PHOTOS, SOSA!

WHERE IS THIS?

SAN MIGUEL DE ALLENDE. A LITTLE UNDER 300 KILOMETRES AWAY, IN THE NORTH OF MEXICO.

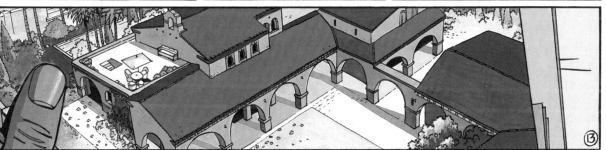

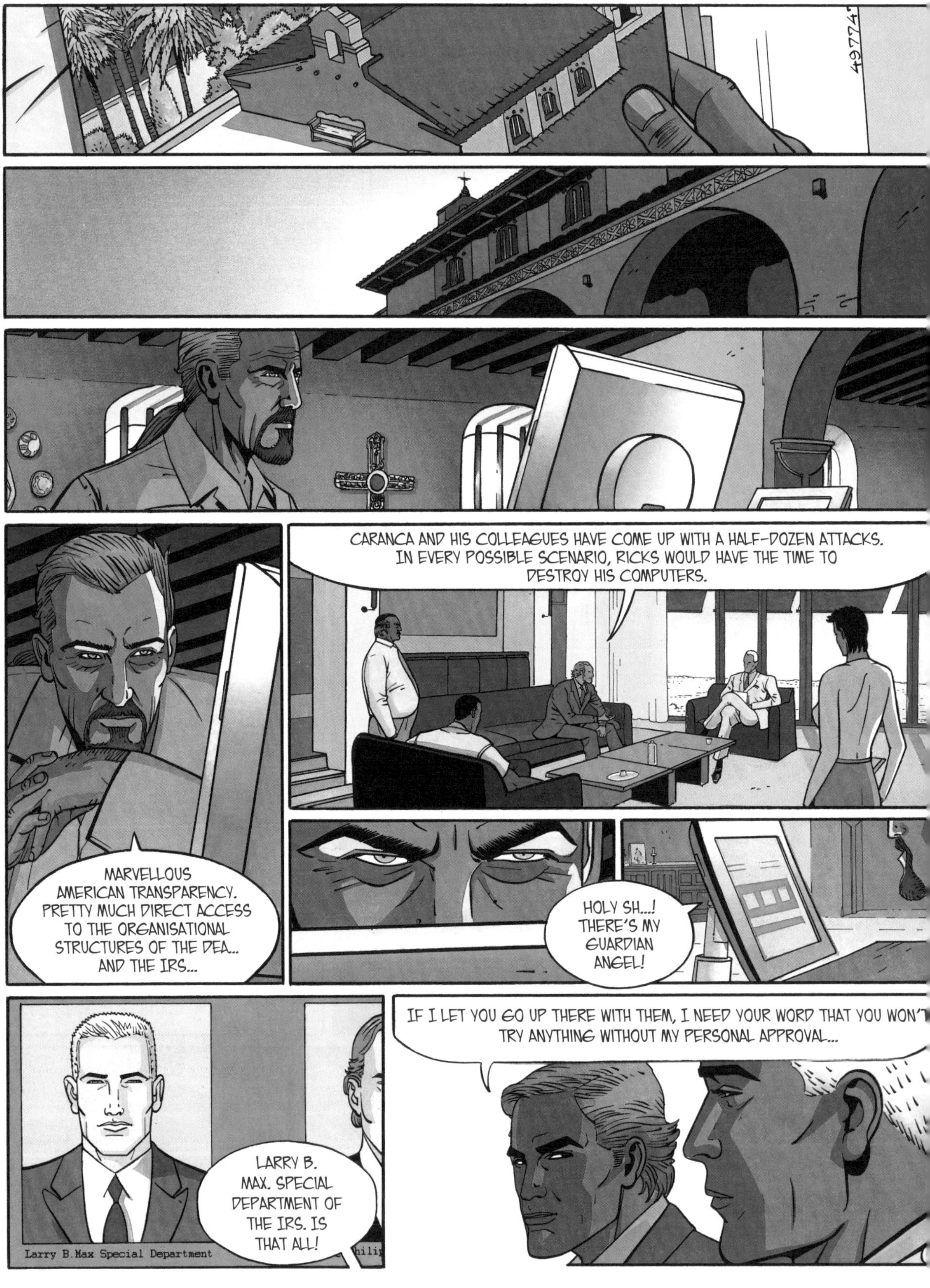
49774
CARANCA AND HIS COLLEAGUES HAVE COME UP WITH A HALF-DOZEN ATTACKS. IN EVERY POSSIBLE SCENARIO, RICKS WOULD HAVE THE TIME TO DESTROY HIS COMPUTERS.
MARVELLOUS AMERICAN TRANSPARENCY. PRETTY MUCH DIRECT ACCESS TO THE ORGANISATIONAL STRUCTURES OF THE DEA... AND THE IRS...
HOLY SH...! THERE'S MY GUARDIAN ANGEL!
Larry B.Max Special Department
LARRY B. MAX. SPECIAL DEPARTMENT OF THE IRS. IS THAT ALL!
IF I LET YOU GO UP THERE WITH THEM, I NEED YOUR WORD THAT YOU WON'T TRY ANYTHING WITHOUT MY PERSONAL APPROVAL...

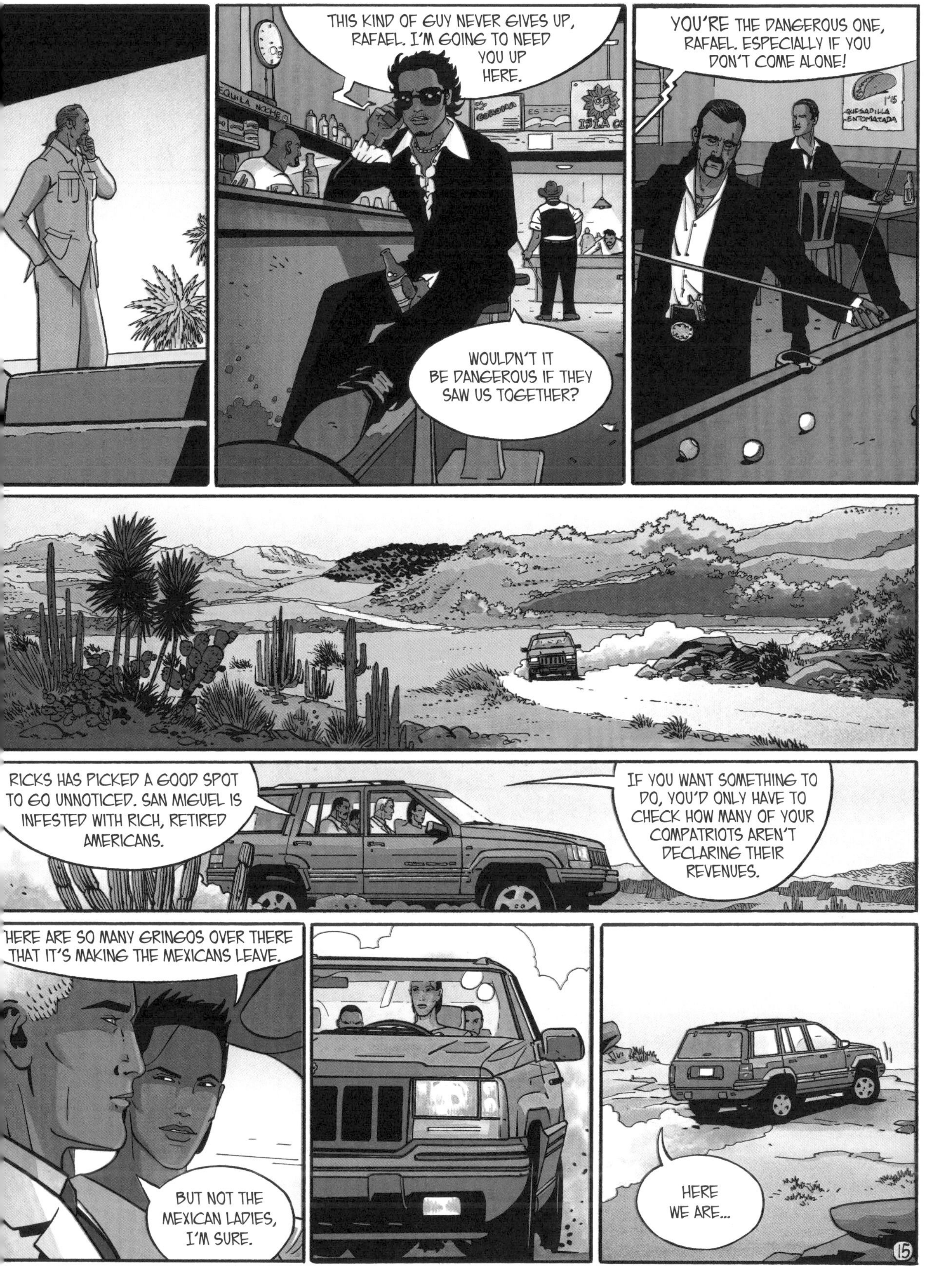
THIS KIND OF GUY NEVER GIVES UP, RAFAEL. I'M GOING TO NEED YOU UP HERE.
WOULDN'T IT BE DANGEROUS IF THEY SAW US TOGETHER?
CORONA
ISLA
QUESADILLA ENTOMATADA
YOU'RE THE DANGEROUS ONE, RAFAEL. ESPECIALLY IF YOU DON'T COME ALONE!
RICKS HAS PICKED A GOOD SPOT TO GO UNNOTICED. SAN MIGUEL IS INFESTED WITH RICH, RETIRED AMERICANS.
IF YOU WANT SOMETHING TO DO, YOU'D ONLY HAVE TO CHECK HOW MANY OF YOUR COMPATRIOTS AREN'T DECLARING THEIR REVENUES.
HERE ARE SO MANY GRINGOS OVER THERE THAT IT'S MAKING THE MEXICANS LEAVE.
BUT NOT THE MEXICAN LADIES, I'M SURE.
HERE WE ARE...
15

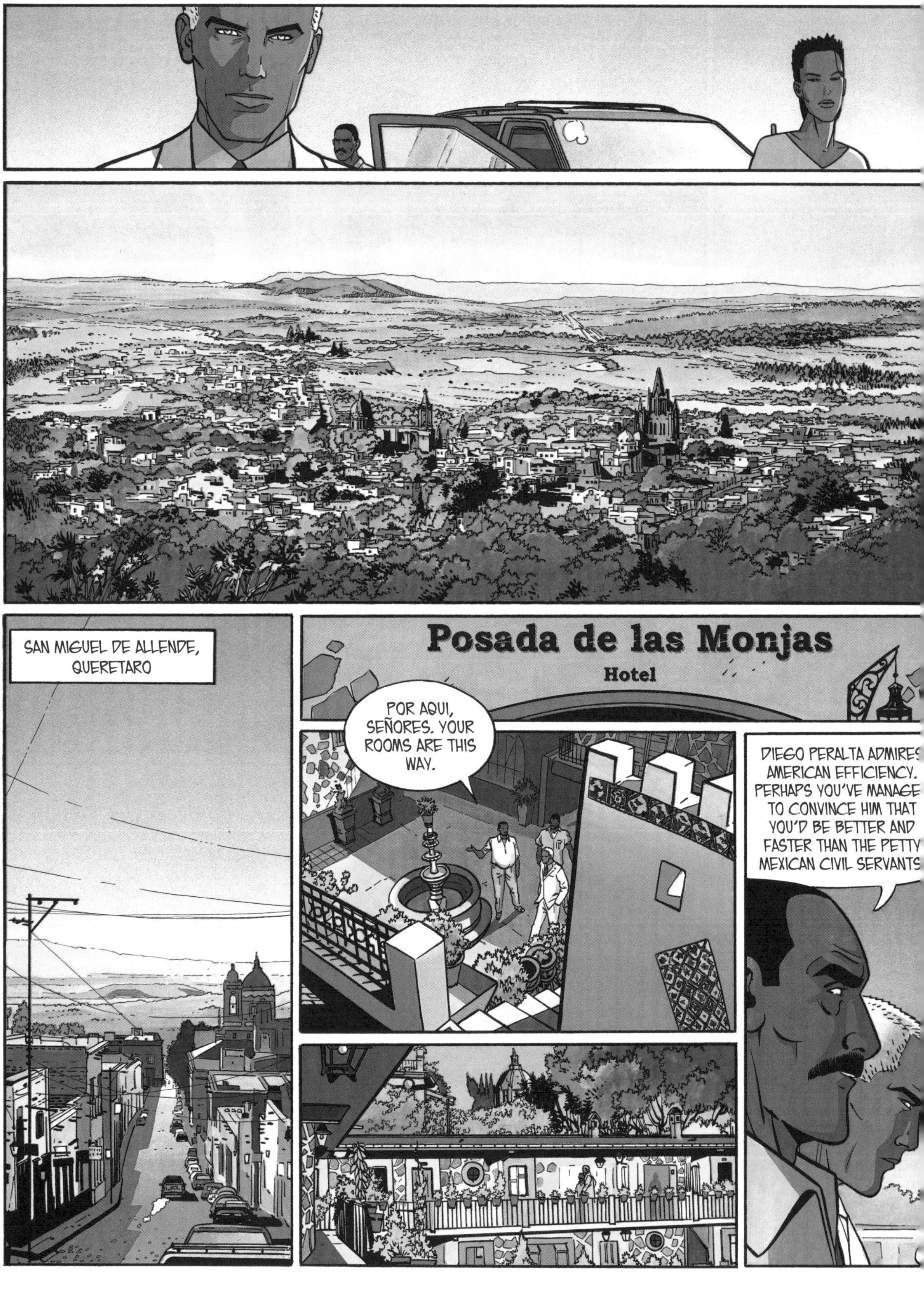
SAN MIGUEL DE ALLENDE, QUERETARO
Posada de las Monjas
Hotel
POR AQUI, SEÑORES. YOUR ROOMS ARE THIS WAY.
DIEGO PERALTA ADMIRES AMERICAN EFFICIENCY. PERHAPS YOU'VE MANAGE TO CONVINCE HIM THAT YOU'D BE BETTER AND FASTER THAN THE PETTY MEXICAN CIVIL SERVANTS

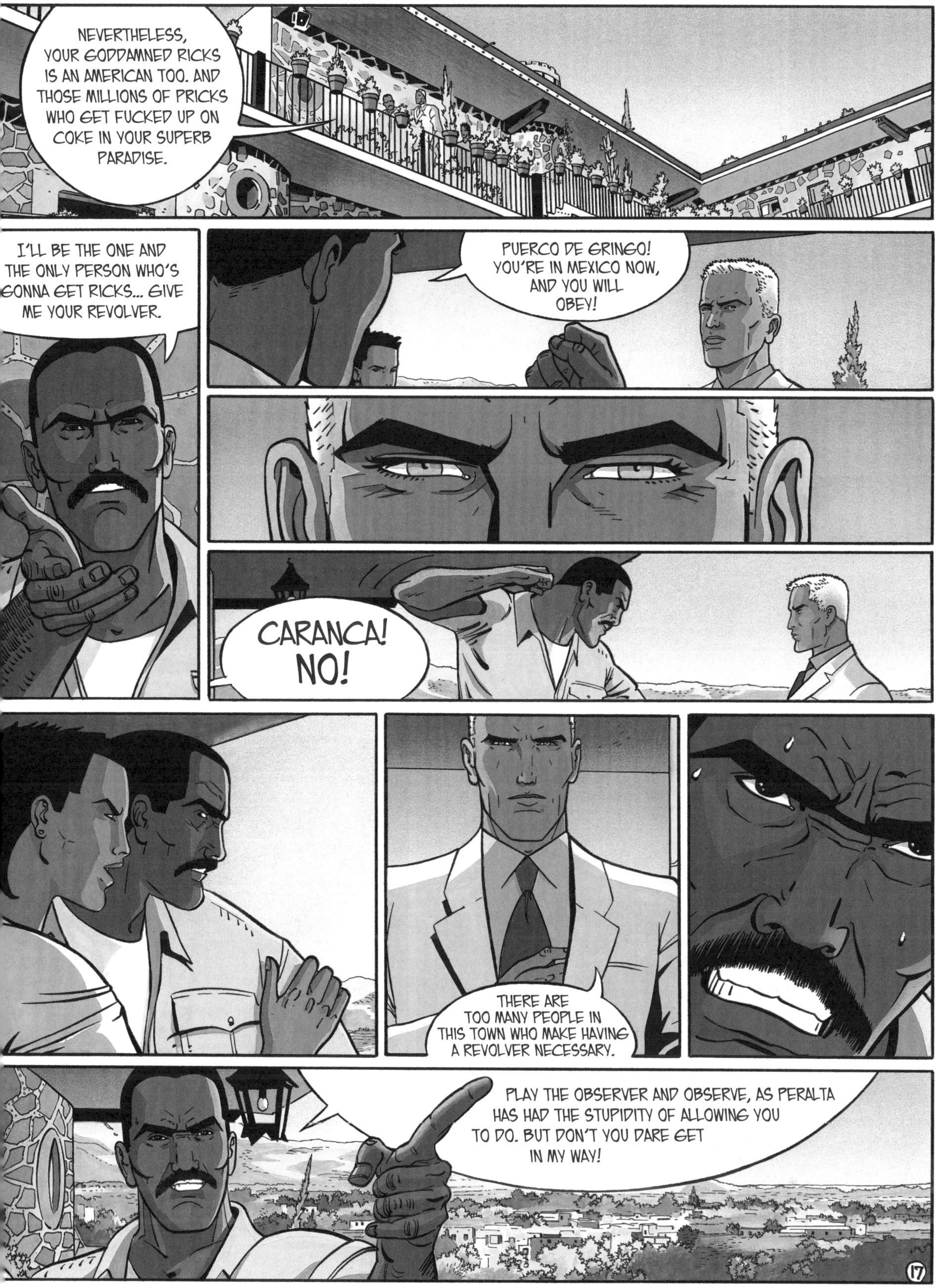
NEVERTHELESS, YOUR GODDAMNED RICKS IS AN AMERICAN TOO. AND THOSE MILLIONS OF PRICKS WHO GET FUCKED UP ON COKE IN YOUR SUPERB PARADISE.
I'LL BE THE ONE AND THE ONLY PERSON WHO'S GONNA GET RICKS... GIVE ME YOUR REVOLVER.
PUERCO DE GRINGO! YOU'RE IN MEXICO NOW, AND YOU WILL OBEY!
CARANCA! NO!
THERE ARE TOO MANY PEOPLE IN THIS TOWN WHO MAKE HAVING A REVOLVER NECESSARY.
PLAY THE OBSERVER AND OBSERVE, AS PERALTA HAS HAD THE STUPIDITY OF ALLOWING YOU TO DO. BUT DON'T YOU DARE GET IN MY WAY!
17

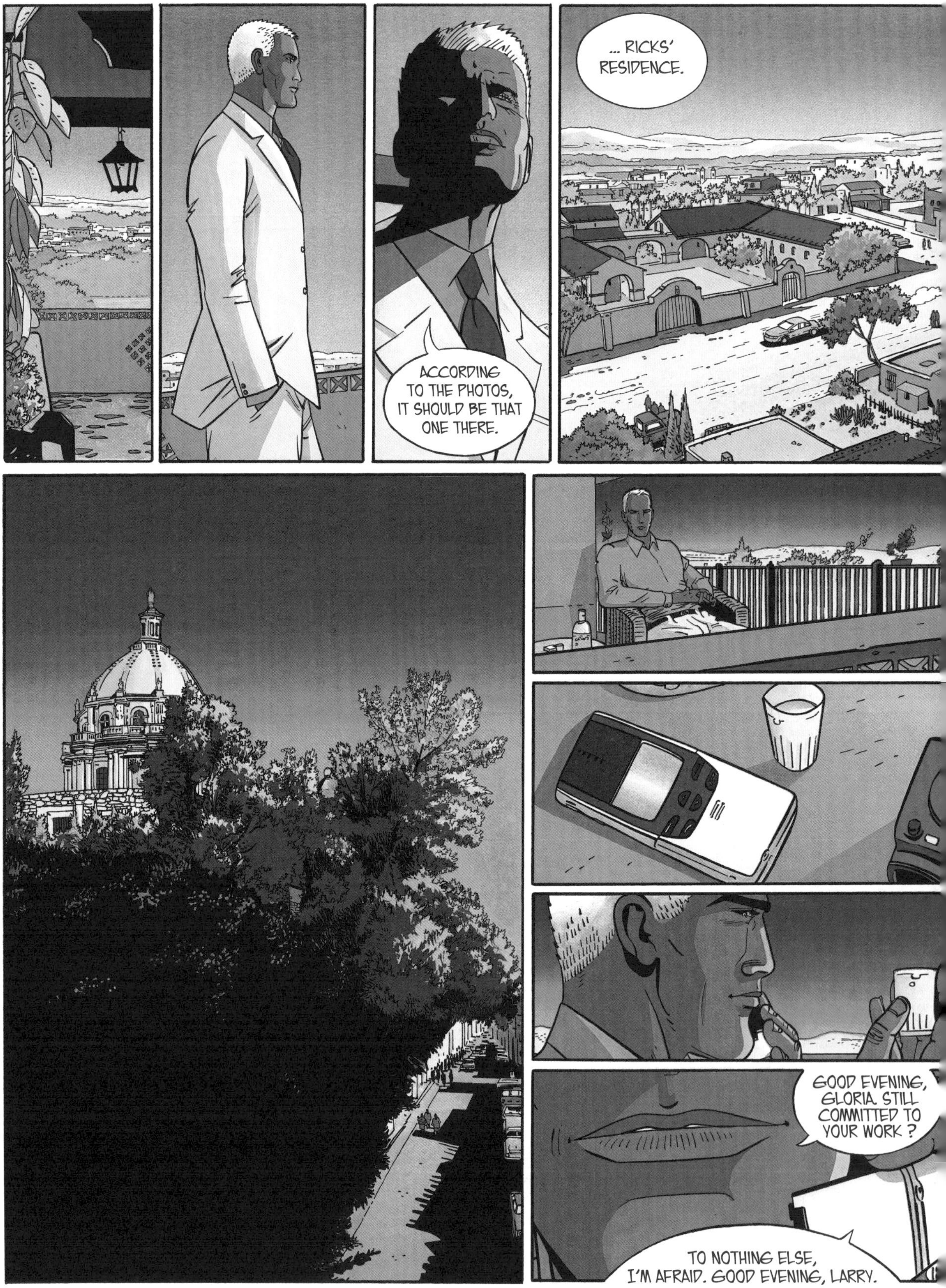
ACCORDING TO THE PHOTOS, IT SHOULD BE THAT ONE THERE.
... RICKS' RESIDENCE.
GOOD EVENING, GLORIA. STILL COMMITTED TO YOUR WORK ?
TO NOTHING ELSE, I'M AFRAID. GOOD EVENING, LARRY.

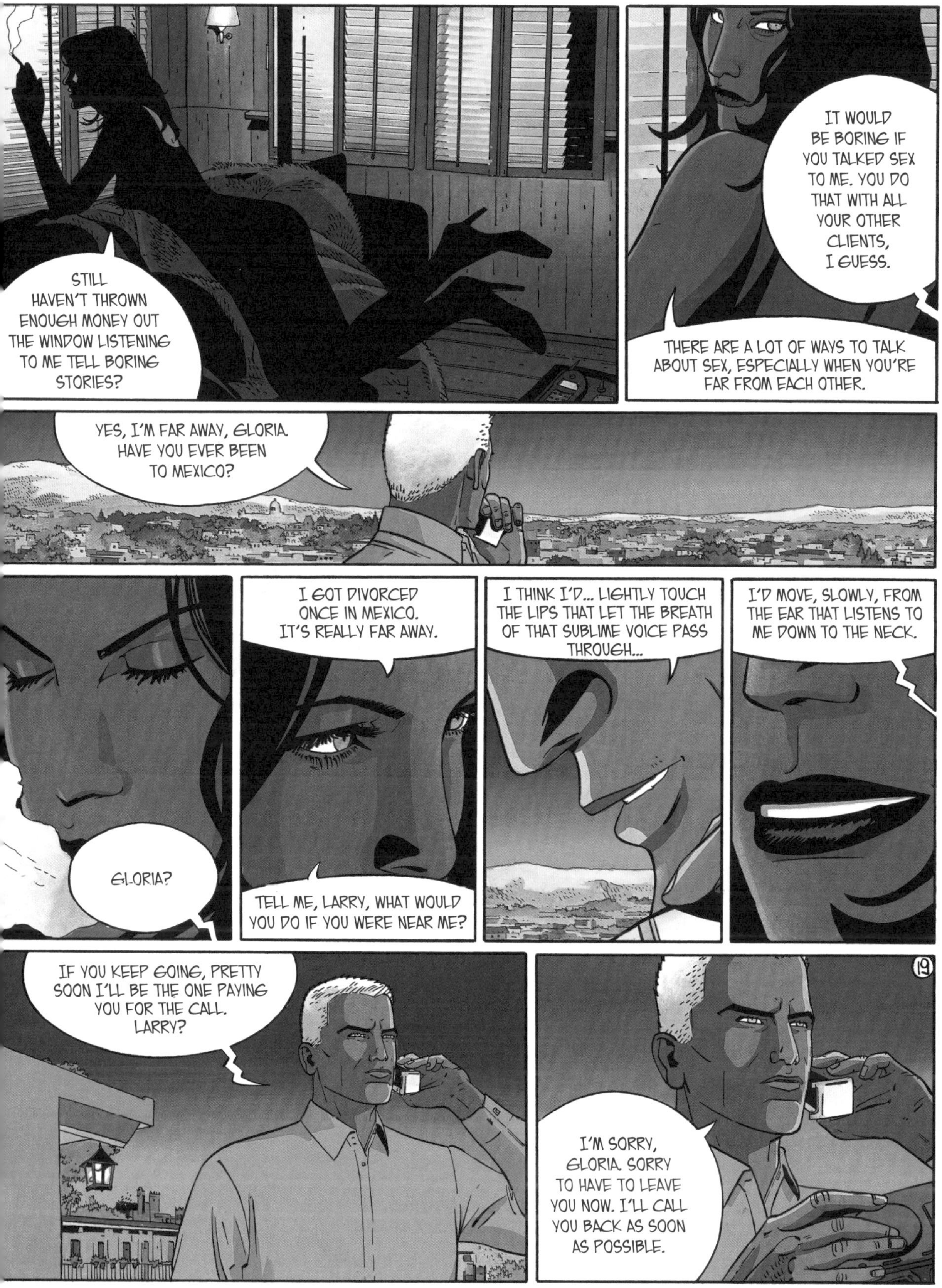
STILL HAVEN'T THROWN ENOUGH MONEY OUT THE WINDOW LISTENING TO ME TELL BORING STORIES?
IT WOULD BE BORING IF YOU TALKED SEX TO ME. YOU DO THAT WITH ALL YOUR OTHER CLIENTS, I GUESS.
THERE ARE A LOT OF WAYS TO TALK ABOUT SEX, ESPECIALLY WHEN YOU'RE FAR FROM EACH OTHER.
YES, I'M FAR AWAY, GLORIA. HAVE YOU EVER BEEN TO MEXICO?
GLORIA?
I GOT DIVORCED ONCE IN MEXICO. IT'S REALLY FAR AWAY.
TELL ME, LARRY, WHAT WOULD YOU DO IF YOU WERE NEAR ME?
I THINK I'D... LIGHTLY TOUCH THE LIPS THAT LET THE BREATH OF THAT SUBLIME VOICE PASS THROUGH...
I'D MOVE, SLOWLY, FROM THE EAR THAT LISTENS TO ME DOWN TO THE NECK.
IF YOU KEEP GOING, PRETTY SOON I'LL BE THE ONE PAYING YOU FOR THE CALL. LARRY?
19
I'M SORRY, GLORIA. SORRY TO HAVE TO LEAVE YOU NOW. I'LL CALL YOU BACK AS SOON AS POSSIBLE.

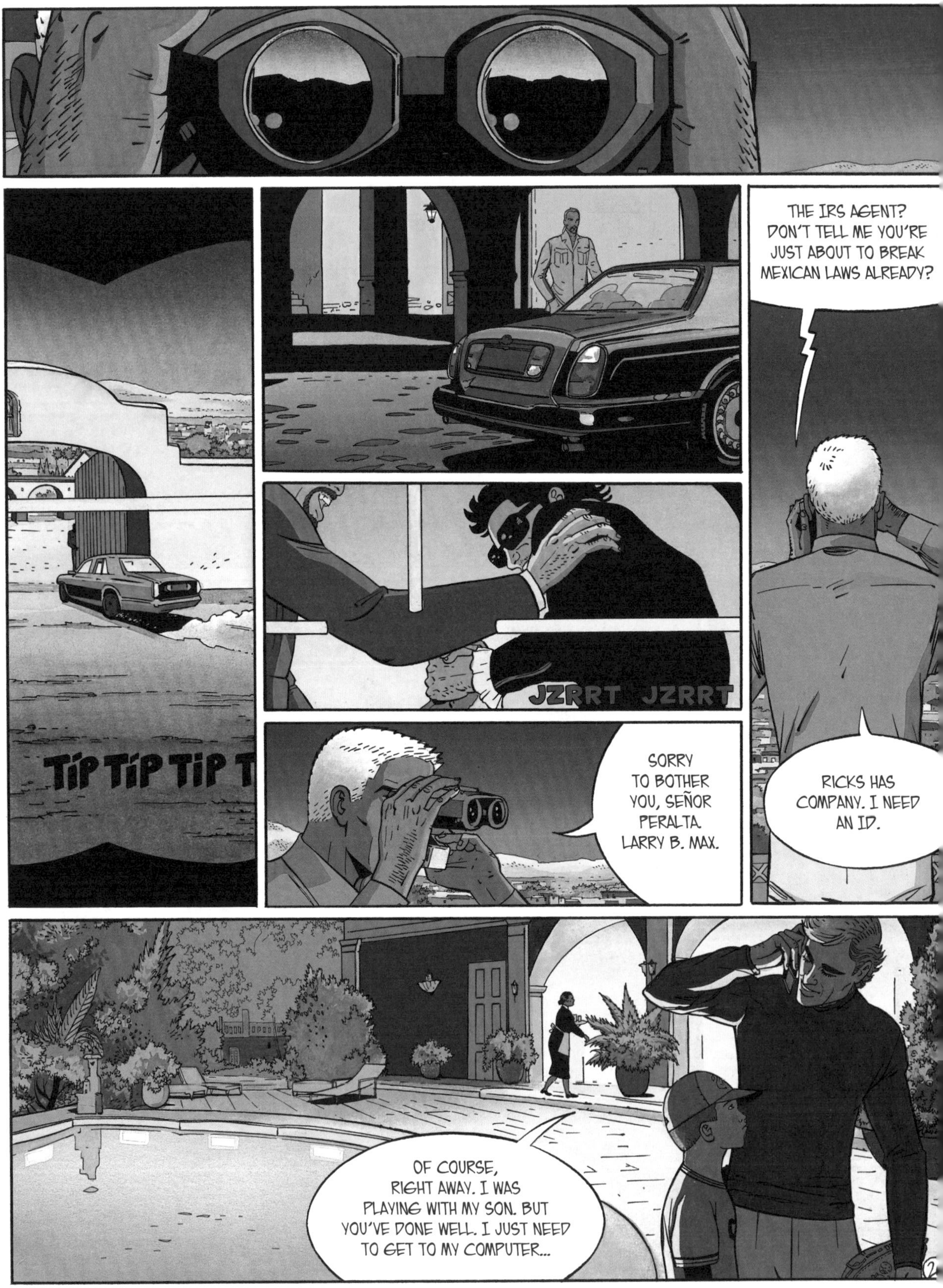
TIP TIP TIP T
JZRRT JZRRT
SORRY TO BOTHER YOU, SEÑOR PERALTA. LARRY B. MAX.
THE IRS AGENT? DON'T TELL ME YOU'RE JUST ABOUT TO BREAK MEXICAN LAWS ALREADY?
RICKS HAS COMPANY. I NEED AN ID.
OF COURSE, RIGHT AWAY. I WAS PLAYING WITH MY SON. BUT YOU'VE DONE WELL. I JUST NEED TO GET TO MY COMPUTER...

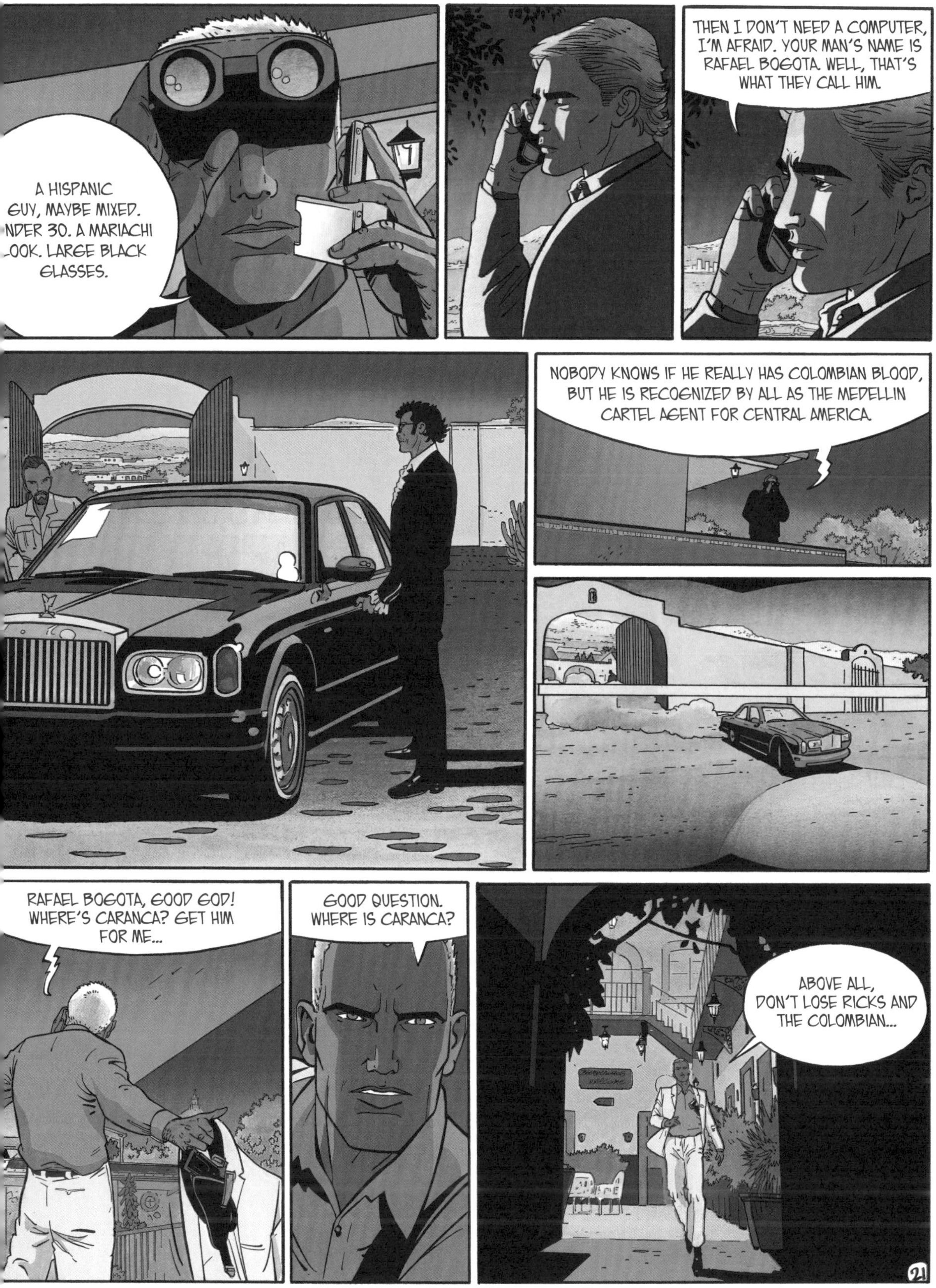
A HISPANIC GUY, MAYBE MIXED. NDER 30. A MARIACHI OOK. LARGE BLACK GLASSES.
THEN I DON'T NEED A COMPUTER, I'M AFRAID. YOUR MAN'S NAME IS RAFAEL BOGOTA. WELL, THAT'S WHAT THEY CALL HIM.
NOBODY KNOWS IF HE REALLY HAS COLOMBIAN BLOOD, BUT HE IS RECOGNIZED BY ALL AS THE MEDELLIN CARTEL AGENT FOR CENTRAL AMERICA.
RAFAEL BOGOTA, GOOD GOD! WHERE'S CARANCA? GET HIM FOR ME...
GOOD QUESTION. WHERE IS CARANCA?
ABOVE ALL, DON'T LOSE RICKS AND THE COLOMBIAN...
21

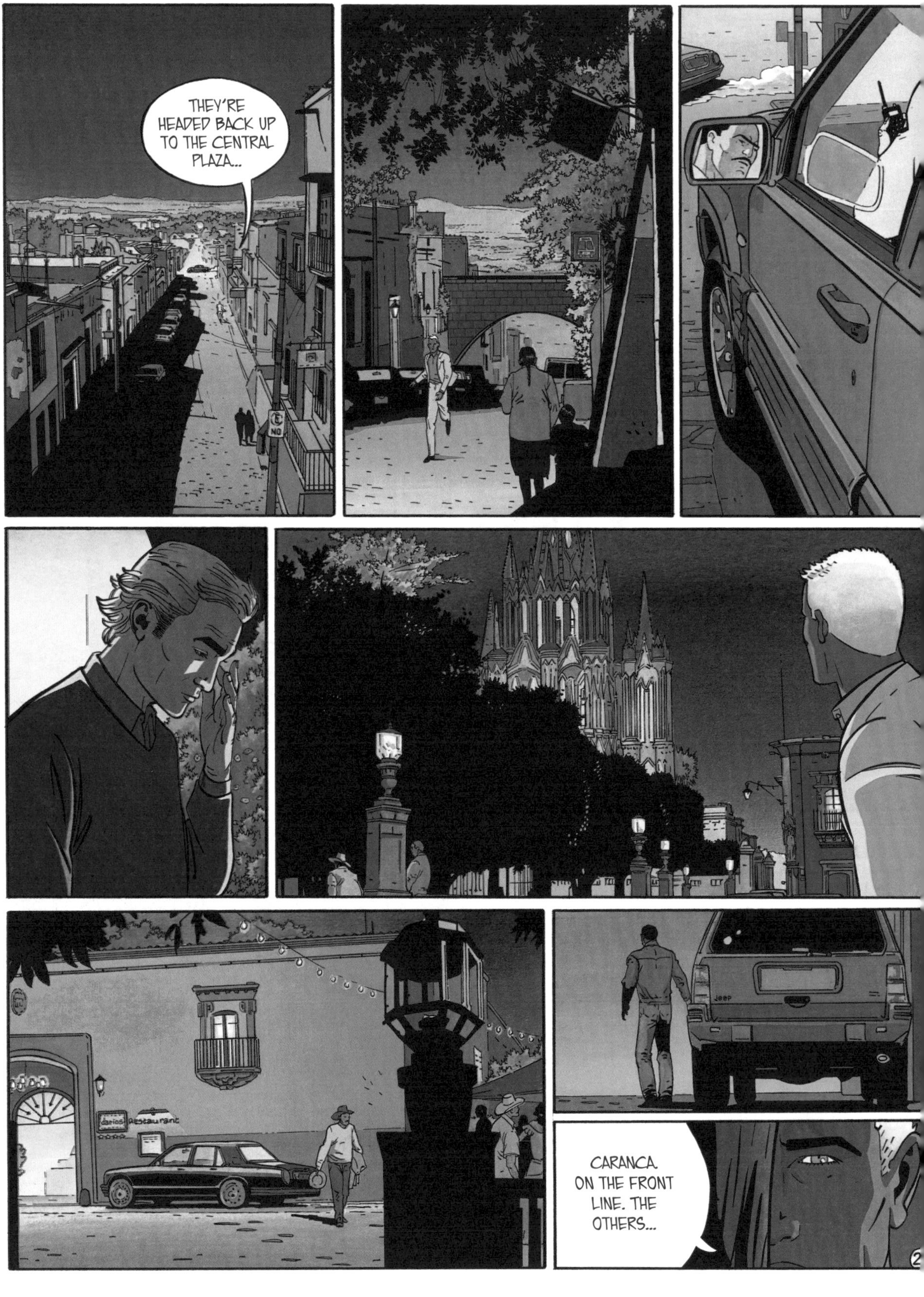
THEY'RE HEADED BACK UP TO THE CENTRAL PLAZA...
NO
Restaurant
CARANCA ON THE FRONT LINE. THE OTHERS...

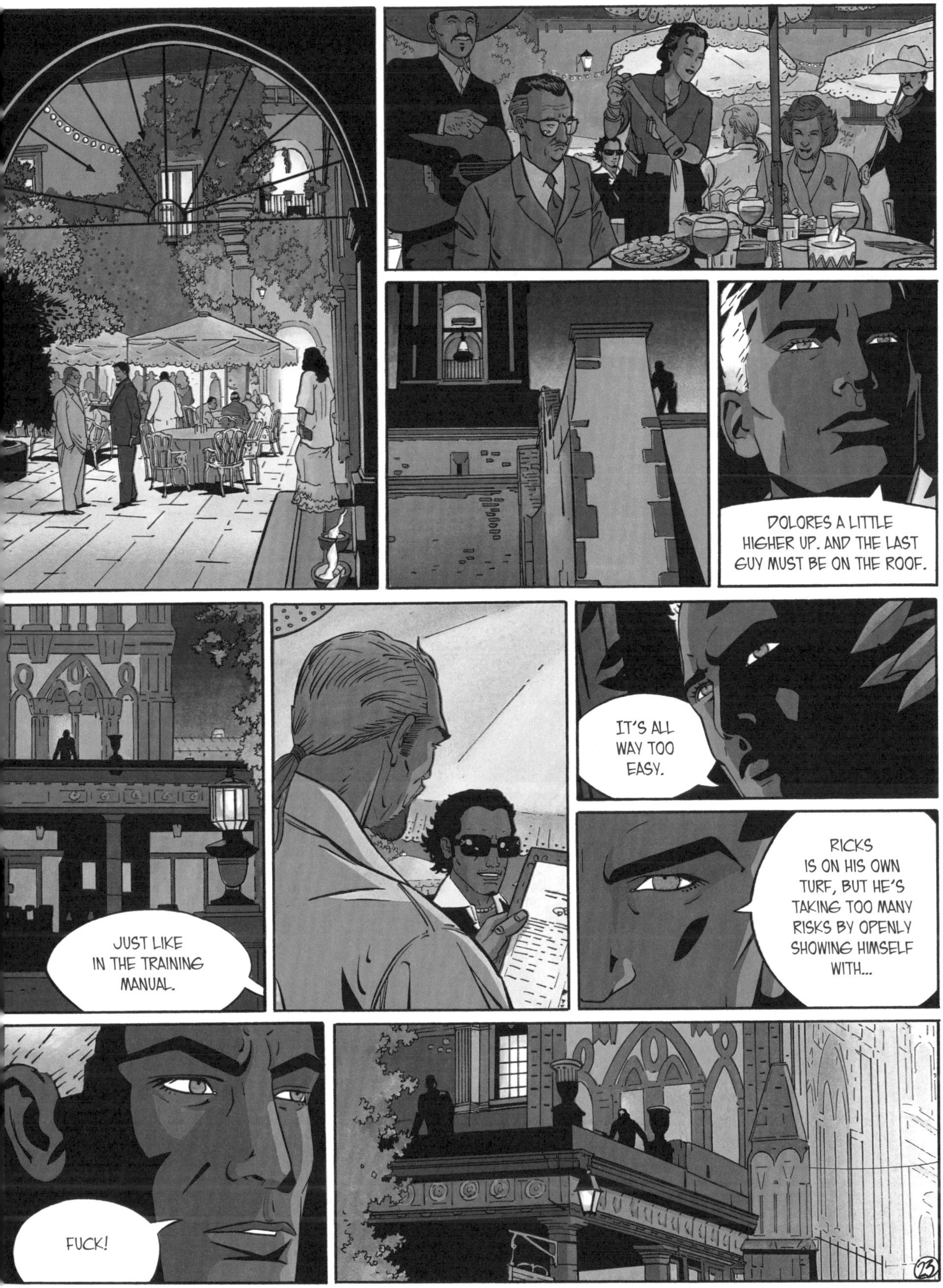
DOLORES A LITTLE HIGHER UP. AND THE LAST GUY MUST BE ON THE ROOF.
JUST LIKE IN THE TRAINING MANUAL.
IT'S ALL WAY TOO EASY.
RICKS IS ON HIS OWN TURF, BUT HE'S TAKING TOO MANY RISKS BY OPENLY SHOWING HIMSELF WITH...
FUCK!
23

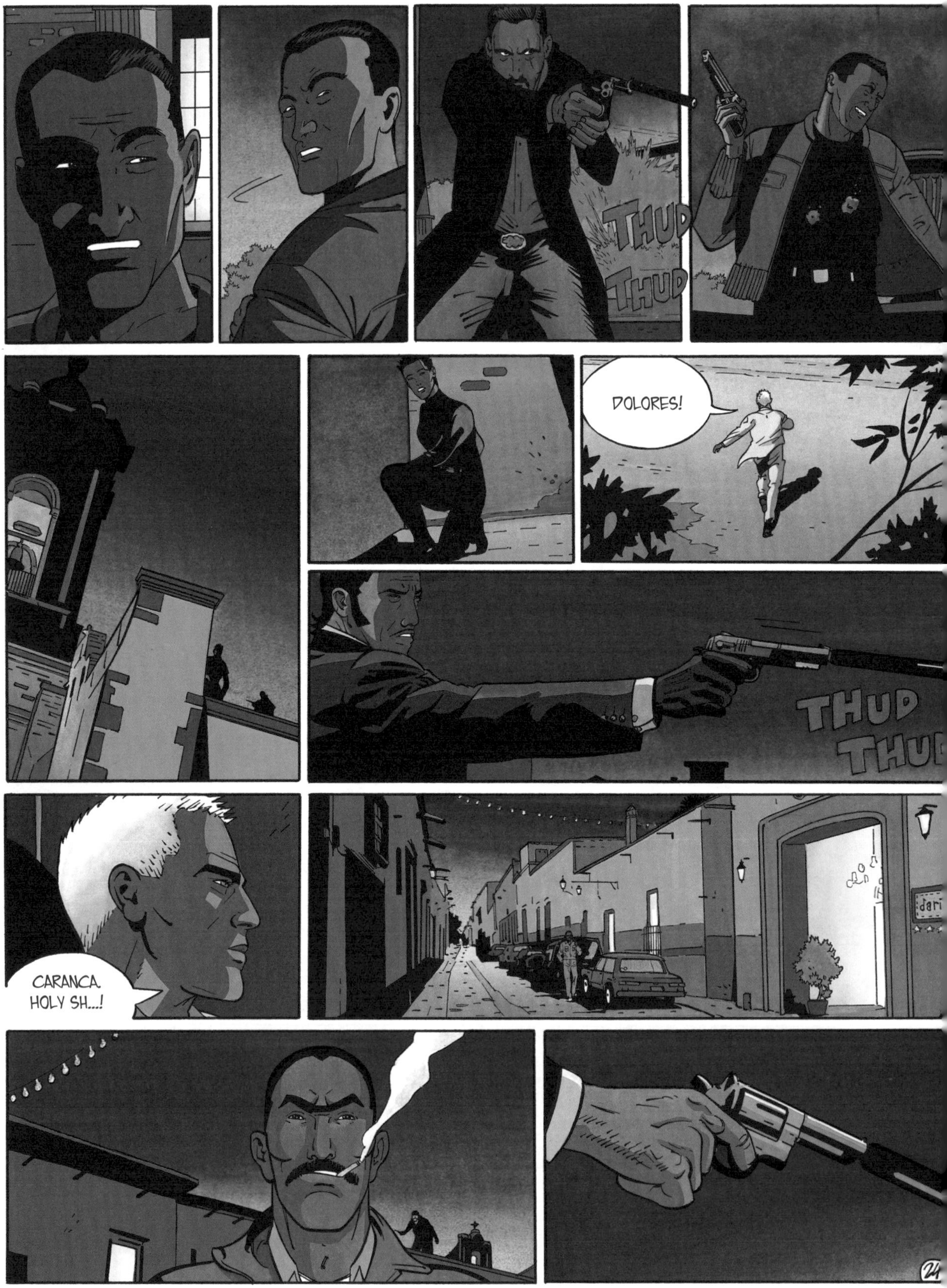
THUD
THUD
DOLORES!
THUD
CARANCA.
HOLY SH...!

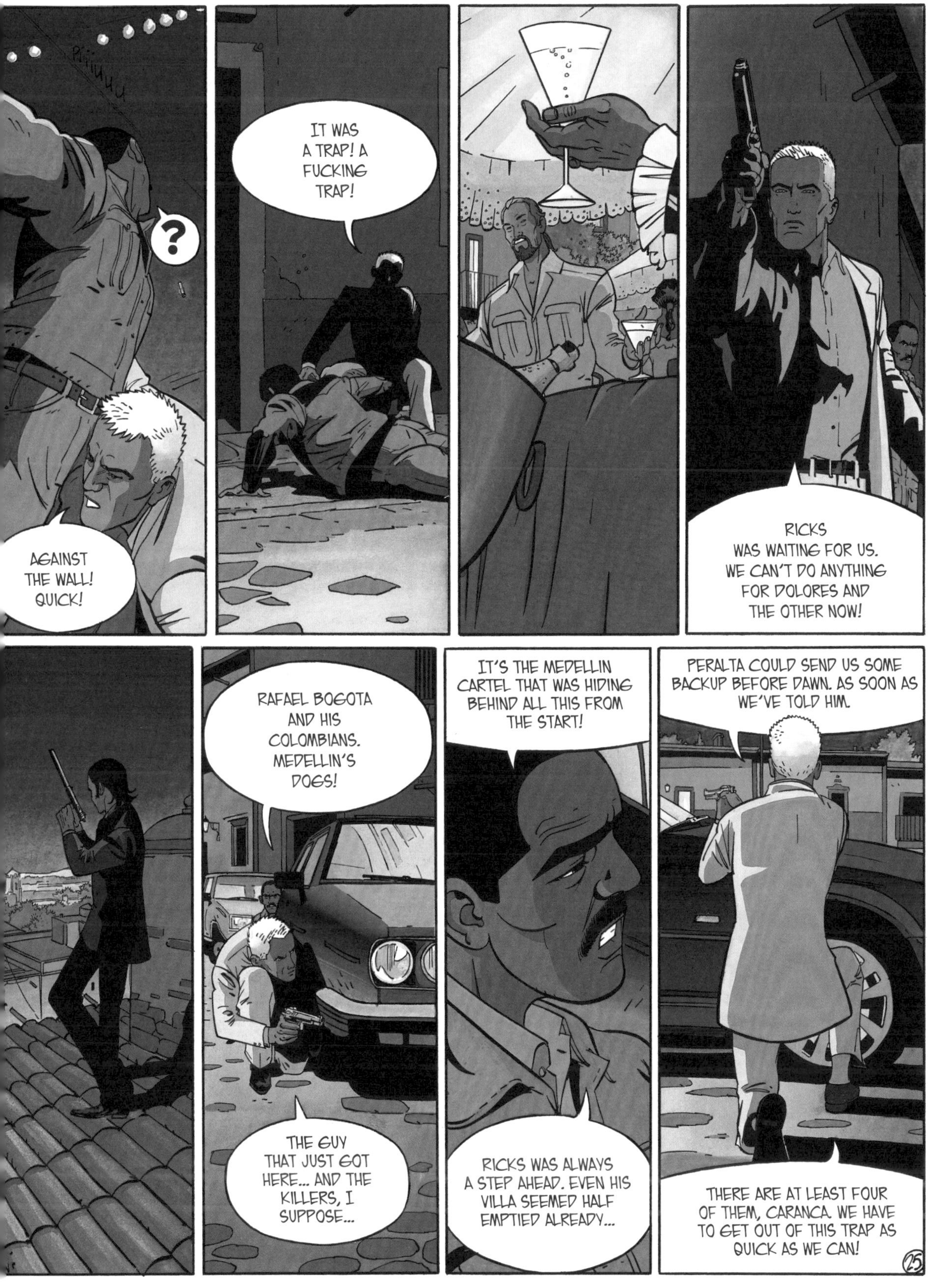
PIIIIUUU
?
AGAINST THE WALL! QUICK!
IT WAS A TRAP! A FUCKING TRAP!
RICKS WAS WAITING FOR US. WE CAN'T DO ANYTHING FOR DOLORES AND THE OTHER NOW!
RAFAEL BOGOTA AND HIS COLOMBIANS. MEDELLIN'S DOGS!
THE GUY THAT JUST GOT HERE... AND THE KILLERS, I SUPPOSE...
IT'S THE MEDELLIN CARTEL THAT WAS HIDING BEHIND ALL THIS FROM THE START!
RICKS WAS ALWAYS A STEP AHEAD. EVEN HIS VILLA SEEMED HALF EMPTIED ALREADY...
PERALTA COULD SEND US SOME BACKUP BEFORE DAWN. AS SOON AS WE'VE TOLD HIM.
THERE ARE AT LEAST FOUR OF THEM, CARANCA. WE HAVE TO GET OUT OF THIS TRAP AS QUICK AS WE CAN!
25

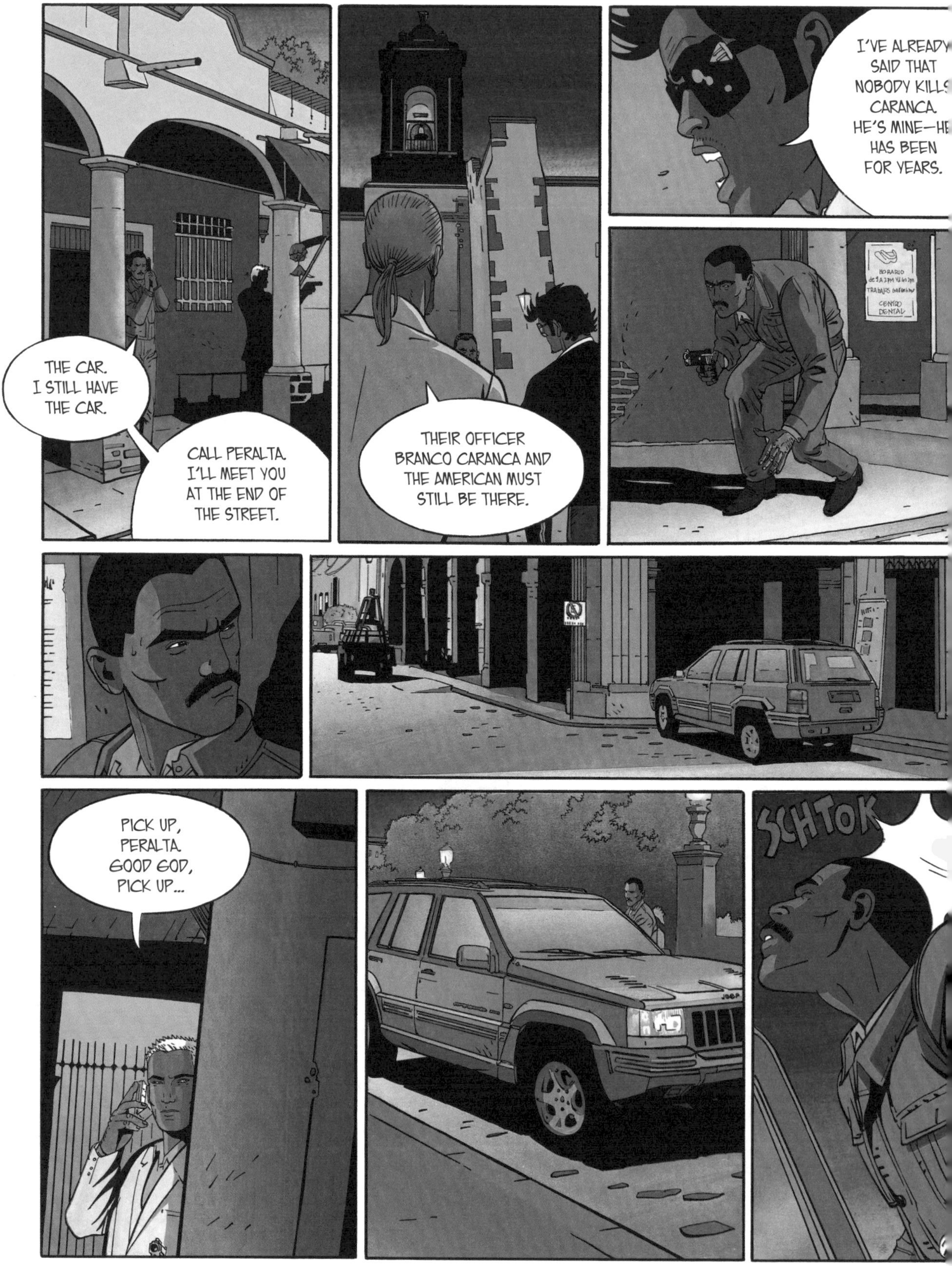
THE CAR. I STILL HAVE THE CAR.
CALL PERALTA. I'LL MEET YOU AT THE END OF THE STREET.
THEIR OFFICER BRANCO CARANCA AND THE AMERICAN MUST STILL BE THERE.
I'VE ALREADY SAID THAT NOBODY KILLS CARANCA. HE'S MINE—HE HAS BEEN FOR YEARS.
PICK UP, PERALTA. GOOD GOD, PICK UP...
SCHTOK

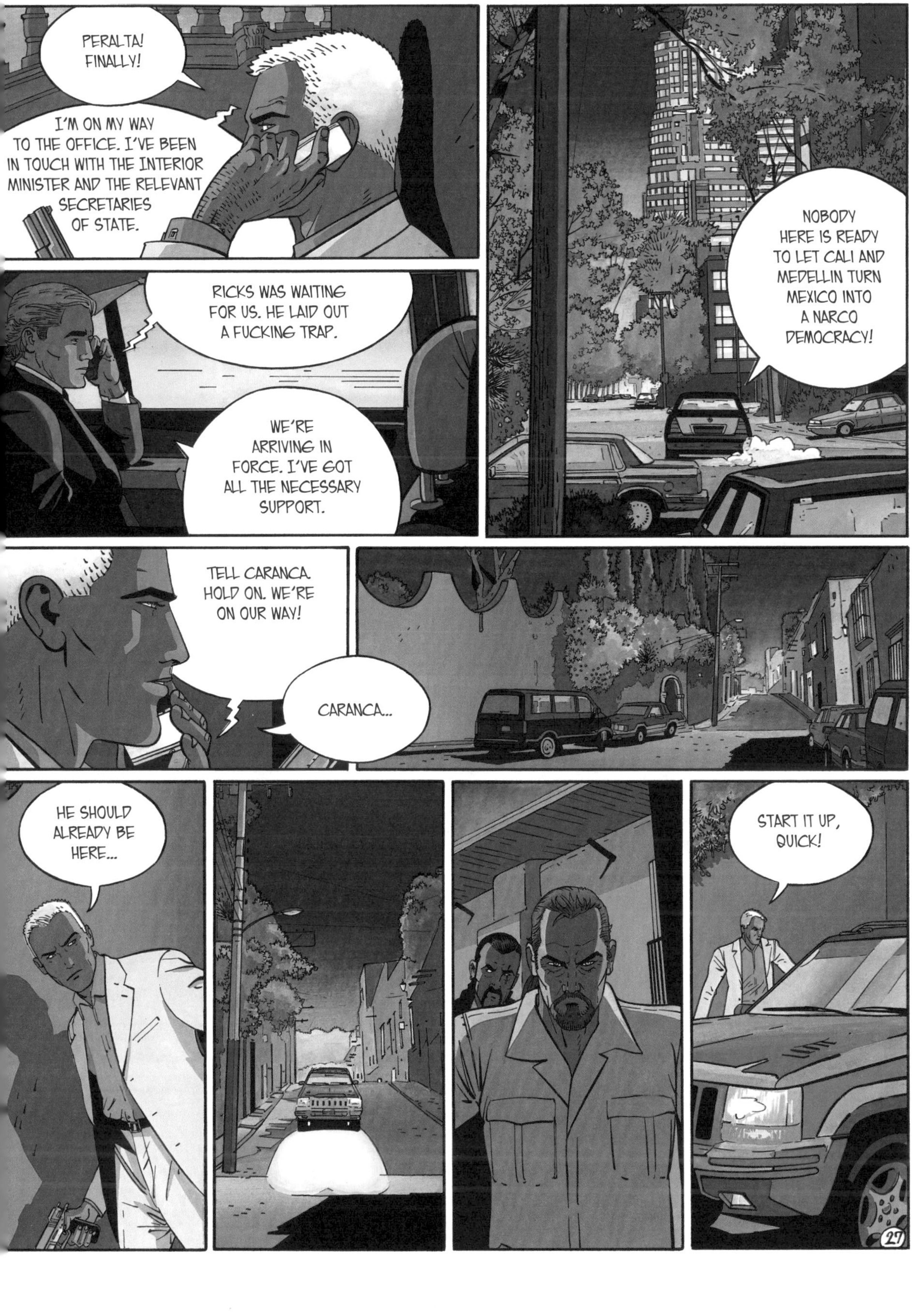
PERALTA! FINALLY!
I'M ON MY WAY TO THE OFFICE. I'VE BEEN IN TOUCH WITH THE INTERIOR MINISTER AND THE RELEVANT SECRETARIES OF STATE.
NOBODY HERE IS READY TO LET CALI AND MEDELLIN TURN MEXICO INTO A NARCO DEMOCRACY!
RICKS WAS WAITING FOR US. HE LAID OUT A FUCKING TRAP.
WE'RE ARRIVING IN FORCE. I'VE GOT ALL THE NECESSARY SUPPORT.
TELL CARANCA. HOLD ON. WE'RE ON OUR WAY!
CARANCA...
HE SHOULD ALREADY BE HERE...
START IT UP, QUICK!
27

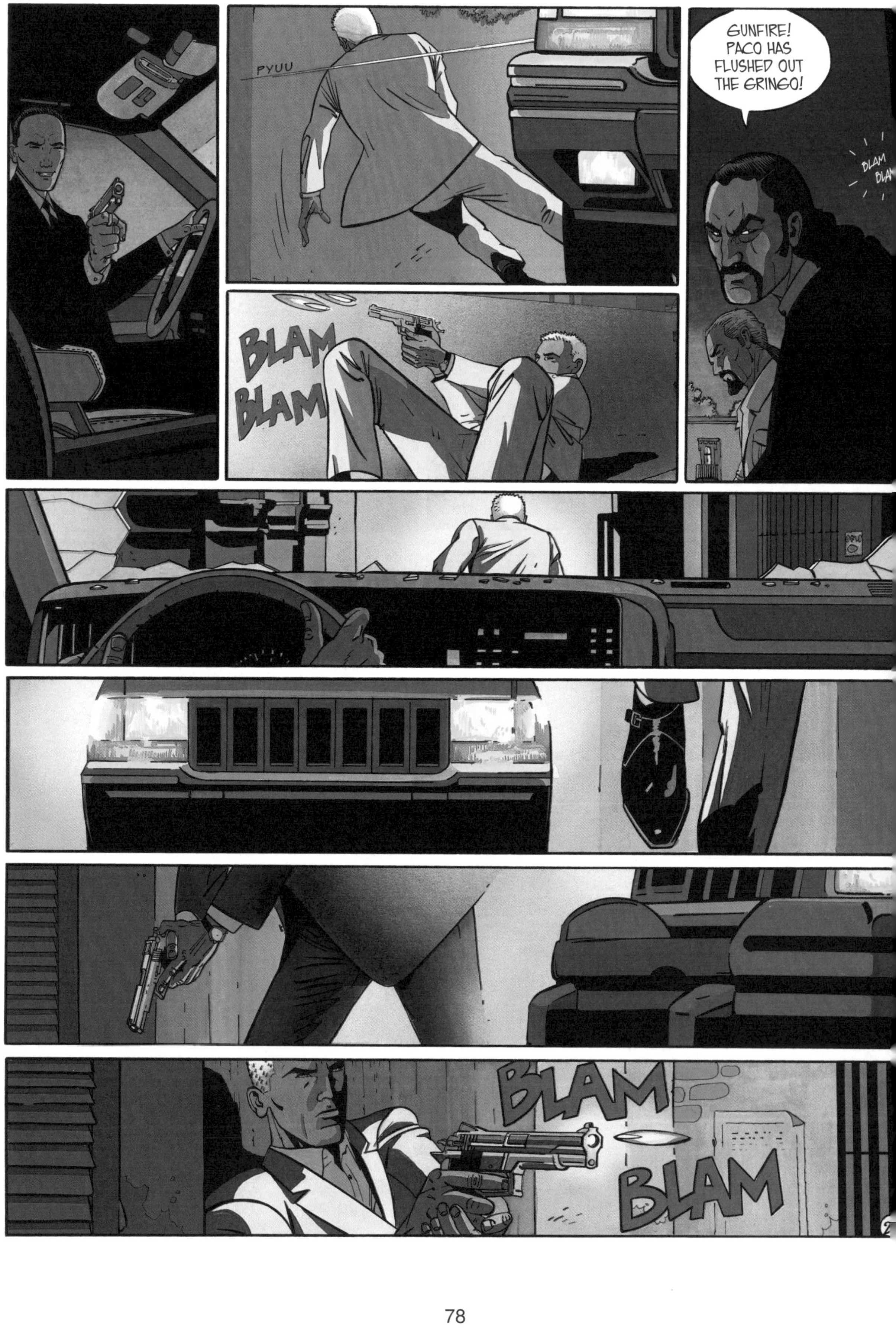
PYUU
BLAM
BLAM
GUNFIRE! PACO HAS FLUSHED OUT THE GRINGO!
BLAM
BLAM
BLAM

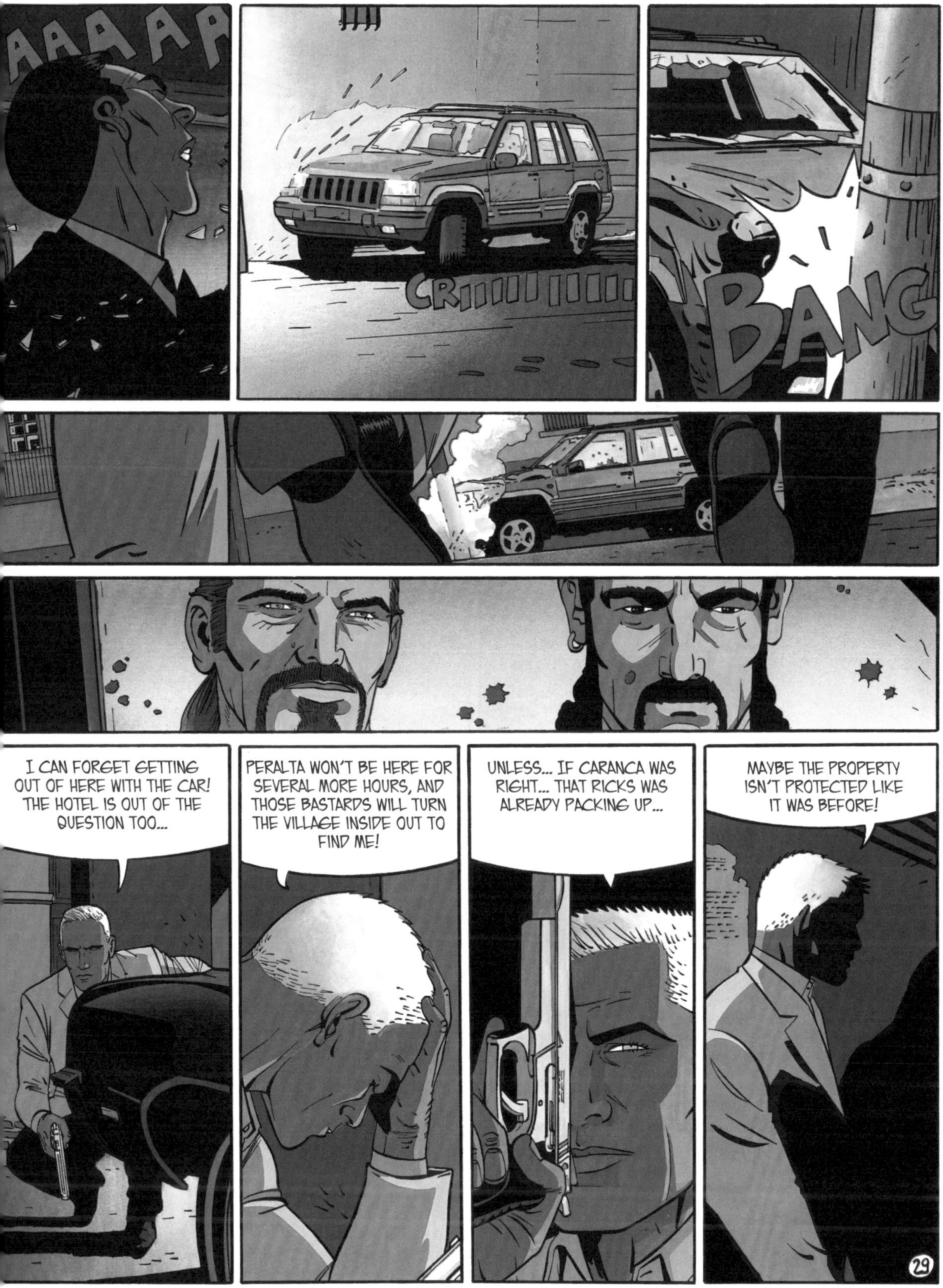
AAAAA
CRIIIII IIIIII
BANG
I CAN FORGET GETTING OUT OF HERE WITH THE CAR! THE HOTEL IS OUT OF THE QUESTION TOO...
PERALTA WON'T BE HERE FOR SEVERAL MORE HOURS, AND THOSE BASTARDS WILL TURN THE VILLAGE INSIDE OUT TO FIND ME!
UNLESS... IF CARANCA WAS RIGHT... THAT RICKS WAS ALREADY PACKING UP...
MAYBE THE PROPERTY ISN'T PROTECTED LIKE IT WAS BEFORE!
29

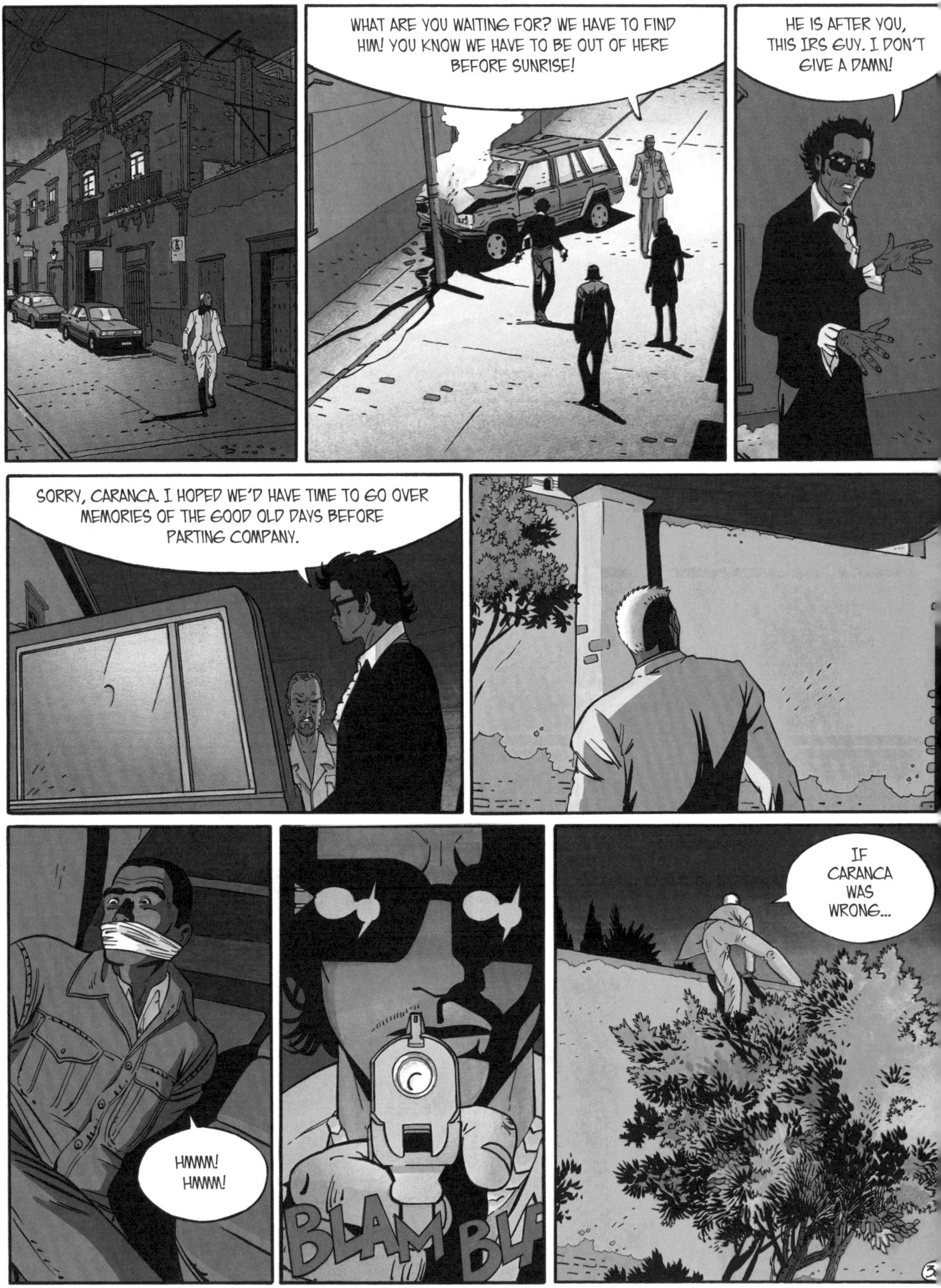
WHAT ARE YOU WAITING FOR? WE HAVE TO FIND HIM! YOU KNOW WE HAVE TO BE OUT OF HERE BEFORE SUNRISE!
HE IS AFTER YOU, THIS IRS GUY. I DON'T GIVE A DAMN!
SORRY, CARANCA. I HOPED WE'D HAVE TIME TO GO OVER MEMORIES OF THE GOOD OLD DAYS BEFORE PARTING COMPANY.
HMMM! HMMM!
BLAM BL
IF CARANCA WAS WRONG...

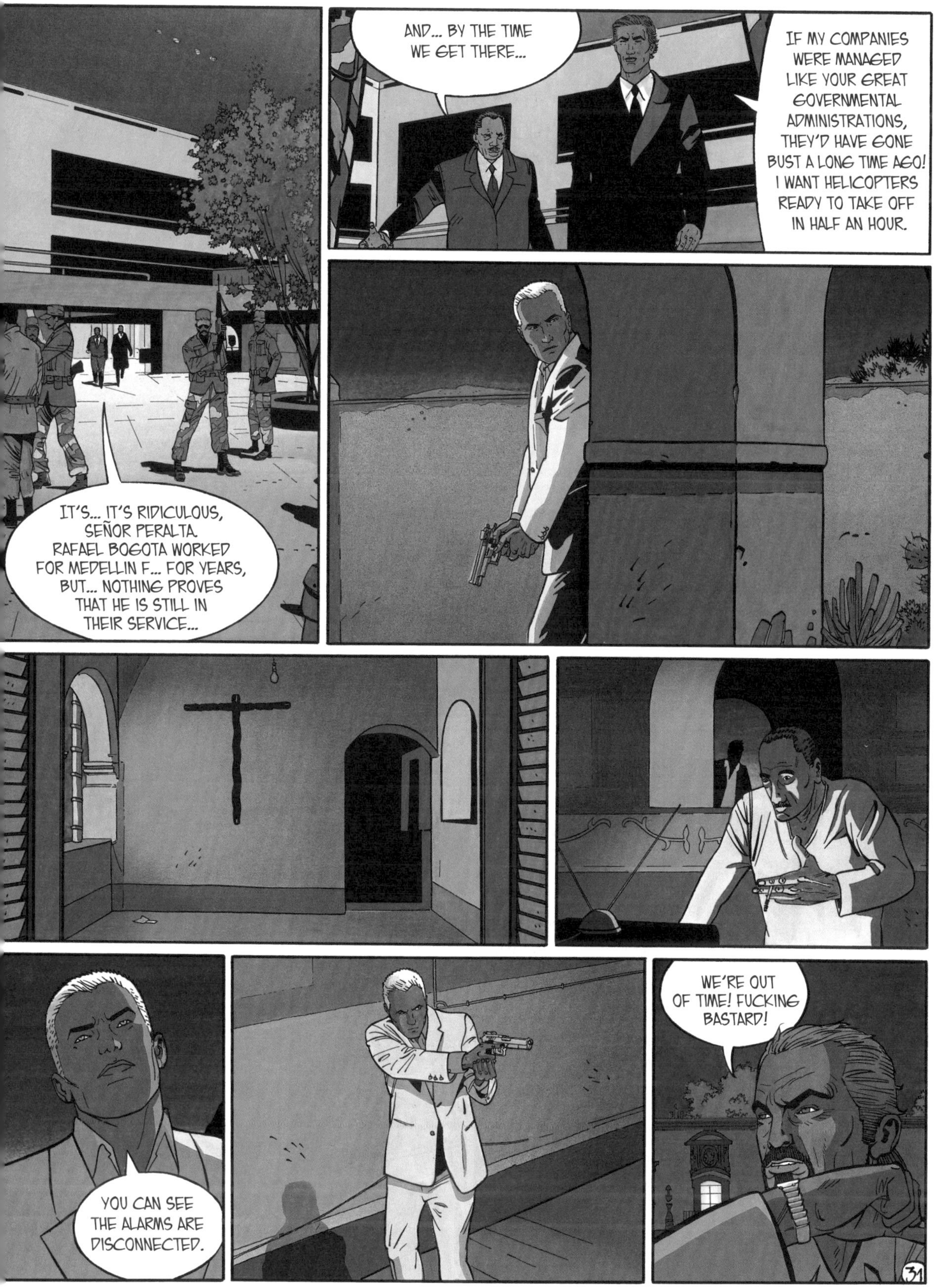
IT'S... IT'S RIDICULOUS, SEÑOR PERALTA. RAFAEL BOGOTA WORKED FOR MEDELLIN F... FOR YEARS, BUT... NOTHING PROVES THAT HE IS STILL IN THEIR SERVICE...
AND... BY THE TIME WE GET THERE...
IF MY COMPANIES WERE MANAGED LIKE YOUR GREAT GOVERNMENTAL ADMINISTRATIONS, THEY'D HAVE GONE BUST A LONG TIME AGO! I WANT HELICOPTERS READY TO TAKE OFF IN HALF AN HOUR.
YOU CAN SEE THE ALARMS ARE DISCONNECTED.
WE'RE OUT OF TIME! FUCKING BASTARD!
31

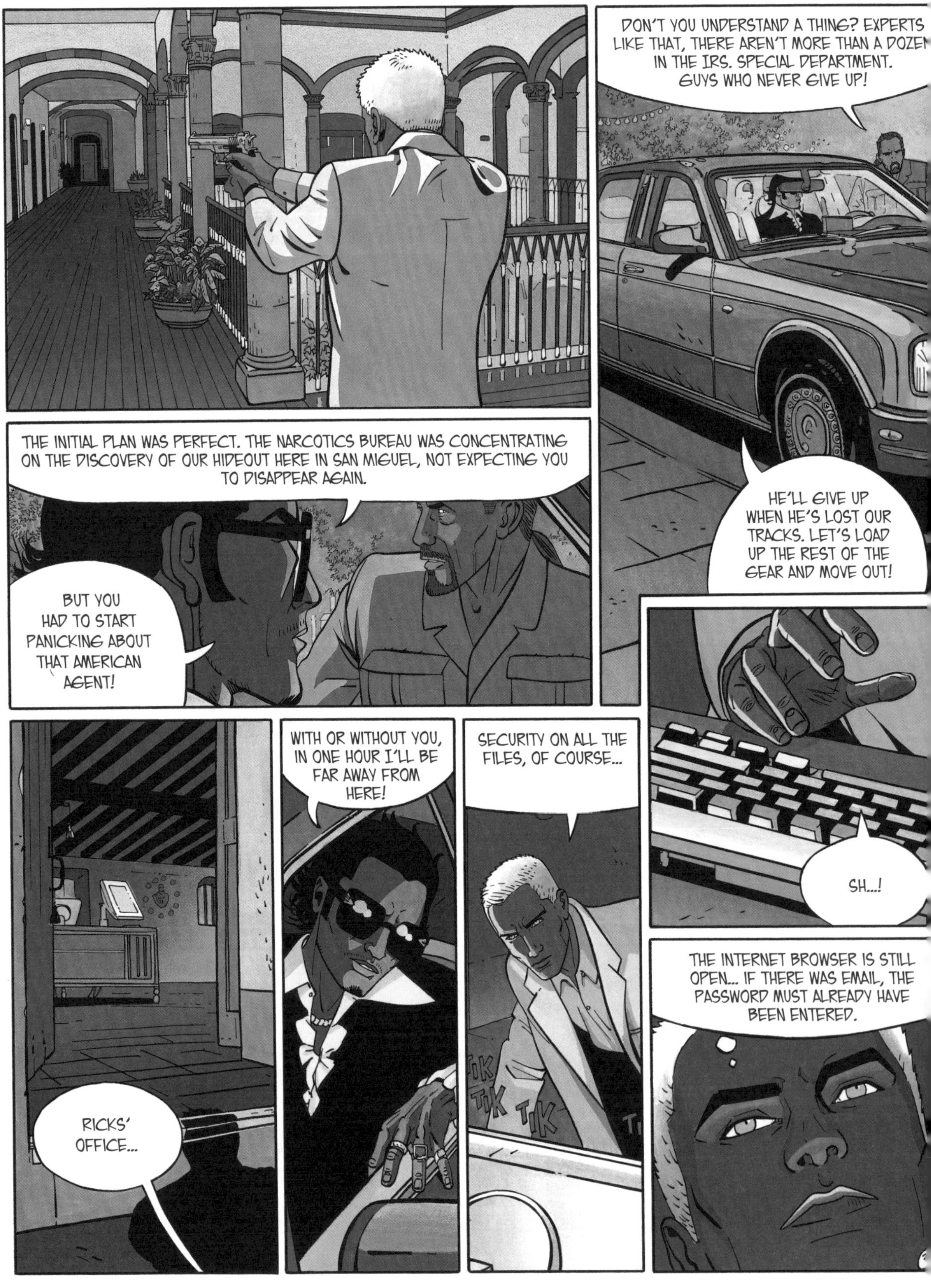
DON'T YOU UNDERSTAND A THING? EXPERTS LIKE THAT, THERE AREN'T MORE THAN A DOZEN IN THE IRS. SPECIAL DEPARTMENT. GUYS WHO NEVER GIVE UP!
THE INITIAL PLAN WAS PERFECT. THE NARCOTICS BUREAU WAS CONCENTRATING ON THE DISCOVERY OF OUR HIDEOUT HERE IN SAN MIGUEL, NOT EXPECTING YOU TO DISAPPEAR AGAIN.
BUT YOU HAD TO START PANICKING ABOUT THAT AMERICAN AGENT!
HE'LL GIVE UP WHEN HE'S LOST OUR TRACKS. LET'S LOAD UP THE REST OF THE GEAR AND MOVE OUT!
RICKS' OFFICE...
WITH OR WITHOUT YOU, IN ONE HOUR I'LL BE FAR AWAY FROM HERE!
SECURITY ON ALL THE FILES, OF COURSE...
TIK
TIK
TIK
SH...!
THE INTERNET BROWSER IS STILL OPEN... IF THERE WAS EMAIL, THE PASSWORD MUST ALREADY HAVE BEEN ENTERED.

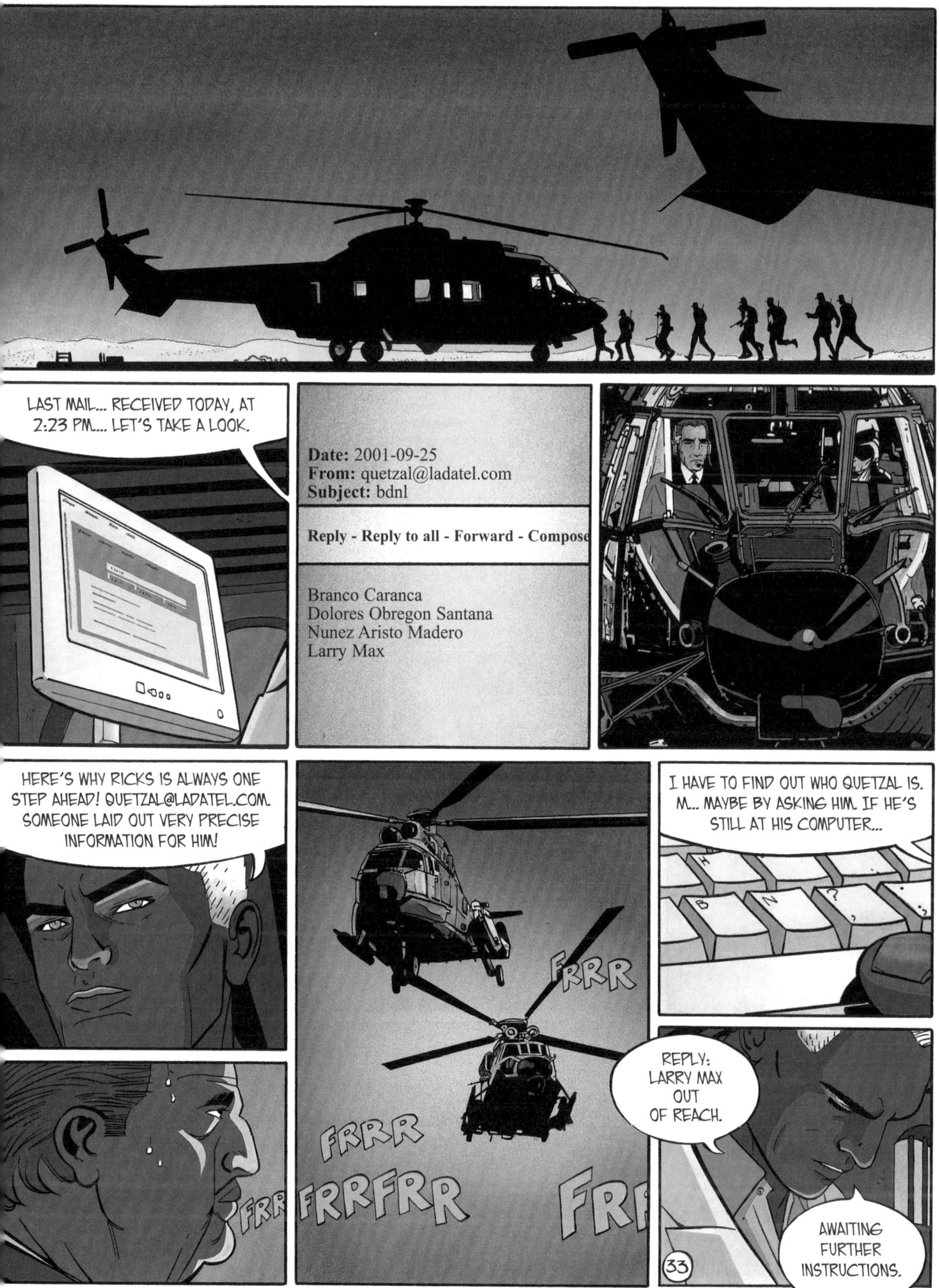
LAST MAIL... RECEIVED TODAY, AT 2:23 PM... LET'S TAKE A LOOK.
Date: 2001-09-25
From: quetzal@ladatel.com
Subject: bdnl
Reply - Reply to all - Forward - Compose
Branco Caranca
Dolores Obregon Santana
Nunez Aristo Madero
Larry Max
HERE'S WHY RICKS IS ALWAYS ONE STEP AHEAD! QUETZAL@LADATEL.COM SOMEONE LAID OUT VERY PRECISE INFORMATION FOR HIM!
FRR
FRRR
FRRR
FRRFRR
FRR
I HAVE TO FIND OUT WHO QUETZAL IS. M... MAYBE BY ASKING HIM. IF HE'S STILL AT HIS COMPUTER...
REPLY: LARRY MAX OUT OF REACH.
AWAITING FURTHER INSTRUCTIONS.
33

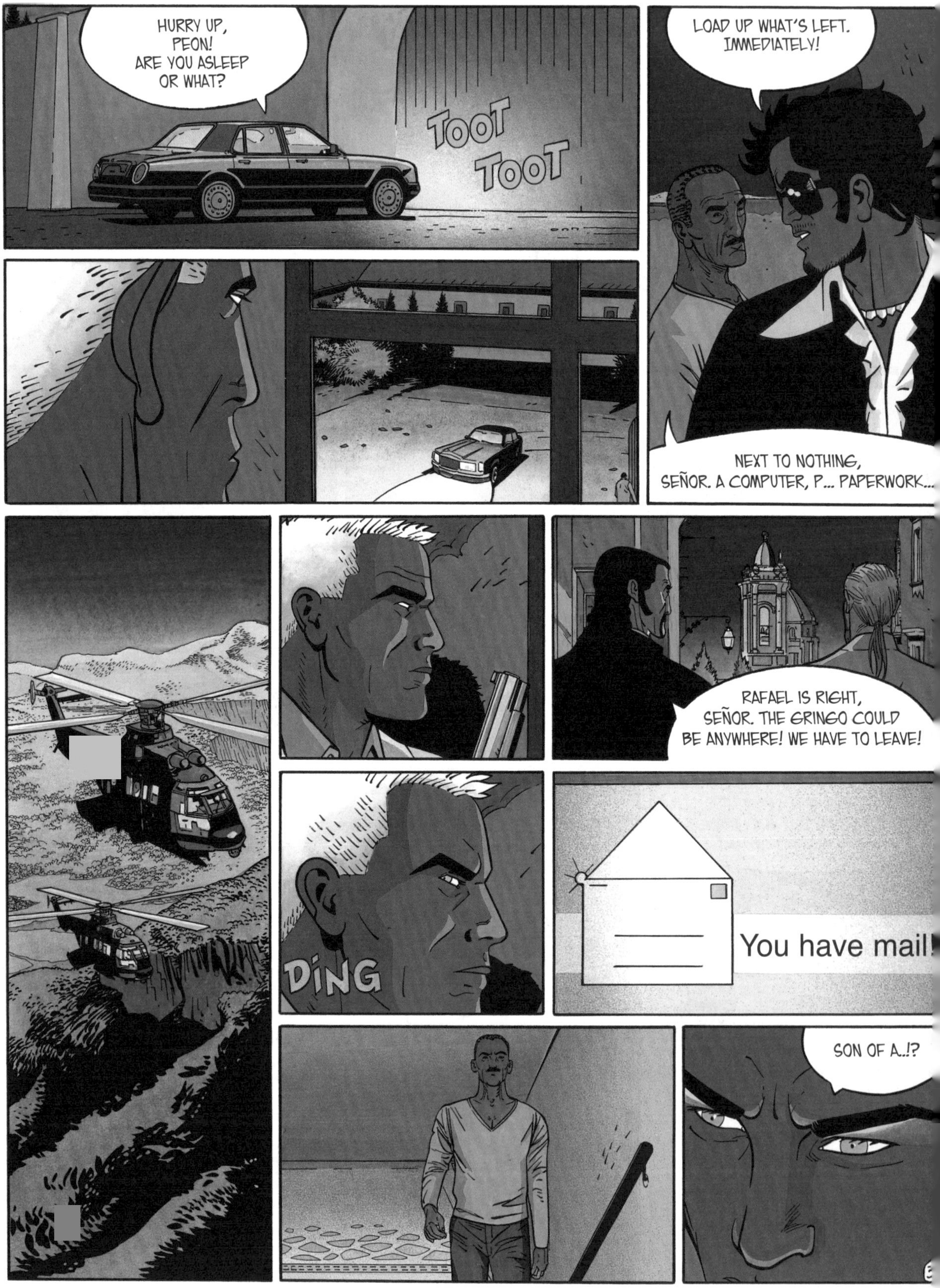
HURRY UP, PEON! ARE YOU ASLEEP OR WHAT?
TOOT TOOT
LOAD UP WHAT'S LEFT. IMMEDIATELY!
NEXT TO NOTHING, SEÑOR. A COMPUTER, P... PAPERWORK...
RAFAEL IS RIGHT, SEÑOR. THE GRINGO COULD BE ANYWHERE! WE HAVE TO LEAVE!
DING
You have mail!
SON OF A..!?

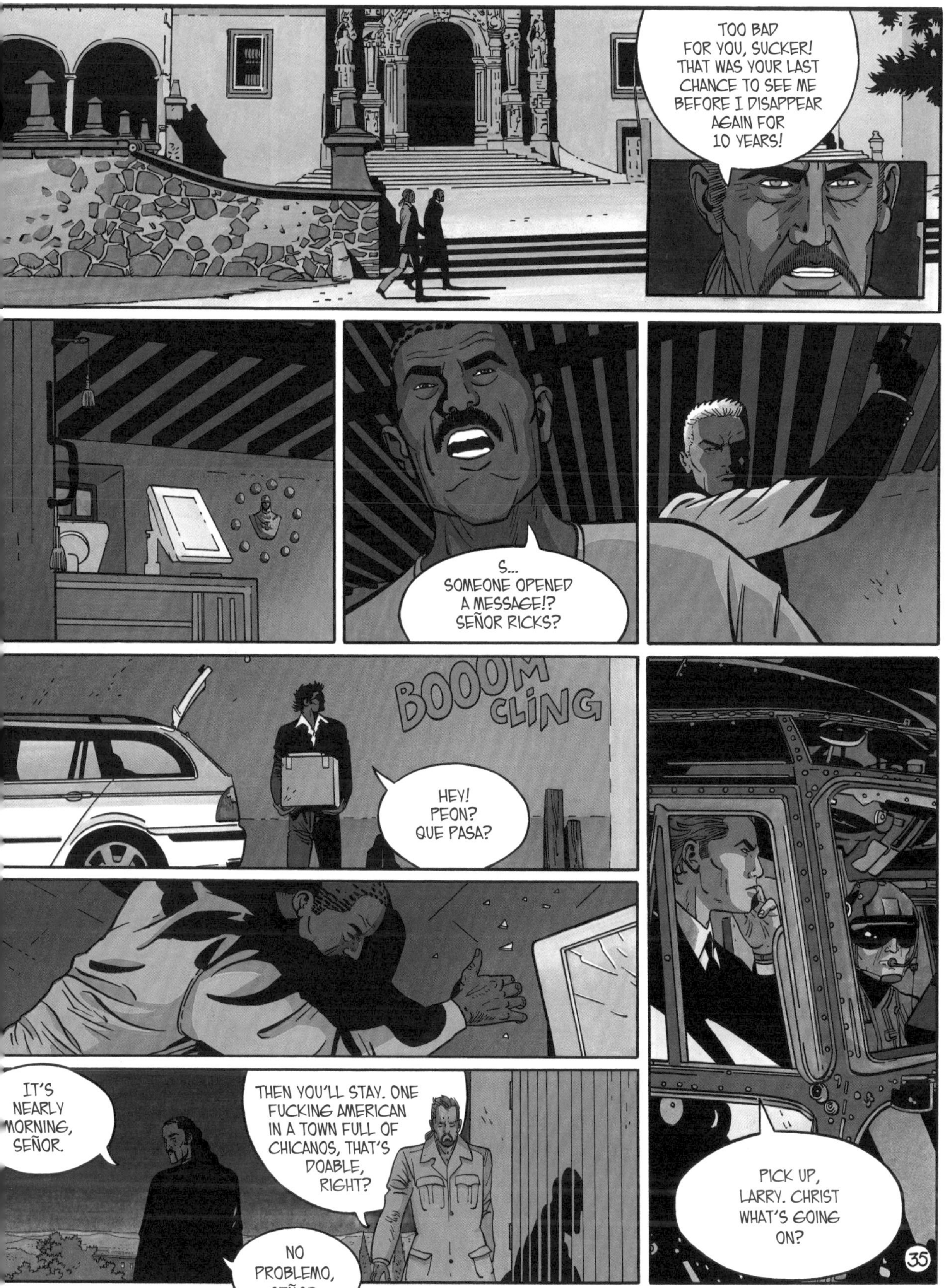
TOO BAD FOR YOU, SUCKER! THAT WAS YOUR LAST CHANCE TO SEE ME BEFORE I DISAPPEAR AGAIN FOR 10 YEARS!
S... SOMEONE OPENED A MESSAGE!? SEÑOR RICKS?
BOOOM
CLING
HEY! PEON? QUE PASA?
IT'S NEARLY MORNING, SEÑOR.
THEN YOU'LL STAY. ONE FUCKING AMERICAN IN A TOWN FULL OF CHICANOS, THAT'S DOABLE, RIGHT?
NO PROBLEMO, SEÑOR.
PICK UP, LARRY. CHRIST WHAT'S GOING ON?
35

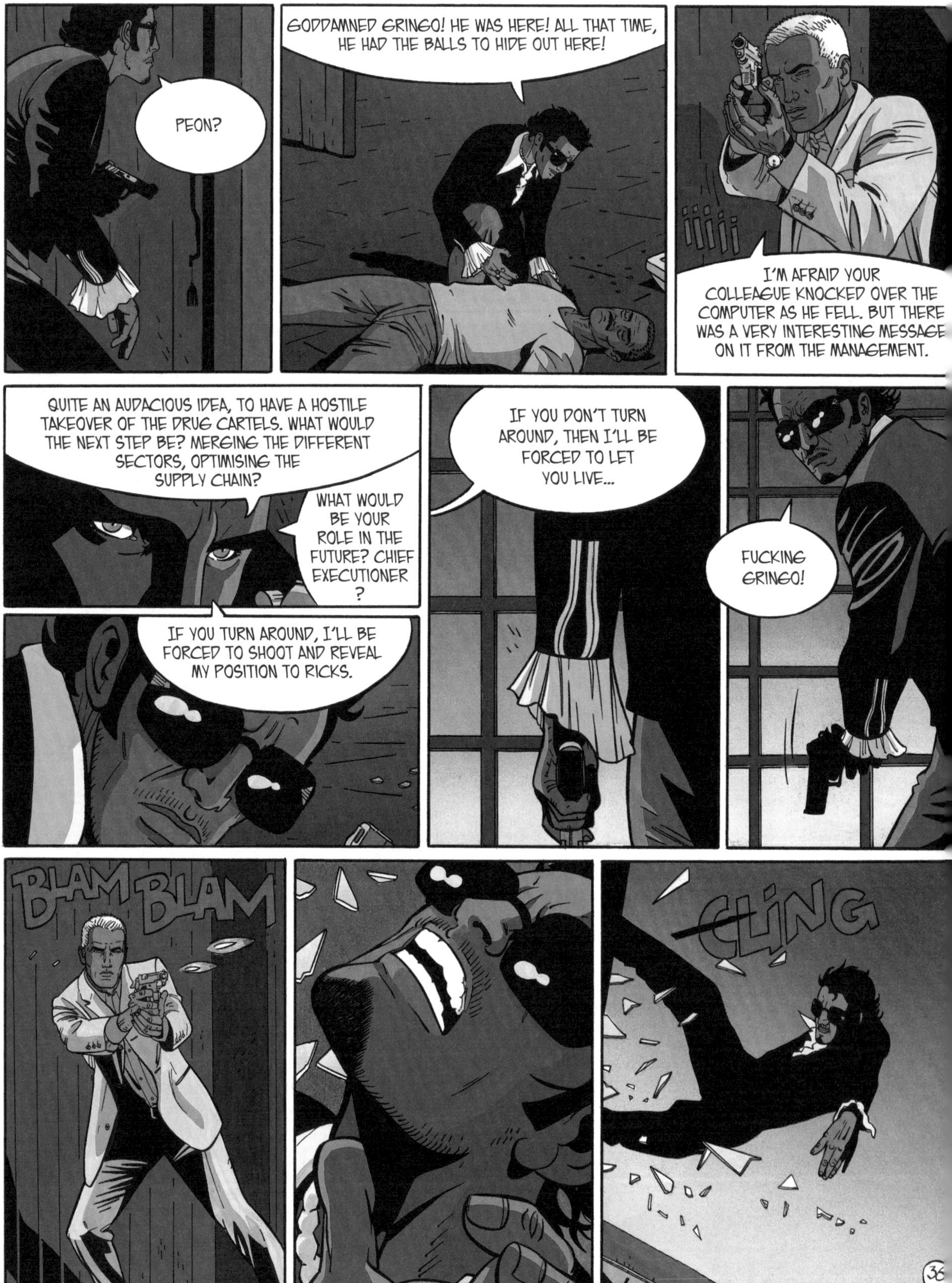
PEON?
GODDAMNED GRINGO! HE WAS HERE! ALL THAT TIME, HE HAD THE BALLS TO HIDE OUT HERE!
I'M AFRAID YOUR COLLEAGUE KNOCKED OVER THE COMPUTER AS HE FELL. BUT THERE WAS A VERY INTERESTING MESSAGE ON IT FROM THE MANAGEMENT.
QUITE AN AUDACIOUS IDEA, TO HAVE A HOSTILE TAKEOVER OF THE DRUG CARTELS. WHAT WOULD THE NEXT STEP BE? MERGING THE DIFFERENT SECTORS, OPTIMISING THE SUPPLY CHAIN?
WHAT WOULD BE YOUR ROLE IN THE FUTURE? CHIEF EXECUTIONER ?
IF YOU TURN AROUND, I'LL BE FORCED TO SHOOT AND REVEAL MY POSITION TO RICKS.
IF YOU DON'T TURN AROUND, THEN I'LL BE FORCED TO LET YOU LIVE...
FUCKING GRINGO!
BLAM BLAM
CLING
36

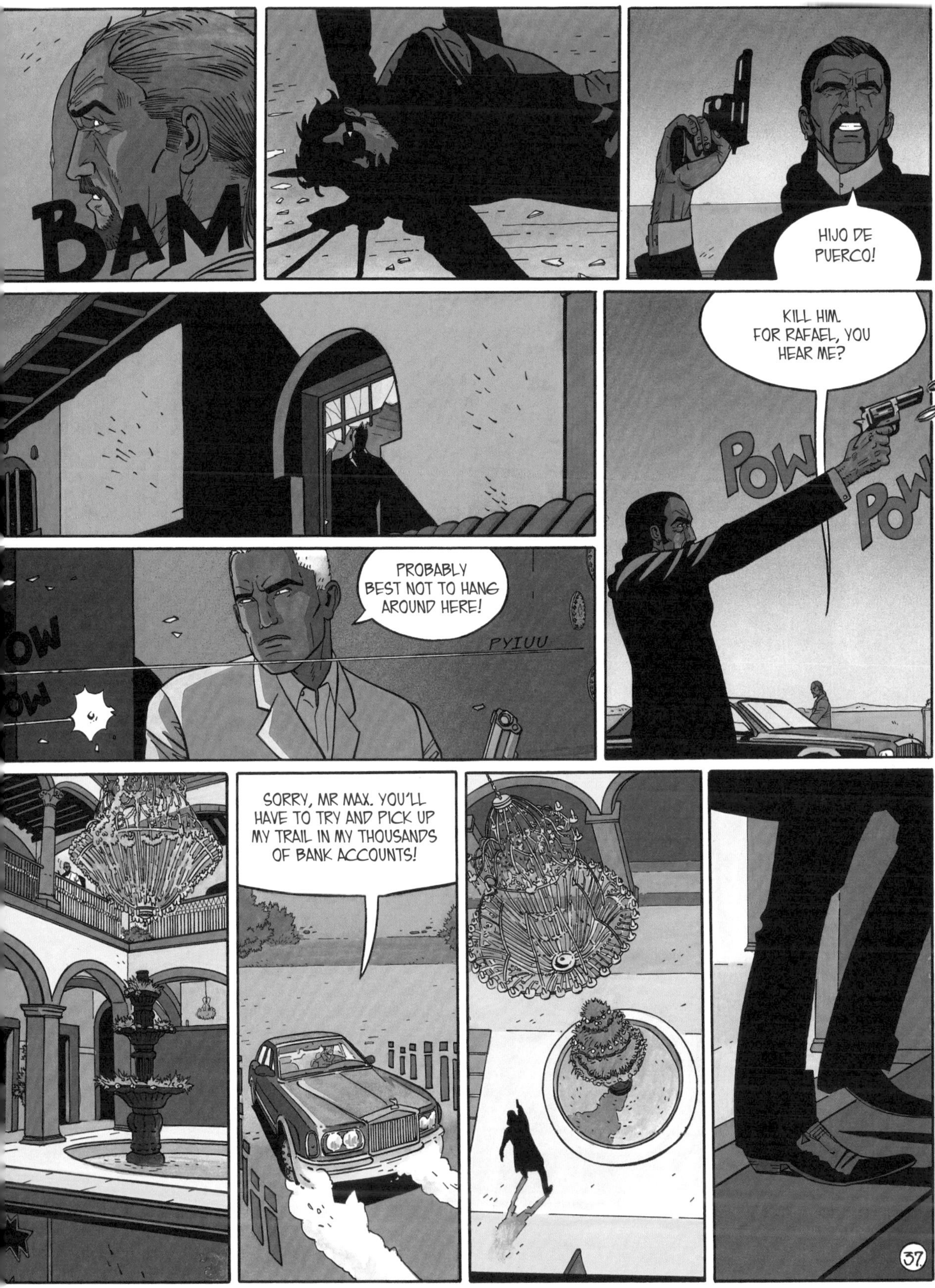
BAM
HIJO DE PUERCO!
KILL HIM. FOR RAFAEL, YOU HEAR ME?
POW
POW
PROBABLY BEST NOT TO HANG AROUND HERE!
PYIUU
SORRY, MR MAX. YOU'LL HAVE TO TRY AND PICK UP MY TRAIL IN MY THOUSANDS OF BANK ACCOUNTS!
37

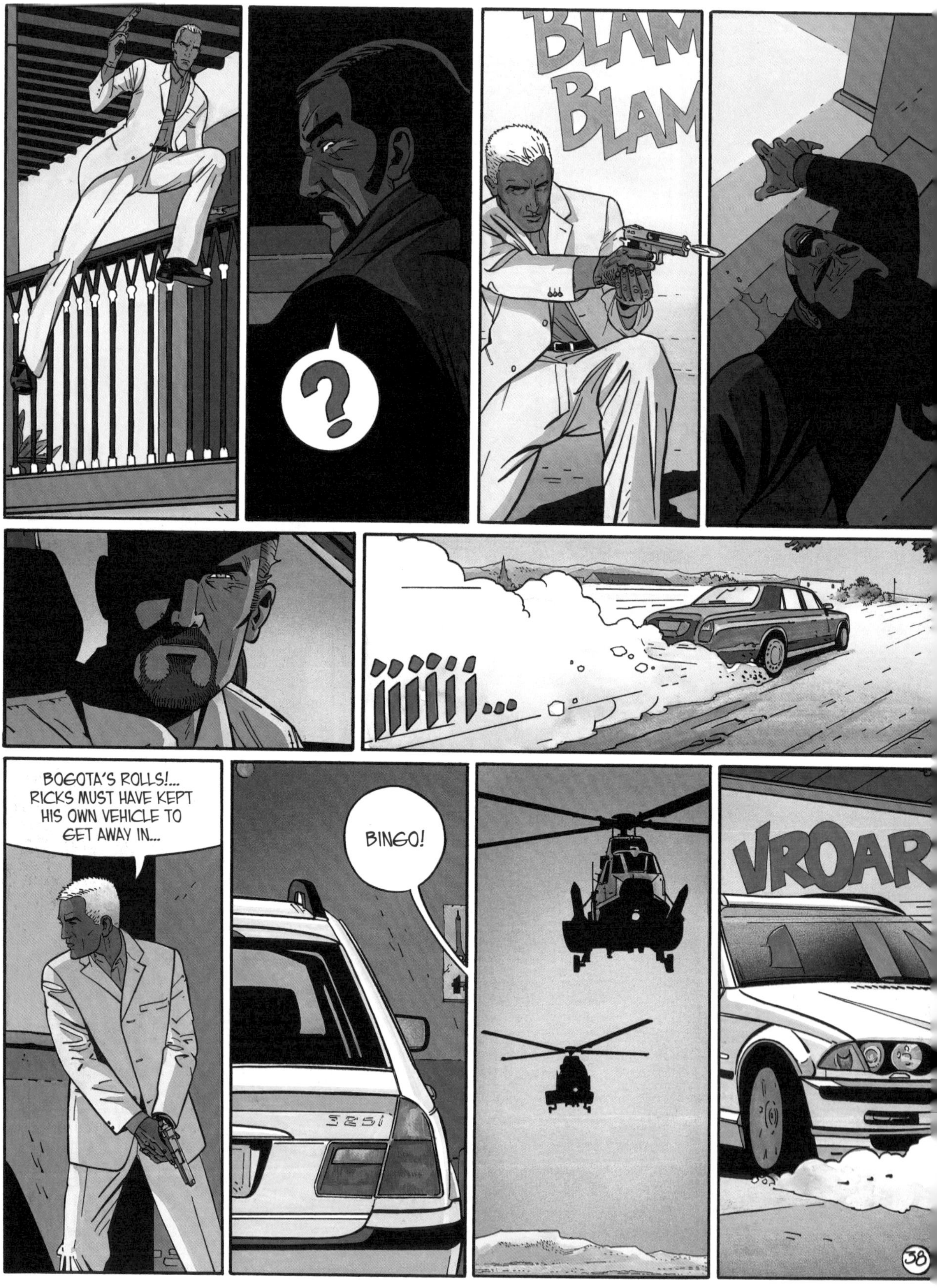
?
BLAM
BLAM
BLAM
IIIIII...
BOGOTA'S ROLLS!... RICKS MUST HAVE KEPT HIS OWN VEHICLE TO GET AWAY IN...
BINGO!
325i
VROAR
38

THERE CAN'T BE THAT MANY WAYS OUT OF THIS TOWN...

VROAR

LARRY MAX! I DON'T KNOW HOW MANY TIMES I'VE TRIED TO REACH YOU! WHERE THE HELL YOU AT?

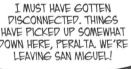

I MUST HAVE GOTTEN DISCONNECTED. THINGS HAVE PICKED UP SOMEWHAT DOWN HERE, PERALTA. WE'RE LEAVING SAN MIGUEL!

W... WITH CARANCA? IN WHICH DIRECTION?

ONLY RICKS AND I. I SEE A SIGN... WE'RE ON ROUTE FOR... CELAYA.

CELAYA. TO THE WEST? WE'RE RIGHT BEHIND YOU!

CAN YOU SEE US? I REPEAT, CAN YOU SEE US?

89

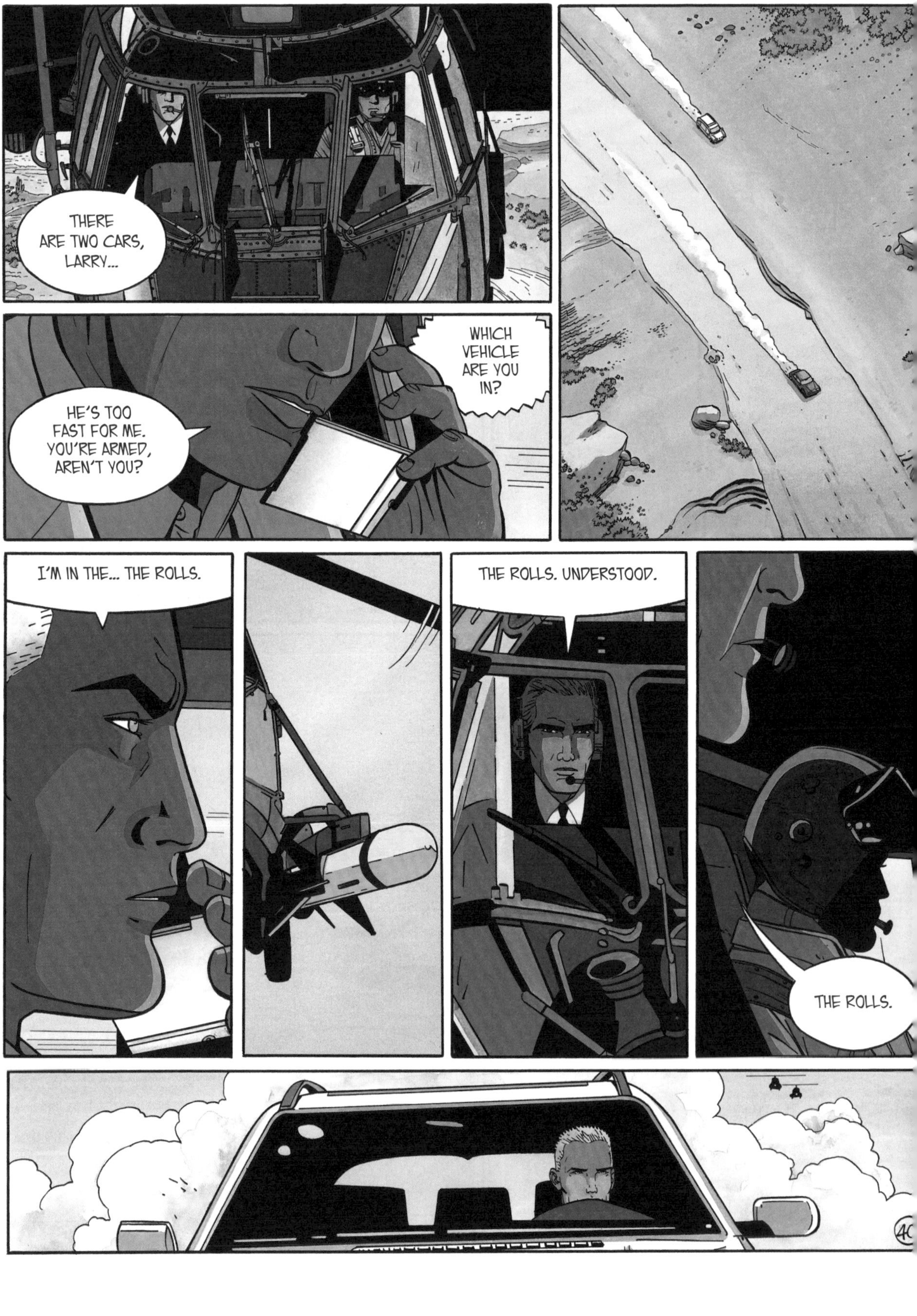
THERE ARE TWO CARS, LARRY...
WHICH VEHICLE ARE YOU IN?
HE'S TOO FAST FOR ME. YOU'RE ARMED, AREN'T YOU?
I'M IN THE... THE ROLLS.
THE ROLLS. UNDERSTOOD.
THE ROLLS.
40

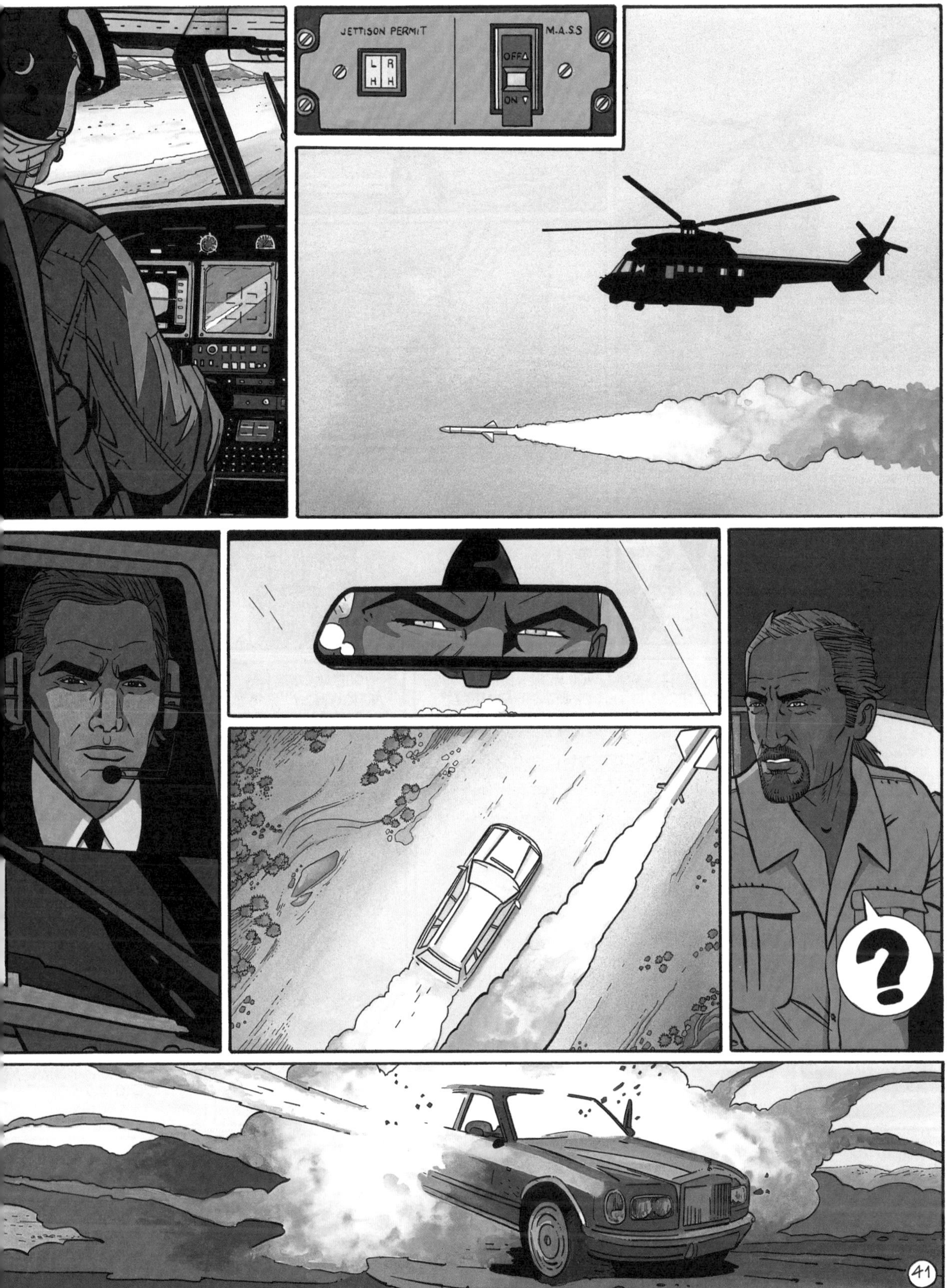
JETTISON PERMIT
M.A.S.S
OFF
ON
?
41

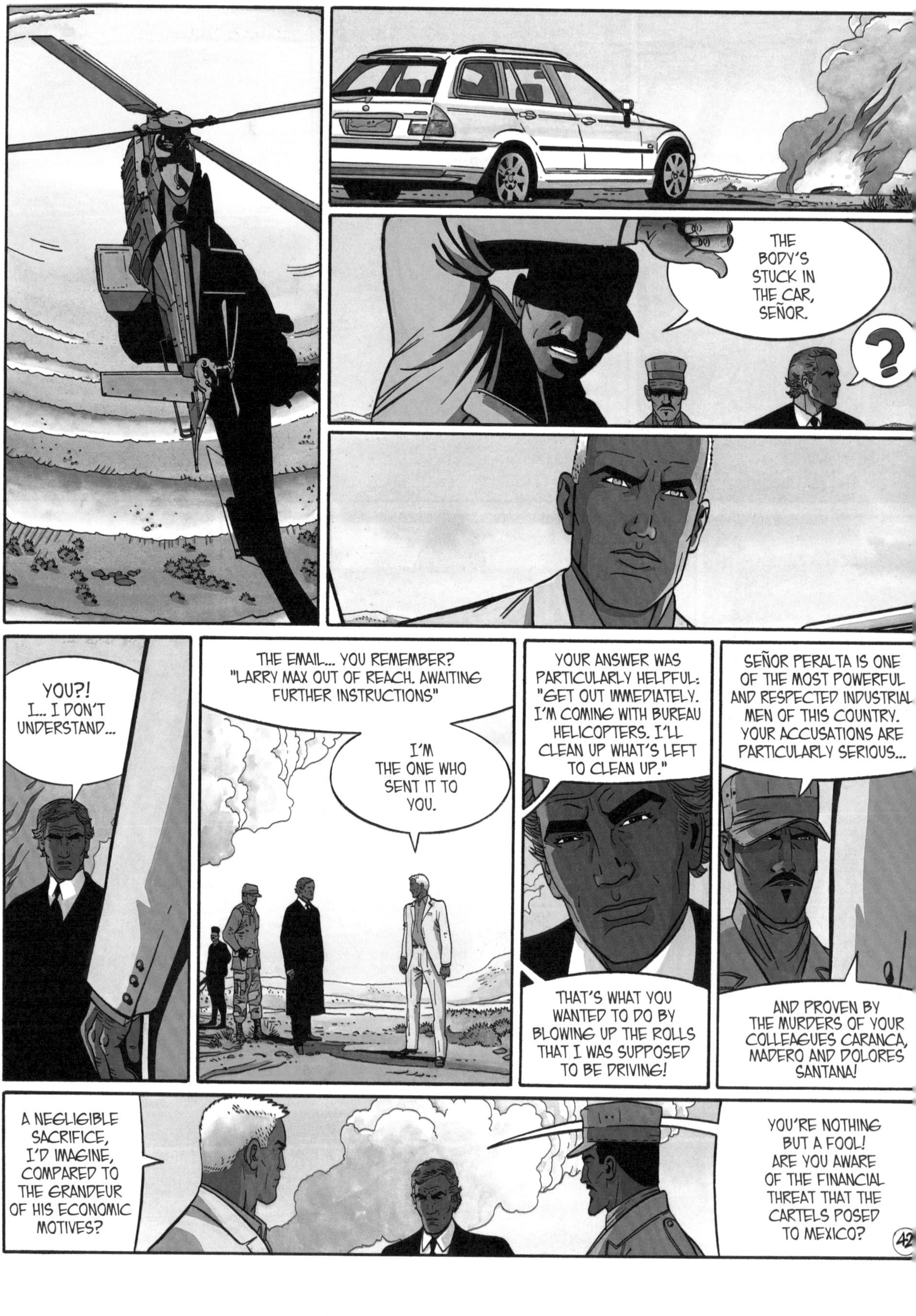

THE BODY'S STUCK IN THE CAR, SEÑOR.
?
YOU?! I... I DON'T UNDERSTAND...
THE EMAIL... YOU REMEMBER? "LARRY MAX OUT OF REACH. AWAITING FURTHER INSTRUCTIONS"
I'M THE ONE WHO SENT IT TO YOU.
YOUR ANSWER WAS PARTICULARLY HELPFUL: "GET OUT IMMEDIATELY. I'M COMING WITH BUREAU HELICOPTERS. I'LL CLEAN UP WHAT'S LEFT TO CLEAN UP."
THAT'S WHAT YOU WANTED TO DO BY BLOWING UP THE ROLLS THAT I WAS SUPPOSED TO BE DRIVING!
SEÑOR PERALTA IS ONE OF THE MOST POWERFUL AND RESPECTED INDUSTRIAL MEN OF THIS COUNTRY. YOUR ACCUSATIONS ARE PARTICULARLY SERIOUS...
AND PROVEN BY THE MURDERS OF YOUR COLLEAGUES CARANCA, MADERO AND DOLORES SANTANA!
A NEGLIGIBLE SACRIFICE, I'D IMAGINE, COMPARED TO THE GRANDEUR OF HIS ECONOMIC MOTIVES?
YOU'RE NOTHING BUT A FOOL! ARE YOU AWARE OF THE FINANCIAL THREAT THAT THE CARTELS POSED TO MEXICO?
42

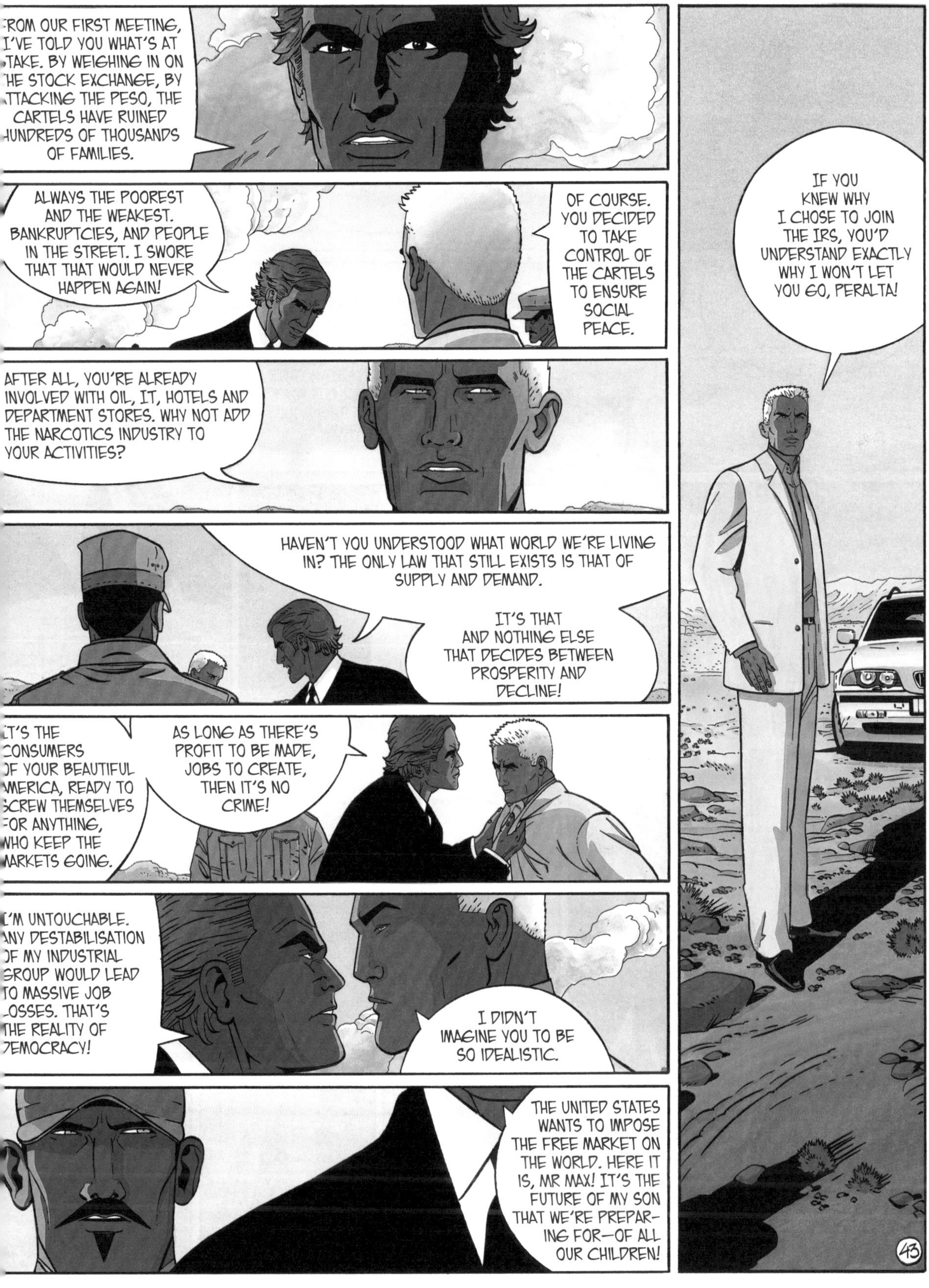

ROM OUR FIRST MEETING, I'VE TOLD YOU WHAT'S AT TAKE. BY WEIGHING IN ON HE STOCK EXCHANGE, BY TTACKING THE PESO, THE CARTELS HAVE RUINED UNDREDS OF THOUSANDS OF FAMILIES.
ALWAYS THE POOREST AND THE WEAKEST. BANKRUPTCIES, AND PEOPLE IN THE STREET. I SWORE THAT THAT WOULD NEVER HAPPEN AGAIN!
OF COURSE. YOU DECIDED TO TAKE CONTROL OF THE CARTELS TO ENSURE SOCIAL PEACE.
AFTER ALL, YOU'RE ALREADY INVOLVED WITH OIL, IT, HOTELS AND DEPARTMENT STORES. WHY NOT ADD THE NARCOTICS INDUSTRY TO YOUR ACTIVITIES?
HAVEN'T YOU UNDERSTOOD WHAT WORLD WE'RE LIVING IN? THE ONLY LAW THAT STILL EXISTS IS THAT OF SUPPLY AND DEMAND.
IT'S THAT AND NOTHING ELSE THAT DECIDES BETWEEN PROSPERITY AND DECLINE!
T'S THE CONSUMERS F YOUR BEAUTIFUL MERICA, READY TO CREW THEMSELVES OR ANYTHING, WHO KEEP THE ARKETS GOING.
AS LONG AS THERE'S PROFIT TO BE MADE, JOBS TO CREATE, THEN IT'S NO CRIME!
'M UNTOUCHABLE. NY DESTABILISATION F MY INDUSTRIAL GROUP WOULD LEAD TO MASSIVE JOB OSSES. THAT'S THE REALITY OF EMOCRACY!
I DIDN'T IMAGINE YOU TO BE SO IDEALISTIC.
THE UNITED STATES WANTS TO IMPOSE THE FREE MARKET ON THE WORLD. HERE IT IS, MR MAX! IT'S THE FUTURE OF MY SON THAT WE'RE PREPARING FOR—OF ALL OUR CHILDREN!
IF YOU KNEW WHY I CHOSE TO JOIN THE IRS, YOU'D UNDERSTAND EXACTLY WHY I WON'T LET YOU GO, PERALTA!
43

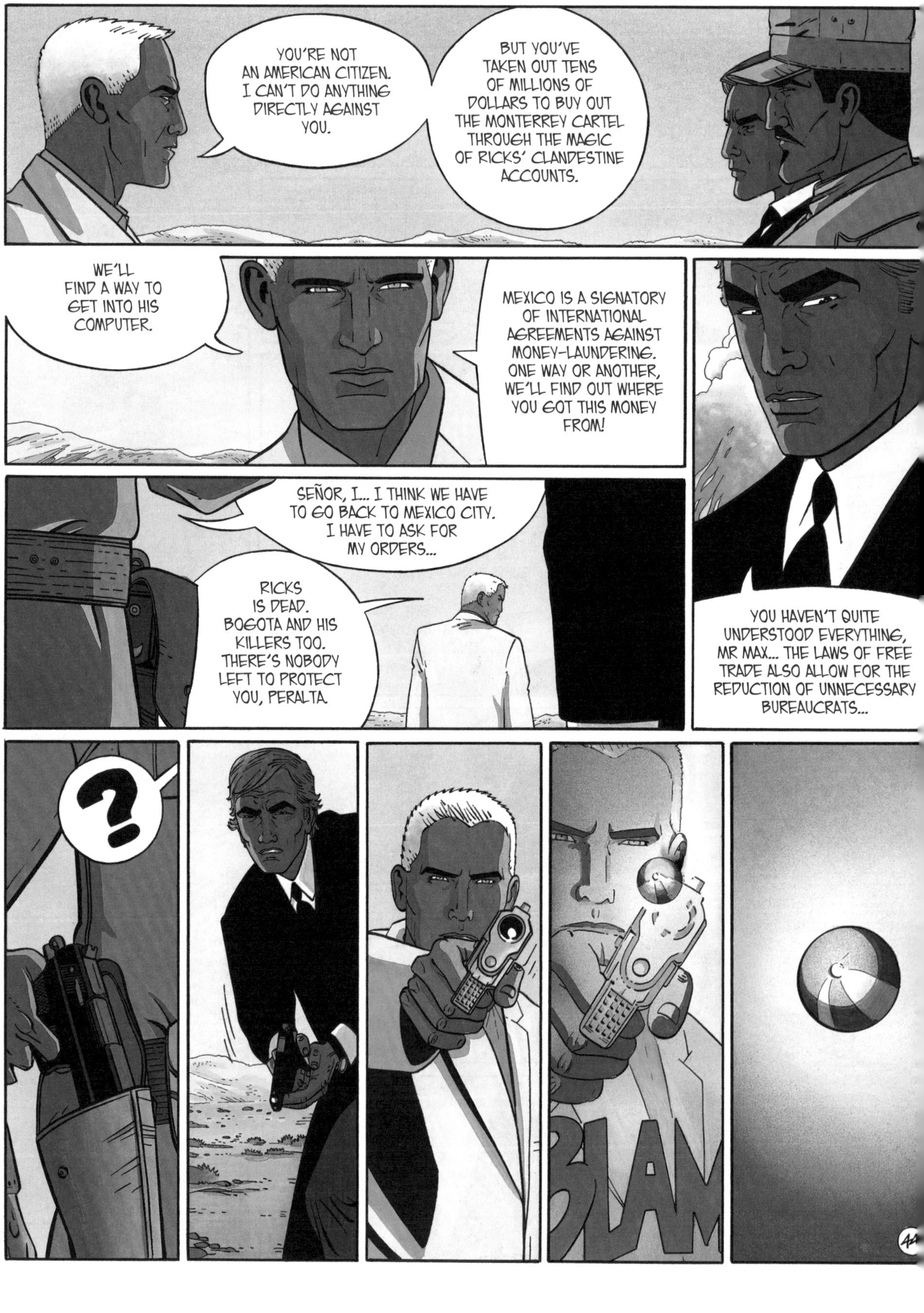
YOU'RE NOT AN AMERICAN CITIZEN. I CAN'T DO ANYTHING DIRECTLY AGAINST YOU.
BUT YOU'VE TAKEN OUT TENS OF MILLIONS OF DOLLARS TO BUY OUT THE MONTERREY CARTEL THROUGH THE MAGIC OF RICKS' CLANDESTINE ACCOUNTS.
WE'LL FIND A WAY TO GET INTO HIS COMPUTER.
MEXICO IS A SIGNATORY OF INTERNATIONAL AGREEMENTS AGAINST MONEY-LAUNDERING. ONE WAY OR ANOTHER, WE'LL FIND OUT WHERE YOU GOT THIS MONEY FROM!
SEÑOR, I... I THINK WE HAVE TO GO BACK TO MEXICO CITY. I HAVE TO ASK FOR MY ORDERS...
RICKS IS DEAD. BOGOTA AND HIS KILLERS TOO. THERE'S NOBODY LEFT TO PROTECT YOU, PERALTA.
YOU HAVEN'T QUITE UNDERSTOOD EVERYTHING, MR MAX... THE LAWS OF FREE TRADE ALSO ALLOW FOR THE REDUCTION OF UNNECESSARY BUREAUCRATS...
?
BLAM

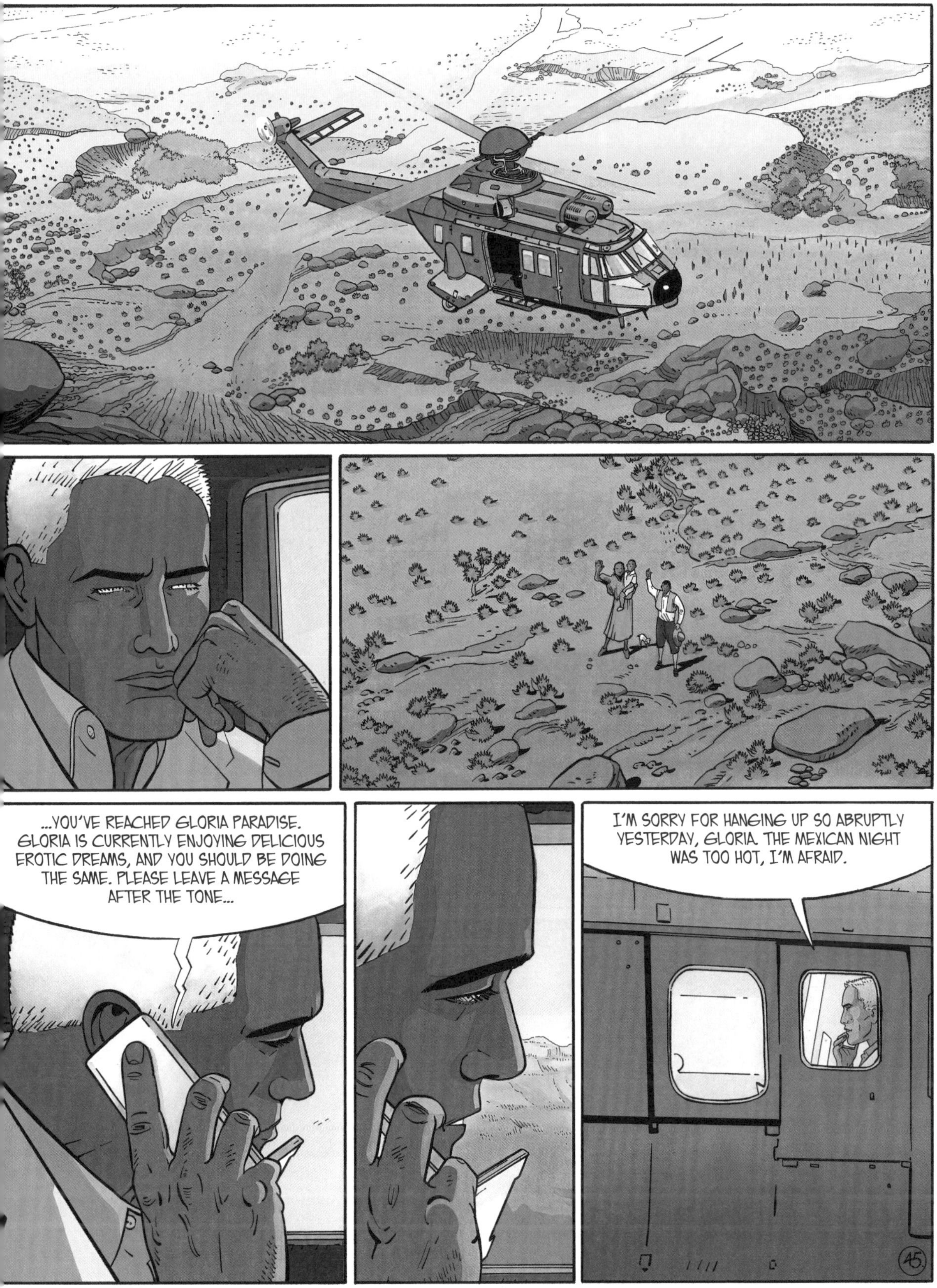
...YOU'VE REACHED GLORIA PARADISE. GLORIA IS CURRENTLY ENJOYING DELICIOUS EROTIC DREAMS, AND YOU SHOULD BE DOING THE SAME. PLEASE LEAVE A MESSAGE AFTER THE TONE...
I'M SORRY FOR HANGING UP SO ABRUPTLY YESTERDAY, GLORIA. THE MEXICAN NIGHT WAS TOO HOT, I'M AFRAID.
45

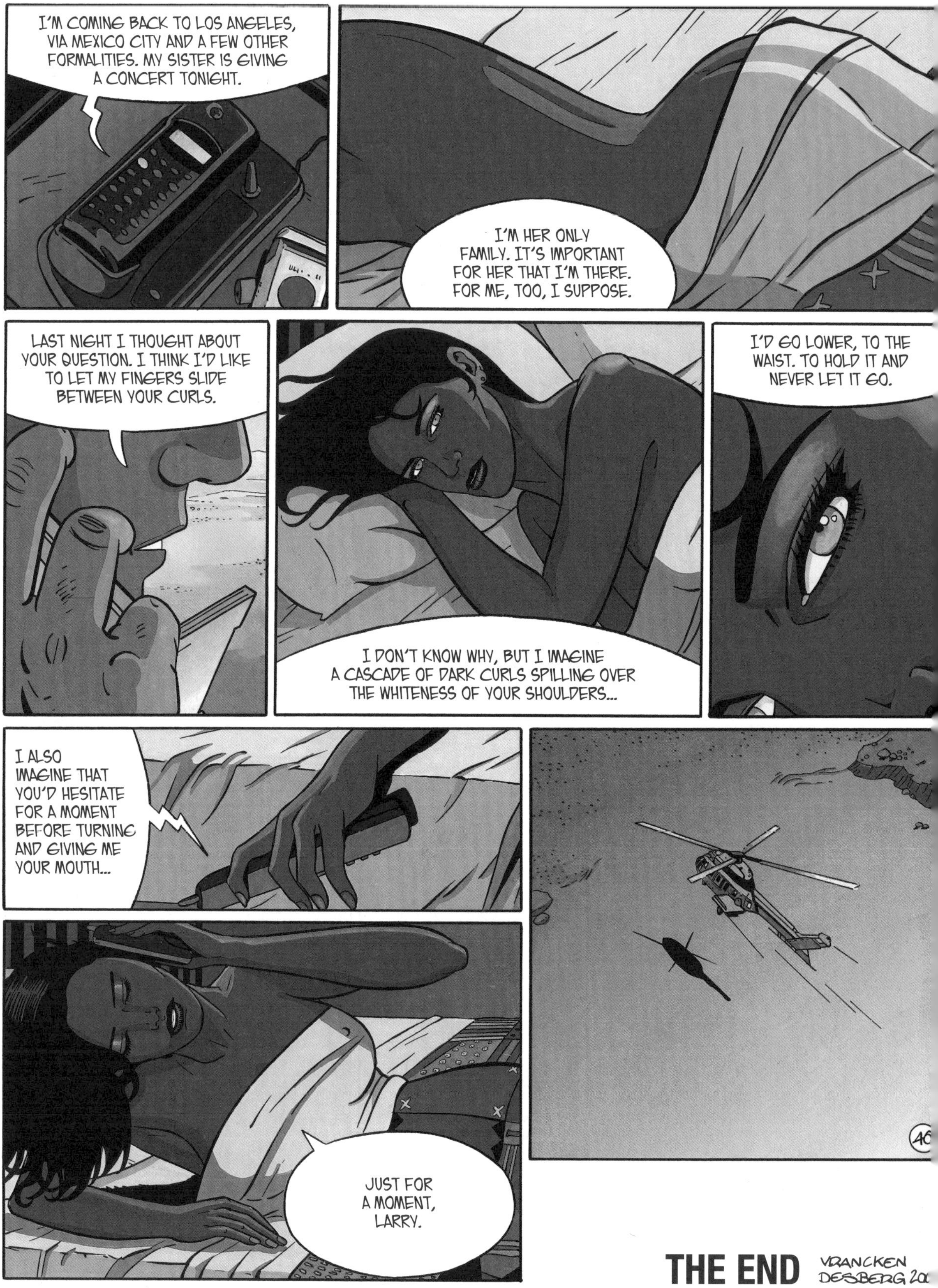
I'M COMING BACK TO LOS ANGELES, VIA MEXICO CITY AND A FEW OTHER FORMALITIES. MY SISTER IS GIVING A CONCERT TONIGHT.
I'M HER ONLY FAMILY. IT'S IMPORTANT FOR HER THAT I'M THERE. FOR ME, TOO, I SUPPOSE.
LAST NIGHT I THOUGHT ABOUT YOUR QUESTION. I THINK I'D LIKE TO LET MY FINGERS SLIDE BETWEEN YOUR CURLS.
I DON'T KNOW WHY, BUT I IMAGINE A CASCADE OF DARK CURLS SPILLING OVER THE WHITENESS OF YOUR SHOULDERS...
I'D GO LOWER, TO THE WAIST. TO HOLD IT AND NEVER LET IT GO.
I ALSO IMAGINE THAT YOU'D HESITATE FOR A MOMENT BEFORE TURNING AND GIVING ME YOUR MOUTH...
JUST FOR A MOMENT, LARRY.
THE END
VRANCKEN DESBERG